How Not to Let Having Kids Ruin Your Sex Life

Dr Karen Gurney is a consultant clinical psychologist and certified psychosexologist, and is a recognised national expert in the theory and practice of therapy around all aspects of sexual wellbeing and function. She is currently Head of Wellbeing Services at the award winning sexual health clinic 56 Dean Street (Chelsea and Westminster Hospital NHS Foundation Trust), as well as Director of The Havelock Clinic, an independent sexual problems service based in London. Dr Gurney regularly writes and is featured in publications such as *Vogue* and *Marie Claire* as well as appearing on podcasts, radio and TV. Dr Gurney has given two TED talks, the latter of which has had over 1.6 million views. Dr Gurney is on Instagram as @thesexdoctor. She is the author of *Mind the Gap* and *How Not to Let Having Kids Ruin Your Sex Life*.

How Not to Let to Let Having Kids Ruin Your Sex Life

DR KAREN GURNEY

First published in 2024 by HEADLINE HOME
An imprint of HEADLINE PUBLISHING GROUP

1

Cataloguing in Publication Data is available from the British Library

Trade Paperback ISBN 978 1 0354 0511 4
eISBN 978 1 0354 0512 1

Diagrams by Louise Turpin

Typeset in 12/16pt Dante MT Std by Jouve (UK), Milton Keynes

Printed and bound in Great Britain by Clays Ltd, Elcograf S.p.A.

HEADLINE PUBLISHING GROUP
An Hachette UK Company
Carmelite House
50 Victoria Embankment
London EC4Y 0DZ

www.headline.co.uk
www.hachette.co.uk

Contents

Preface
All at Sea

I began learning to sail at the age of twelve. My beloved next-door neighbour, Jim, had a small boat he had built himself, which he took out on a local lake. I was his crew for many years, spending evenings after school and Sundays gliding through the water, my mouth watering from the aroma of the local bakery making tomorrow's loaves as it drifted across the lake. I developed a love of the terminology, the adrenaline and the clanking of the halyards on the mast in calm water. Then, as a teenager, I was lucky enough to be selected for a few weeks at sea on a 150-foot three-masted schooner in the Atlantic ocean with thirty other teenagers (NB: imagine a pirate ship and you're picturing it right). We were pushed to the limits with seasickness, terrifying storms and rewarded with camaraderie, escorts of playful dolphin families and a thirst for more. As part of this experience, I met Sir Robin Knox-Johnston, a British sailor who was the first person to perform a single-handed non-stop circumnavigation of the globe in 1969. Knox-Johnston gave a jaw-dropping account of his trip and the vast amount of knowledge one needs to survive the ocean.* Inspired by this, as I got older, my

---

* If all this sailing talk has piqued your interest, Sir Robin Knox-Johnstone's bestselling book, *A World of My Own* (Cassell, 1969), is an incredible account of the isolation, exhilaration and psychological hurdles of his round-the-world trip.

interest turned to the more technical aspects of the sea as well as the practical: tides, weather, navigation, boat maintenance, chart reading. Learning about sailing fitted with my love of the sea and my nature (I like to know the technical aspects of things inside out, which is a bit of a running joke in my family). I went on to pass my skipper theory and practical exam as the only woman in the class, and continued to race small boats and skipper large sailing boats over the decades that followed.

Now, every good sailor knows that the power of the sea should never be underestimated. A boat navigating stormy seas must bow to the sea's strength and accept that, in open water, any boat is insignificant in comparison to the natural forces acting upon it. The captain and crew are not powerless, however, even though it may appear this way at times. They have the ability to recognize and accept the weather, understand the direction of the wind and predict the pull of the tide. They can make decisions to take action, by spilling wind from their sails, changing course or weathering the storm.

Some parts of the voyage will be more intense and will require efforts of preservation only. Fierce storms will lead sailors to 'batten down the hatches' – sailing speak for protecting the boat and focusing on staying afloat only until the storm passes, accepting that they will be tossed around by its force for some time. Other parts of the voyage may encounter choppy seas, but will allow the crew to take more control of their vessel, and navigate purposefully through them, albeit without much grace. There will also be periods of plain sailing where the weather is fine and the sea is calm; at this point the crew can take care of any damage the boat has endured or make good progress with their journey.

No sailor enters into the sea without a purpose or a final destination in mind, and an awareness of the best course or trajectory is essential to a successful voyage. After a period of bad weather, sailors might ask themselves: 'How did that knock us off course?', and right this as soon as is within their power. Good sailors have an awareness that, particularly with long voyages, a very small change in trajectory caused by bad weather, or a change of tide, can lead to an entirely different destination if this course is left uncorrected over a long distance. It is important, therefore, to carefully take stock of your position regularly and use this knowledge to make small changes of trajectory, or adjust the sails as needed. Making such checks and righting trajectories prevents sailors and their vessels ending up unexpectedly at a final destination that is quite different to where they intended. This is not about discounting the power of the sea, or feeling exempt from its force, but accepting its power and working with it respectfully. At some point the weather will pass, and clearer skies will emerge.

To my mind, as a sailor *and* as a parent, there is no better metaphor to guide us through the subsequent chapters than this one. The force that parenthood exerts on your relationship and sex life is beyond your control, and at times you will feel powerless against it. Getting through it relatively unscathed will be the best you can do at times, and there are ways to do this that will allow you to preserve the boat (your relationship) in a good state until the storm passes. At other times, taking stock of the course you are currently on and making small tweaks to adjust your trajectory will allow you to find yourself at a destination that is favourable, maybe years down the line. And this is possible even in the choppy waters of fatigue, and with huge waves of life admin crashing down on the boat that is your relationship.

As a clinical psychologist specializing in helping people get the sex lives they want, I see the impact of an unfavourable trajectory and unwanted destination in the couples who come to see me when their kids are teens or adults, wondering how they ended up where they did. They weren't to blame for the storm: the storm is part of the deal. What they weren't given were the skills to navigate the boat when the sea was rough – the skills to weather the storm, preserve the boat and emerge safely and happily into calmer seas and then onward to a sunnier destination. This is the purpose of this book. I'm looking forward to joining you on your voyage and supporting your safe passage to sunnier climes, whatever weather you currently find yourself in, and no matter where you are on your journey.

Introduction

There's a certain irony in the fact that the very act that leads to having children for many of us is often, ultimately, ruined by it also. It's true that we shouldn't expect the same sex life that we had before, when all-day brunches were still easy to organize and lie-ins were ten-a-penny. It's also true that your sex life *can* survive having kids, and may even (dare I say it) end up being better off for it. So let me tell you how to weather the storm and emerge feeling more connected and satisfied than ever.

Having children is a colossal life event and, understandably, for a period of time takes our attention and focus away from other important parts of our identity, including our sexual selves. For many people sex fades out of focus for a while, and then gets back on track without a sense of urgency or problem, weeks, months or years later. For others, a change in their sex lives feels more pressing, either because their sexual expression is a really pivotal part of their identity, so the loss feels greater, or because its absence presents challenges for their relationship. Sex can be a pursuit that, when we access it, allows us to relax and truly feel like ourselves. This can feel even more needed in the transition to parenthood, as it can feel so exhausting, and so easy to lose oneself in it. Some of you may be worrying about relationship security – especially now you have a family – and so making sure sex is okay can be part of protecting the relationship for the sake of the whole family. For others, the changes your body has been through with pregnancy and birth, or, in contrast, being the person who did not give birth and perhaps feels a little excluded, might have made you feel insecure, and sex is a way you can feel wanted and prioritized by each other. The key thing is that sex means different things to each of us, but is often integral to our psychological wellbeing, or the health of our relationship. For this reason keeping our sexual relationship boat seaworthy even in these choppy seas can be invaluable.

I wrote this book because you asked me to. My first book, *Mind The Gap: The Truth About Desire and How to Futureproof Your Sex Life* (Headline Home, 2020), was about the challenges of maintaining desire in long-term relationships, and although the sex lives of parents featured, there was too much to say about desire to focus on the specific challenges of parenthood in a meaningful way as well. My online course on this topic is *extremely* popular, but my inbox was full of requests to write a follow-up book specifically based on how to not let having kids ruin your sex life, so here it is.

This book is for *all* parents, not just women. I mention this as women are often positioned as the default captains of the boat, too often bearing the brunt of parenthood tasks when in relationships with men. I don't want 'fixing our sex life' to be yet another item on the mental to-do list they have to deal with, with their needing to read the book then being the sole implementer of all they have learned. But the other reason I mention the fact that this book is for all genders is that many men are struggling with their sex lives after becoming parents and tell me they don't know where to turn. People of *all* genders are affected when sex isn't going to plan.

Before we get much further, a note at this point about language and inclusivity. I'll be talking about birth parents and non-birth parents at times, to be inclusive of all families, but I'll mention gender specifically when relevant to the research. Parents in same gender/sex relationships are subject to the same parenting stressors as opposite sex couples (with some unique differences, which I'll mention where relevant). There is a lack of research into sex for trans and non-binary parents, however, so although much of this info will fit just as well, please accept my apologies for the lack of further specific mention at points. I'm well aware of the binary nature of sex science and the over focus of cisheterocentric research into parenthood.*

You will benefit from reading this book from start to finish, as there is a chronological story of our sex lives to be understood, with each new phase we begin informed by the last. Though I've tried to keep each chapter succinct and practical to acknowledge that the very reason you are reading this book is that you are time-poor. If you can, try to encourage each other to read this book together, or in parallel. It takes two people's understanding and efforts to make changes to get the sex life they both want, so this book is for both partners equally.† You'll find many of the tasks I set are for you to discuss together. There is a reason for this, which is that often in these discussions great changes can happen. But don't feel too disheartened if you

* You may see the prefix 'cis' before man and woman in the book from time to time. Cis means you identify as the same gender/sex you were assigned at birth. Cis is the opposite of trans. I use this term to be clear about who I'm referring to at times, as sometimes *all* women will be under the same pressures – so cis and trans women will share the same experiences – and I'll just refer to 'women' to reflect this. Other times sex research or specific sexual experiences will be different for different groups and I will use a prefix to be more specific.

† My language about 'two people' throughout this book is not intended to ignore those of you in polyamorous or open relationships who are also co-parents. The reality is that maintaining a good sex life is more challenging for people in monogamous relationship structures, so this book is written with them in mind. You may be a step-parent, blended family or have another family set up than the two parents who conceived at least one child and stayed together. I encourage you to adapt my language to suit your circumstances wherever you need to.

haven't got buy-in from your partner on this just yet. There may be a small change suggested in this book that you can get them to agree to try out, and seeing the difference this makes may give them the nudge they need to pick up this book too and engage with it further.

I'll start with an introduction to why sex matters to relationships and also give you an opportunity to take stock of where things are at for you currently, alongside examining the history behind your personal journey so far. I will then take you through the unique features of the different 'weather and sea conditions' that you will go through in your sexual relationship as parents, and how each of them will contribute to the trajectory of your sex life in their own, distinct way. Within most chapters you'll find tasks to aid your thinking, communication or problem solving for you and your partner to do separately or together. Each section aims to encourage you, where needed, to make the smallest change of course possible to have the biggest impact on your future destination. I've written the book this way as I know you have a busy life, with much to juggle (I'm a parent of two myself – I get it!). I also know, as a therapist supporting people with their sex lives, that the least time investment for the biggest reward is always a fruitful way to make change. Parenting is a long journey, so drastic changes of course are rarely necessary. But taking a position and being aware of your current trajectory and potential future destination almost certainly is.

Finally, a word on hope.

One of the hardest things people tell me they feel they have to deal with when their sex life isn't going so well is feeling clueless about being able to fix it. I want you to know that the power to make changes sits entirely within you and your relationship, and I will show you how. I also want you to know that even if you can't make a practical change just now, knowing that what's happening is normal, and finding ways to get through it without it reducing your relationship satisfaction is an achievable goal with considerable psychological benefit.

Having a great sex life after having kids is challenging but *absolutely* possible.

1

Learning the ropes
Why does sex matter anyway?

Parenthood can be a rollercoaster of joy *and* resentment. One minute you are watching your partner making your child giggle in a scene of family bliss and wondering how you got so lucky. The next you are watching them drop their socks on the floor and asking yourself *'When did they last get up in the night or put a load of washing on?'* In my clinic, I notice that sex can be another irritation that gets added to the ever-growing list of irksome things in this phase of life. Sex, when it's not going so well, can be just another source of increasing frustration, chipping away at relationship satisfaction over time.

There are numerous studies detailing the psychological and relationship consequences of an unhappy sex life. We know that, among other things, sexual problems in monogamous relationships are associated with decreased relationship quality, thoughts of infidelity and lower personal wellbeing.[1] Not being happy with sex in a monogamous relationship can lead to resentment, feeling disconnected, or can leave one or both partners vulnerable to the idea of meeting their sexual needs elsewhere.

In my work, I notice we lack understanding as a society about how and why sex matters in relationships. Sex is often positioned as merely a physical pursuit, diminishing its psychological and relational importance in our lives. Research tells us that, when couples have sex, they are more likely to report a better mood and relationship satisfaction on that day and for the next day or two afterwards.[2] [3] Studies have also shown that sexual satisfaction is a good predictor of overall relationship quality,[4] and can predict relationship satisfaction years down the line.[5] There is also strong evidence that having a good sex life is associated with boosts to our mood and relationship stability,[6] so, as much as we might like to think of sex as a frivolous recreational pursuit, there are some clear reasons why we might want to nurture our sex lives if we hope for a final destination of a happy life, and a happy relationship with the same partner over time.

Something less well known, and I would argue less utilized as a tool at our disposal, is the protective impact that feeling sexually connected can have more broadly on new parents' relationship satisfaction over time. It's not just about preventing problems from occurring. Sex itself – as long as it's a source of satisfaction and joy – can actually act as a sort of glue that holds your relationship together when other cracks may start to appear in times of stress, such as having young children. Research tells us that sexual satisfaction can improve the emotional climate of our relationship, helping us feel more connected and more like a team.[7] Think of it as strengthening the structure of the boat. Also relevant to parenthood is the fact that relationship quality is strongly connected to sexual satisfaction, and relationship quality has been shown to influence the psychological wellbeing of children raised by those parents.[8]

What does sex mean to you, your partner and your relationship?

In the past, you may have assumed that sex is just something you should feel like and should be doing in a 'normal' relationship with someone you love, but have you ever examined it beyond this? Why does it actually matter to you? Does it? What do you get from it? Do you know why it matters to your partner? Are you right about this? How does it impact your relationship? It's likely that you and your partner might have different reasons why sex matters to you and that's okay. Understanding each other's reasons is important, and having differences here can be the first problem we encounter in our sex lives when things don't go to plan. One of the keys to getting the sex life you want post kids is to look a little deeper and figure out why it matters.

Take Ben and Jo as an example. Ben was unhappy with the amount of sex he and Jo had been having since their first child, Rohan, was born. He frequently let Jo know this, and Jo felt irritated and harassed by the frequency with which he brought this up. When I saw them for therapy, they had reached a stalemate around this topic (this is usually what brings people to see me, and by the time we meet, sex has often become a subject that is hard to discuss without high emotion). We started to delve into the meaning of sex for each of them personally, and what they felt it signified for the relationship. Jo described that she felt sex was something she did for fun, at times out of obligation, and when she wanted to feel close to Ben. At this point in their life, she told me that sex was less important to her than it had ever been. From Jo's perspective, they had just had their first child and become a family of three, and she had never felt more settled and secure in their relationship. She didn't feel she had time for fun, and whereas before she may have felt obligated to have sex at times she knew Ben wanted it, she simply couldn't take on another person's needs right now. 'He's an adult,' she told me, 'he can cope and sort himself out if he's not okay. I just can't take on another person's needs with everything else I've got to deal with.'

Ben's constant talk of sex actually *threatened* her sense of closeness and contentment. She couldn't understand why he had to keep bringing it up and she found it irritating and insensitive. She told me, 'It's like he can't see how busy and tired I am, which I find deeply insulting.'

Ben, meanwhile, described that sex, to him, felt like an affirmation of their partnership, and he had always felt more secure in their relationship after they had sex. 'It's when I feel most loved and close to her,' Ben said. 'I know it's a cliché, but I see her with Rohan and it's beautiful, but I feel that I'm left to one side sometimes.' Ben shared that his own parents had split when he was six, and later in life they had cited the stress of having children as the reason. He described that his biggest fear was parenthood putting distance between them in a way they could never recover from. 'It's so important to me that we have a stable family for Rohan,' he said. 'I don't know what I'd do without them both.'

Arguments about it made this worse and (ironically) disharmony made the need for sex even more important to Ben, creating a circular pattern that they had become stuck in. Jo was unable to see the meaning that sex had for Ben, as she had a different association with sex. Jo saw sex as more frivolous and a 'nice to have' rather than the essential glue for their relationship and a conduit for closeness. She was also affected by reductive gendered narratives in society that 'men are always thinking about sex',* so it was hard for her to spot a deeper meaning for Ben than the physical act. Ben was unable to communicate why it mattered so much, as he himself was unaware of this, and instead communicated his dissatisfaction and desperation by sarcastic digs about how long it had been, which, due to how they came out, just strengthened Jo's hypothesis over time.

The arguments that ensued over sex based on this misunderstanding meant that any desire for being sexual with each other felt further and further away, and also affected their relationship satisfaction. They began to argue more about other things and found co-parenting a challenge, characterized by constant bickering about who was doing more. The more Ben felt distance between them, the more he raised the issue with sex. This is what therapists such as myself call a 'circular problem'.[9] Neither Ben nor Jo is wrong or to blame, but their lack of understanding of each other, different experiences and expectations, and patterns of communicating are keeping them stuck in a pattern of distance and dissatisfaction. At the foundation of this misunderstanding is their lack of awareness of the function of sex for each of them and for the relationship. Their relationship, and their personal wellbeing, was suffering as a result.

What is needed for Jo and Ben (and perhaps for you) is a new lens, and a deeper understanding, to break any unhelpful patterns that may have been inadvertently created, bringing a different perspective and a more nourishing experience.

---

* You may have heard the widely held idea that there is scientific evidence that men think about sex every seven seconds. Interestingly, recent research has shown that there isn't a significant difference between how often people of all genders think about sex, and the slightly higher reported expression of sexual thoughts by men is also seen in how often they think about hunger and sleep. This suggests that men have a lower threshold for thinking about *all physical needs* more, rather than there being something unique about sex. The median daily tally count of thoughts about sex for men was about nineteen thoughts per day, and ten per day for women, significantly less than the 8,000 a day every seven seconds would amount to.

TASK: What do we want?

Consider the following questions separately, then sit down together and share your answers with each other. If saying what you want out loud feels tricky (talking about sex can be difficult!), can you text or email your answers to each other instead?

Take it in turns answering each of these questions and *really* listening to each other's perspective. You don't need to have similar answers, so try not to be swayed (or irritated) by your partner's response. There are no right or wrongs here. This task is about understanding each other, not about being on the same page or agreeing. Keep your answers somewhere you can refer back to, if you want, as we will touch on these reasons again later.

Try not to half answer the question. *'I would like our sex life to be better'* tells us nothing! *'I would like us to feel sexually connected and to know that you still fancy me even when we're not having sex'* is more useful.

Similarly, *'I would feel happier'* is not a full answer that helps us to understand the situation fully. You need to add in the 'why', i.e. *'I would feel happier, as it would make me feel that we are a really strong couple and we still have that spark'* would lead to more understanding.

In an ideal world, how would you like your sex life to be?
   I would like our sex life to be _____

What would be the impact of this on you, personally?
   I would feel _____

What would be the impact on your relationship, if your sex life were as you imagined?

We would _____

What if we don't want the same thing?

Just a little note here on the first question you answered, on how you want your sex lives to be.

I mentioned that you don't have to have the same answers, and you really don't. But it can be useful to see if both of your needs can be met by noting each other's answer, and factoring in some element of compromise into a new, *shared* answer. Make sure to listen well and try to avoid familiar but less helpful conversations about this topic that you've had many times before. After all, they probably haven't helped so far.

I need you to try to merge, as best as you can, both of your answers to the first question – *'In an ideal world, how would you like your sex life to be?'* – to find something that works for you both.

It doesn't need to be perfect, as actually what you will find is that, as things start to improve between you, and your satisfaction grows, things that feel more challenging now will feel easier to achieve. The peak of the mountain always looks higher from ground level. But I do need you to be working as a team towards a mutual goal you can both agree on. If this feels really challenging, and talking together about this stuff feels too hard, don't be ashamed to seek out more face-to-face sex therapy. But, for now, if you can reach some kind of middle ground you both agree on regarding what you want, that will see you well for the rest of this book.

So go back to that first question. *In an ideal world, how would you like your sex life to be?* Rewrite both statements into one statement that you both agree on. As an example, below are Ben and Jo's individual answers, plus their merged one.

> **Ben:** *'I'd like our sex life to be regular and to feel connected sexually to Jo again so I feel strong in the relationship.'*
>
> **Jo:** *'I'd like sex to take a back seat for a bit, but for that not to feel like an issue and diminish how strong we feel as a couple.'*
>
> **Merged goal**: *'We would like to find a way to feel sexually connected that doesn't rely solely on frequency, so that we can feel like a strong couple in this time where sex feels challenging.'*

Can you see how the merged or compromise answer to the ideal world question factors in both of their needs? Ben has asked for regular sex, and Jo has asked for it to take a back seat. Although their answers sound all about frequency, I can tell you frequency here is a red herring. What they are really saying is that they want more of *something* (connection for Ben) or less of *something* (pressure for Jo). Making some time for sexual connection, whatever that is for them (and it doesn't have to be a traditional idea of sex) is the key to what they really want. To feel strong as a couple, and for sex to not be a source of discontentment. This is a course they can set for now, until the direction of the tide or the wind changes again.

In my clinic I have to invite couples to trust me on this, that what they think they want may in fact be a symptom of the 'circular problem', not what their relationship *actually* needs. For example, I've met many people like Ben, who feel that their issues with sex as a couple can only be solved if the other person just starts wanting sex much more than they do now. I've also met many people like Jo, who are so sick of feeling pressure around sex that they feel they could never have sex again and be quite happy. Both of these positions are ones that the individual people have been recruited into by the circular problem intensifying, not necessarily by what they actually want or need. Something I see happening over and over again with couples as we make small changes, and sex starts to be less of an issue, is that the person in Ben's position starts to notice frequency is less important than they once thought, and the person in Jo's position starts to notice that, actually, they do have their own desire and interest in sex, but it had just been stifled by pressure.

TOP TIP: Frequency is almost always a red herring

What I mean by this is that the desire for frequency is often not about missing the regularity of sex, but missing the benefits we get from it. As you'll learn later on, our motivations for sex are much more likely to be about meeting psychological needs, such as wanting to feel desired, special, wanted, connected, like a good couple, close, alive. Try to rewrite your statement to reflect this. For example, instead of '*In our ideal sex life we'd be having sex X number of times per week/month/year*', you might write: '*In our ideal sex life, initiation would be easy for each of us, and we would flirt/kiss more and feel sexually connected and like having sex more often. This would leave us both feeling that the other desires us and in touch with our sexuality.*'

Take the time now to rewrite that ideal sex life question, incorporating what both of you need, if you haven't already. This will be important later when we discuss small changes that will make a big difference.

Our ideal sex life would be _____

TOP TIP: Avoid the familiar

Generally, conversations which are 'known and familiar', such as the same old argument again and again, aren't useful and can do more harm than good. If you notice that you are having a discussion that you've had many times before, it might be worth giving each other permission to stop and say: *'We've been here before, haven't we? Shall we not go there? Why don't we both calm down and come back to this later and try to find another way to discuss it?'* This can stop you both in your tracks and prevent you from going down a rabbit hole of animosity or conflict.

Help! One of us cares about sex, but the other doesn't!

This is a very common experience and it's often not as straightfor-ward as it looks initially. It can often be a statement about people's differing experiences of desire at that point in their lives. And it might well be the case that one of you could take or leave sex at the moment quite happily, but is a relationship without sex in the long term actu-ally what you want? What would be the impact of this? Are there benefits of having sex that you desire, if not the sex itself? Perhaps you have no desire for sex just now, but you still wish to have a sex life together, as you feel it would be good for each of you, or good for the relationship. A lack of feeling desire throughout the day, week or month is not the same as not wanting to feel desire or not wanting a sex life. It is common to feel that it is partly due to how we've been socialized to think about desire as society, in essence as something that we should feel out of the blue for our partner. As you will learn in Chapter 3 (if you don't know this already), desire often doesn't function like this in long-term relationships.

There are plenty of people whose sexual orientation is such that they don't wish to be sexual with another person (asexuality), and so would happily have a relationship without sex (or with very little sex) without this causing distress for them or feeling that anything is missing. This is perfectly fine as long as it is something that works for you both. It's also the case that our physical attraction to a person we hoped to always maintain a physical attraction to can wane, and this can (obviously) make having sex with them extremely difficult. For some people, having children temporarily masks a lack of attraction, as it can be easier to explain a lack of sex as about convenience or tiredness, rather than have a more challenging conversation about a loss of attraction and what this means for the relationship. Physical attraction or sexuality are not aspects of ourselves that we can easily change on demand, even if we wanted to, and a lack of attraction or a clash of sexual orientations can obviously make it hard to fix a troubled sex life.

If you find yourselves in either of these positions, your conversations might look quite different to the conversations in the rest of this book, but they are still important to have. Have you always felt like this about being able to take or leave sex with others, but perhaps have only just allowed yourself to lean into it? What would it mean for the two of you if physical attraction never came back? How long would you wait to see? Is having mutual sexual attraction in your relationship a dealbreaker for you, or not? Although talking about this can feel terrifying, opening up options, such as separating amicably but co-parenting, staying together and co-parenting without sex, or staying together, co-parenting and opening up your relationship, might be a better solution than years of arguing about sex in these circumstances and the psychological impact of this on the whole family.

Help! We have totally different ideas about what we want!

More middle-ground hunting is required here. Hold in mind the purpose of this discussion of creating a merged goal that works for you both rather than insisting all your needs are met from the get-go. Often this means looking for the commonality between you and weaving back and forward between the two of you to create something that connects the two, a bit like we did with Jo and Ben. I would suggest, in the true spirit of battening down the hatches and just getting through each phase as best you can, that a best-fit-is-better-than-nothing rule applies here. If you find a temporary fix that isn't perfect but partially meets both your needs for a time, this can be a much easier position from which to improve things further, later down the line. It gets easier and easier to get on the same page with sex as you improve things more generally, and you can set a new goal in six months, or whenever. You don't have to build Rome in a day.

Help! We can't do this without arguing!

If this is you, put this conversation on hold for now, and read Chapter 7 on communication. It may be that you need to do a little work here first before you can have this discussion. This may be as sex has become a subject that's too fraught, or as really listening to each other has become too difficult. Come back to this task when you feel you've had some time to work on communication more generally. Don't worry that you haven't been able to do it yet, as you've still hopefully learned something that you didn't know before – that sex might need to be *understood more* first, and *done more* second.

Why does sex matter anyway?

So why is sex important to us, our partners or our relationship and why does it matter if we don't have it? Well, we've already outlined what we know from sex and relationship science about how staying connected sexually is good for your relationship satisfaction, psychological wellbeing and relationship climate. It also makes seeking sex with someone outside the relationship on the grounds of dissatisfaction (for those who are monogamous) less likely. Feeling sexually satisfied doesn't just help us with our own mood and wellbeing, but can act a bit like 'relationship savings', which we can dip in to when needed, perhaps when we're vulnerable to feeling a bit ratty with each other. It's there to draw on when times are tough.

It's not hard to deduce why this gets more important when you have kids, as the stress of being a parent can take its toll on even the best of relationships. Research tells us that new parents have steeper declines in relationship satisfaction compared to nonparents over the same relationship period,[10] meaning that having kids can create challenges in your relationship that you wouldn't have faced without kids. Doing what we can to buffer against this by topping our relationships up with sexual satisfaction can really be make or break for some relationships.

So good sex is protective for our relationships, but why does it matter to us personally? Why do we bother? Well, partly the answer to this is linked with the reasons we have sex in the first place. Ideas in the media will have you believe that sexual activity is a behaviour that naturally follows feeling horny, but actually that is not necessarily the case for many of us. Yes, sometimes we are motivated to be sexual as we notice feeling turned on in our bodies or minds, and feeling like engaging in the act of sex as we are feeling 'horny' in this way is referred to in sex science as a 'sexual motivation'. Where it gets interesting is that it's often not sexual motivations, such as horniness, that prompt us to seek out and engage in the behaviour of 'sex'; it's something else instead.

For many of us in a long-term relationship, this horniness is not there in the beginning when we first have a thought to have sex – it grows over time and as we start to engage in physical intimacy with someone else. There's another need being met at the beginning that it's important we are paying attention to. We call these 'non-sexual motivations', and they are often what trigger us into being sexual with someone else. They include being motivated to engage in the behaviour of sex to gain other things we need for ourselves and our relationships, such as connection, expressions of love or fun.

It's both the sexual and non-sexual motivations, meeting psychological needs for us that, without sex, we or our partners feel we are missing out on that cause us distress. Let's explore this in a bit more detail, as it will be crucial to the success of your sex life moving forward.

In 2007, sex researchers Cindy Meston and David Buss conducted a large-scale piece of research looking at the reasons people engaged in sex. Before this, there had been a few studies citing seven to eight reasons, things like *as I felt horny* or *to relieve sexual tension* or *to be emotionally close'.*[11] Meston and Buss found there was much more to it than this. Two hundred and thirty-seven reasons, in fact, linked with other aspects of our psychological or relational functioning, whether we were referring to casual, regular or outside the relationship partners.

Here's about 10 per cent of them, for you to get a sense of how varied they are.

for pleasure/to meet a physical need

to show desire

to distract myself   to have excitement

to experiment

to express love   **to feel close**

to feel normal

to feel attractive   to make up

to feel confident   I was drunk

to relieve boredom

To have fun

to relieve stress

because the other person wanted to

to feel better

to connect

as it had been a while

Because we feel we should   **to get pregnant**

in exchange for something else

to express my identity

to feel wanted   To show I fancy my partner   To help keep the relationship

Notice how different they are? Some relate to pleasure, some relate to protecting the relationship, some relate to expressing or feeling attractive, some are about placating and some are about obligation, boredom, distraction or similar. Take a minute to consider how motivations to be sexual are represented in films or on TV, one of our primary sources of learning about sex. 'Good' sex or desire is almost always portrayed as the ideal of unbridled sexual passion – the 'out of the blue' horniness I mentioned earlier. What I'd like you to take away from this is that 'sexual motivation' – feeling horny, basically – is often not the driver of sexual activity for many people. And although it may be a key driver at the start of the relationship, when lust is high, it is actually not very realistic as a common motivator in long-term relationships.

What's interesting here, and what I want to make clear to you, is that depending on your key drivers, concerns about what is happening in your sex life post kids might not necessarily be linked with how much sex you are having, but rather that you, and/or your partner, are losing the opportunity to meet these psychological or relational needs in that particular way.

Think back to the three questions I asked you earlier. I asked you what the effect on you personally would be if you were able to have the sex life that you want at the moment. Your answer to this provides the clues to what sex brings for each of you and the relationship, and what you feel you and your relationship might be missing when sex isn't going so well.

Let's return to Jo and Ben to understand this further. To the second question, *'What would be the impact on you personally?'*, Ben answered: *'I would feel attractive and desired.'* This is what Ben is missing at the moment. He has lost the opportunity to be seen in Jo's eyes as attractive, and as an object of desire, and this matters to him. Feeling attractive and desired matters to many of us. It's the reason we flirt with people, the reason we take care over our appearance, the thing that can put a spring in our step. In a monogamous long-term relationship, it can be challenging to continue to experience this from a partner, as a familiar object (a long-term partner) is less likely to be coded by their brain as a novel or exciting stimulus. We also have many overlapping relationships/roles and our role to each other as sexual partners can be diluted by less sexual roles, such as best friends or housemates (and now parents). Lastly, it can be easy for us to be distracted from our partner's needs or prioritizing the relationship when we feel it will always be there without fail (one of the dangerous myths of monogamy), and we can simply be blinded from seeing that nurturing it is needed.

Understanding the impact of sex on each of us personally, as well as on our partners and our relationships, can be the first step in getting to the bottom of what's missing for us and our partners if we're not having the greatest sexual connection at the moment. But even more importantly, it can also give us some great clues around how we can address these needs in other ways – either while we work on sex, instead of it or perhaps as well as it.

I wanted to say a bit about men here for those of you that are men, and/or those of you in relationships with them. Due to societal discourses about men being obsessed with sex, it can be easy for men's feelings about wanting sex to be trivialized as them having 'sex on the brain' or it being a 'biological need'. This does men's desires a disservice, as it implies that their desire for sex isn't linked to any of these non-sexual motivations, such as relationship satisfaction, security, intimacy, self-esteem or psychological wellbeing, which of course it may be. Yes, men often have higher levels of spontaneous desire, and therefore sexual motivations, partly due to the effect of androgens like testosterone, but partly to do with having the reward of their physical needs more often being met by sex in a patriarchal society (see 'orgasm gap' in Chapter 8). In my experience, however, when sex isn't going well, it's not the physical need men feel they are losing out on. It's usually that they feel unwanted, less connected, or inhibited about expressing affection themselves sexually.

Not only is it equally common for men to be the partner expressing lower desire in long-term relationships,[12] but we know that men express the same motivations for feeling desired and emotional connection as women do.[13] Our desire and our motivations across gender/sex are often more similar than they are different, and more similar than the tropes that 'men are from Mars' etc have led us to believe. One study found 88 per cent of men interviewed reported wanting to feel desired more than they currently do in their partnerships with women, and they specified ways they would like to feel that desire across five key themes. These were: through verbal expressions of desire, flirting, romantic non-sexual touch, their partners initiating sex, by being an enthusiastic participant in sex.[14] Interestingly, many of the respondents were clear that this flirting, sexual touch and expression of desire didn't actually have to lead to sex. Ben's need to seek connection in this way is not at all unusual. Research into attachment styles also tells us that some people use sex as a way to feel closer to their partner and get reassurance about their partner's feelings for them.[15] We also know that, in long-term relationships, sex can be used as a means to create and experience intimacy.[16]

What if I only want to do it to keep them happy?

Research has looked at the difference between the experience of sex for people who were motivated to have sex for a positive outcome, such as giving or receiving pleasure to a partner or feeling close (termed 'approach' reasons), compared to those who were motivated to avoid negative outcomes, such as conflict, a partner's disappointment, or to prevent a partner leaving (termed 'avoidance' goals).[17] The results were fascinating. It turns out that having sex for avoidance reasons, such as to avoid a row, is more likely to result in

28

a decline in sexual satisfaction over time. On the other hand, having sex for approach reasons (i.e. to get something positive, not to avoid something negative) is associated with increased sexual satisfaction as well as the person holding a more positive view of sex. What's useful to know from a desire perspective is that not only is having sex for (non-sexual) approach reasons associated with better sex, but it has also been shown to buffer against sexual desire dropping over time.[18] Having sex to gain something positive for your partner, yourself or the relationship, therefore, is generally good for your sex life.

In my work I often meet couples who are having sex as one person wants to (and is annoyed if they don't 'get it') and the other person is feeling little desire to but is having sex to 'keep the peace'. This kind of pattern is likely to further reduce desire over time for the person going along with it. Further still, this same crucial research into the impact of approach or avoidance goals on a partner has found that, despite people often having this type of avoidance sex to please a partner, it doesn't actually have this result, as sexual partners of people having sex for avoidance goals also report less satisfaction after this type of sex. What this means is that while it might feel like it's helping to have sex to avoid a row, it is not actually helping anyone. Instead, it's possibly making the situation worse over time for both of you.

A crucial boundary for all relationships, but especially relevant for parents, is that you won't always be able to, or feel inclined to meet these needs in each other at the exact moment the other person craves them, and you should never be expected to. But understanding what is behind another person's needs, and reflecting on whether there's anything you can do to meet that outside of sex can be an incredible relationship tool at your disposal.

Notice that Ben has equated 'having sex' with 'feeling desired', and as they are having much less sex, he is missing feeling desired, which then impacts on his psychological wellbeing and relationship satisfaction. There are a number of mental leaps here that Ben has made (and we all make these kinds of leaps/associations at times), which require a bit of examination.

It makes sense to me that Ben equates Jo wanting to have sex with him as a marker of her desire or attraction to him, as that's often how sex is sold in society. But it's a very crude and drastic measure of attraction of desire, isn't it? We don't always express attraction or desire this way, and there are plenty of more subtle or nuanced ways we express attraction and desire.

The first question I asked Ben and Jo was about how expressing attraction or desire happened in their relationship in *other ways*, apart from sex. They were able to recount a whole host of ways they do this for each other, and reflected that, since kids came along, they were doing this less. Many of Ben's stories described surprise gestures of attraction from Jo. For example, he described one occasion on their way to a family gathering where, as they got in the lift just the two of them, Jo grabbed him as the lift door shut, pushed him up against the wall and kissed him passionately, her hands all over him for just five seconds until the door opened. He described another occasion when they were at an NCT get together before Rohan was born, when his phone buzzed with a text when he was talking to some new friends, some other parents-to-be. He reached in to his pocket to get it, and noticed Jo looking at him from a break in conversation she was having with another group. *'You are by far the hottest man here'* the text said, signed off with a flame emoji.

Ben described feeling on top of the world in these moments. This conversation opened up some nuance about the importance of feeling attractive or desired. We established that, although they both needed to feel this way, Jo felt desired by Ben pretty much all the time, mainly as Ben expressed it often, and also as it wasn't so much a source of vulnerability for her. We also established that, for Ben, when he felt desired by Jo it put him on cloud nine and made their relationship feel indestructible. This, to him, was connected on a deeper level, to his insecurities about relationships ending based on his early life experience. For better or for worse, he had coded attraction and desire as crucial signs that 'everything is okay'. He hadn't noticed this before we discussed it at length. Lastly, we noticed that signs of attraction and desire from Jo to Ben were around less than they had ever been since the baby had come along. This made sense for two reasons. Firstly, they have a baby, and this has disrupted the time and focus they have for each other, particularly for Jo, who is the one up in the nights due to breastfeeding. Secondly, since sex has become an issue, Jo is wanting to avoid giving Ben any hint that she might want sex, to avoid a row, and avoid his disappointment. As a result, she has stopped making comments about how he looks, flirting or kissing him other than a peck on the cheek. I asked Ben, '*What would be the effect on your sex life if you had no more sex than you were having now, but you got to feel those moments like you felt in the lift, or the NCT meet up?*' Ben reflected that although he hadn't considered it before, it wasn't the sex that he was missing, but that feeling of being wanted or seen by Jo exactly how he wanted to be, albeit briefly, and for this to reassure him about the relationship. In actual fact, he realised that that kiss in the lift had felt more erotic and reassuring to him than any of the sex they had had in the last year.

Jo had some thinking to do here. On the one hand, she felt huge relief that the possibilities for change that were starting to emerge through our conversations weren't about having more sex. She also understood Ben in a way she hadn't before and had to admit she had seen his need for sex as irritating, selfish, and about a physical need, not a psychological one. Reframing his feeling in this way reduced much of her annoyance and, as a result, removed some of the barriers to her feeling able to be sexual with him.

She described that she could now see a solution that might help them meet their overall couple goal for their sex life for the short term. If you remember, their goal was 'To find a way to feel sexually connected that doesn't rely solely on frequency, so that we can feel like a strong couple in this time where sex feels challenging'. In many ways it seemed simple, Jo mused. It just required an injection of noticing Ben and taking a moment to tell him, or show him. But she was also drained of energy, busy and preoccupied, and didn't know if she had the energy or inclination to do this for him along with everything else she had to do. We reflected on this dilemma together, the three of us, and wondered what the effect would be on each of them separately, and on the relationship, if sex became a non-issue at this moment in time, and it was big.

Here was one solution for us to experiment with, which we all agreed could have big effects, but there was one final question: how could we create the mental headspace for Jo to feel present in her thoughts about Ben, at a time when she was already stretched? What would it take for her to be in a psychological place to be able to do this? For Jo, this was easy to answer. 'Don't expect me to flirt when I've had no sleep or have got baby sick on my clothes', 'Don't expect too much from me – we're different now to the people we were before kids', 'Don't expect it to lead anywhere – if I do anything like this, it is NOT a come on!' and 'The more I feel supported by you, the more headspace

I have. Do more to take the pressure off me and I might be more inclined or able to be present for us'.

They decided to experiment with forgetting about sex and prioritizing the moment of expressing attraction or desire, which is fleeting but used to be part of their relationship more. When I saw them again a month later, they had managed to find two moments for this. One was a passionate kiss goodbye in the car when Ben was off on a weekend work trip, akin to the early days of them being together. The other was a moment of appreciation when Ben got out of the shower, when Jo looked at him drying off and pointed out that he 'still had it', and beckoned him over to kiss his slightly damp stomach and seductively run her fingers along the waistband of his boxer shorts, looking him square in the eye. They had had no sex, but the situation between them had dramatically improved. Ben felt great about their relationship, and as a result had stopped worrying about sex and bringing it up. Jo felt less pressure, as Ben was bringing it up less, plus she realized that she actually enjoyed these moments, and if she felt free to do them without Ben expecting them to go anywhere, she actually found them nourishing for their relationship as well. She described how these moments helped her feel they were still a strong couple, and marked them out as being more than parents, at a time when they were all consumed by being parents.

I call these types of interactions 'sexual currency'.[19] This reference has nothing to do with money, but currency as in the *sexual charge* between you. Sexual currency has a powerful impact on sexual satisfaction and desire. I'll be returning to it in Chapter 3, to demonstrate how you can use it to your advantage in your sex life as a parent.

TASK: Understanding your sexual motivations and the needs they meet

Spend some time reflecting on the last year, the last five years and perhaps previous relationships, if you can remember. Separately, write a list of some of your reasons for having sex, or ones you think may have influenced you, even if you can't remember.

Nothing is off limits and nothing is a 'bad reason'. It's about understanding yourself and what needs sex meets for you. It's okay if these are sexual motivations, such as *'I felt turned on in my body'*, or non-sexual motivations, such as *'I wanted to feel close/ alive/connected'*, *'I wanted to express love'*, *'I wanted to feel excitement'*. If you're struggling, think about when sex isn't happening – what is it that you feel you are missing out on?

If you're really struggling, consider what you feel the impact on your relationship might be if you never have sex again. Perhaps investing in the relationship is your motivation to be sexual, rather than a desire to have sex for yourself? This is really okay, and a common reason people give for wanting a sex life. You might write this as *'I want sex to nourish our relationship and keep us close'*.

Once you've done your lists, I want you to set some time to discuss this together, perhaps over dinner, or once the kids are asleep and there are no distractions, and take turns sharing your lists. Here are some pointers for this discussion to ensure it goes well.

1) Do not judge each other's motivations

It's common at this stage in your life/relationship to have something like *'Because I felt that I should'* or *'To make my partner happy*' as a reason. This is okay. The concept of 'sexually giving' in this way to protect the relationship or acquire something positive for the relationship or your partner has been shown to be a helpful quality in long-term sexual satisfaction[20] (there is more about this in Chapter 8). Please take note later, though, when we discuss desire in more detail, as to whether your desire is triggered once you start being sexual together. If it is, great. This is responsive desire working really well as a result of a non-sexual motivation. If it's not, and you feel disconnected during sex, or don't get into a sexual headspace at all, having sex when you're not feeling into it for someone else's benefit will actually diminish your desire over time.

2) Try to understand the motivation

Open-ended questions, such as 'tell me a bit more about that' or 'describe that to me', 'what does it feel like?' or 'how do you feel about us when you get that?' can really help you understand each other more.

3) All motivations are equal

Something I notice in my work is that it can be challenging for a partner to accept non-sexual motivations, such as the need to feel close, as valid and acceptable if they themselves experience higher levels of spontaneous desire and experience sexual motivations, such as feeling turned on, more frequently. The reason for this is that their experience of desire is that it requires little effort or nurturing much of the time. This way of experiencing desire aligns with how desire is portrayed in the media, and so it's easy for this to seem like the 'right' way to experience it. Because of this, partners will need to learn that this being 'normal desire' is not backed up by science. They will need to appreciate that, actually, never experiencing desire out of the blue, and having motivations to be sexual that are driven by other non-sexual reasons *is* how desire works for a lot of people in long-term relationships (particularly, but by no means exclusively, women). You and your partner will need to really understand this for this exercise to be useful and feel valid. You will also need to understand this information to be able to navigate a good sex life over time. We'll talk more about desire in Chapter 3, but if you want to learn more, you might want to read my book, *Mind The Gap: The Truth About Desire and How to Futureproof Your Sex Life* (Headline Home, 2020), which is all about the science of desire in long-term relationships.

The relationships in focus in these years, the ones that take the most from us, cause us the most stress and bring the most joy can often be those with our kids. This is natural and normal. When we are in the eye of the storm of new parenthood, it can be hard to imagine the future, and a time when our kids need us less. We are so absorbed by surviving the weather battering down on us that it can be easy, but dangerous, to lose track of our trajectory and ultimate ideal destination. It can be hard to imagine a time when we might start to separate ourselves slightly from the intense closeness we have with our little people and crave adult connection more. It can be hard to imagine (if we have hopes to stay with our partners long term) how our relationship with our partners may come into focus more, and become the primary relationship in focus once again. For these reasons, we may not consider the importance of maintaining our connection sexually, at a time when we feel pushed to our limits in other ways. It can feel like the easiest ball to drop when we are juggling so much. What I'd like you to take away from this chapter is that sex matters for relationship satisfaction, and relationship satisfaction matters now, perhaps more than ever. I'd like you to think of your sexual connection as a glue that you have available to you to protect the boat from the damage that the storm of new parenthood can cause, and help you survive it unscathed. I'd also like to sow the seed that being sexually satisfied is more in reach than you might have felt it to be. Later on we'll get into how you can make some small practical changes that make a big difference, like Ben and Jo did, but, until then, let's understand how and why the journey that you've been on up until this point matters.

2

Chart your position

What trajectory is your sex life on?

S exual satisfaction often matters in the story of our lives. It matters to people, it matters to relationships, and because of its impact on relationship satisfaction, it matters to parenthood. But it's also true that it is easy to lose our way with our sex lives, and find ourselves on a course we didn't plot, and a trajectory that we didn't choose. Part of the reason for this is that we've been sold an idea that it will take care of itself without effort. Love someone? Well then, you should be having good sex without really needing to talk about it too much. Fancy them? Well then, time for sex should be easy to find – why aren't you?

These things aren't true, of course. Loving your partner and having a good relationship don't automatically lead to good sex or sexual satisfaction, as you heard in Chapter 1. Part of the reason for this is that the foundations needed to build a sex life like this are missing for most of us. Being able to talk about sex is the obvious starting point. Without it, it can be hard to navigate any kind of difference between us and a partner in a relationship that feels important without defensiveness or conflict. Being able to talk, and finding a way forward that feels acceptable to both people sensitively, can take skill. This becomes especially hard with a topic like sex, which is often associated with shame, embarrassment, or not having had much practise (or never having been given permission to) at saying the words out loud or feeling entitled to ask for what you need. Sex, and navigating sexual differences, can feel more challenging compared to other conversations we might have to settle differences, such as attitudes to money. It doesn't have to be, but for many people it's a conversation too far, too difficult or just too exposing. It can often feel easier to just not do it. But try to imagine trying to achieve something as a team without any form of conversation about it in any other area of your life. It's close to impossible.

We've also been sold an idea that humans are monogamous and so we expect that our sexual relationships won't particularly suffer with the passing of time. We *can* be monogamous (and many of us can be successful at it), but it isn't 'natural' for humans in a way that makes it easy for us to succeed at it without any effort. The longer we are with someone, the more at risk our sexual satisfaction can be (without any thought given to nurturing or intentional action). The passing of time *is* a threat to sexual satisfaction, even without having children (but much more dangerous with it, which we'll come on to). Without knowing and acknowledging this, we are behind the curve.

This expectation that long-term monogamy is the norm, and that love is all you need, along with the misplaced idea that the desire for the person you love should be ever present and occur frequently out of the blue creates problems for many of us. Instead of working on our sex life by considering it, as we do our health by considering our diet/exercise and acting accordingly to set ourselves on a trajectory of wellness, we ignore it and hope for the best. The trajectory is set, and the ultimate destination we end up in may be years or decades away, but how often do we stop to consider whether this destination is actually where we want to end up?

If we want sex to be as satisfying as it can be, it's important to pay attention to how the relationship is helping, hindering or stifling our sexual connection. Often in magazines, or in advice columns, the state of the relationship is referenced in connection with crucial dynamics, such as conflict, contentment, communication and respect, and these are all very important and must be examined. But it's easy to muddle this with an assumption that, if the relationship is generally 'good', then sex and desire should work okay, and this isn't necessarily so. To truly nurture desire within a relationship context, we must consider how facilitative or constraining our relationship culture allows our sexual expression to be, how intimacy or distance helps or hinders our desire, how our motivations for sex and the complex and intertwining meanings we make of sex separately and together might be responsible for creating sexual problems, or promoting sexual satisfaction. In this book I'll be referencing some of the key aspects of co-parenting relationship dynamics too, which may also help or hinder sexual satisfaction.

When I meet with couples who consult me around their sex life I can often see that future trajectory in the details they tell me about how their sex life looks currently. I use my clinical experience in this field, professional training as a clinical psychologist, sexologist and relationship therapist, plus what sex research tells us about the factors that help keep a sex life good over time, to form a sort of mental checklist of where the issues are. Spotting these provides important indications of where the opportunities for change will also be. A sort of sex-life barometer, if you like. Before technology advanced to its current form, sailors used barometers as predictors of the weather ahead, and in many ways this is what I'm doing. The question I'm asking myself (and encouraging you to do in this chapter) is 'what's ahead if they (we) continue on this trajectory?'

*

As a rule, I don't rush in to supporting clients to make changes straight away. It's essential that we have a few sessions for us all to understand the issues in detail from all angles, and for me to share with them my ideas of where I feel they may be stuck, how that connects to what we know about sexual function and happiness, and where, if we make changes, the problematic status quo that they are consulting me for may no longer be able to survive. We also look at the potential impact of *not* making changes (essentially, the destination of the current trajectory). This is important, as we're all having an impact on our sex lives, all of the time, even if we are not doing anything. The absence of nurturing is not neutral, it will also take its toll over the years by setting us on a certain course.

Essentially, my clients and I are looking to work as a team to undermine the problem* they have come to see me about. Working as a team is key. It's not a blame game, or about point scoring, or convincing me which of them is right (though these can be tempting patterns for people to fall into in therapy). Instead, it's genuine team work, focusing on the patterns that they have gotten stuck in, how these patterns recruit them both into different roles, and how the roles they are both recruited to play keep the problem going without either of them wanting this to be the case. We look at how these roles may have been easy for them to be recruited into, due to their own individual experiences, psychological make-up or experiences of gender. It's about having a *different* conversation than they have had before.

Many of the relationship culture signs, or ways of being together, I'm looking out for are surface-level indicators that signify a trajectory

---

* 'Undermining the problem' is a concept with its roots in systemic therapy, which suggests that if you address the ways in which the problem is sustained, for example what each person is inadvertently doing to maintain it, you can create a situation where the problem cannot continue to exist.

we might want to disrupt. They are indications that something may be slightly amiss, a bit like when your car shows you an orange light on the dashboard. The light isn't an indication you're going to experience a problem right now, but it's telling you that, without action, trouble might be ahead. These signs must be taken in context, in that for some people and in some circumstances they may be perfectly fine, but for the majority, and when combined with other information, they may tell us something useful. They are an opportunity to spot potential changes, which provide a way of shifting the culture in the sexual relationship to where it needs to be. A way to take stock of our course and adjust as needed.

In this chapter, I'm going to share some of these sex-life barometer indicators, so that you can see how they relate to your own sex life. I'm going to also suggest, as I do with my clients, that you don't rush to action in addressing any of these points. The chapters that follow will be akin to the therapy sessions we might need to really understand the role that each of these things play before we address them. It's also not helpful to be told what to do about your own sex life by someone outside of it if you're not completely sure about why you're being asked to do something, or don't have the knowledge to understand why or how it might help. In my experience that never goes well.

What I will ask of you, if you can, is to complete the sex-life barometer questions, and try to do so as a team – 'the relationship', not as opposing teams of 'me' and 'you'. Try to remember that this is about having a *different* conversation about sex, not the usual ones. After all, isn't that why you picked up this book?

The questions in the sex-life barometer are not exhaustive, and there's more I'll be sharing with you, and alerting you to as we go along. It is a good starting point, however, for some of the most common culprits in maintaining a good sex life, and each of these contributes to a trajectory, one for which you may not necessarily have signed up. You might feel you want to use this book to change course, and changing course does not have to take much time or effort. A small change of bearing can lead to an entirely different destination, over time. We'll be revisiting these ideas later on, and, if you wish, you can also use this barometer again in the future as a way of comparing the changes you've made to your sex life since reading this book.

TASK: Your sex life barometer

Work together and discuss how to answer the questions below. You might have slightly different ideas on how things are, but hopefully you can settle on an answer you both agree on. Please keep your answers to this somewhere – you'll need them later for Chapter 8.

Before you start, it's important to say that this isn't an exercise in blame or criticism. I want you to objectively try to notice the status quo, without getting into why or whose fault it was, as things will be moving from here anyway.

If it's too difficult just now to do this together without conflict, you can complete this separately and perhaps revisit looking at it together after you've read Chapter 7 on communication. Don't worry about it being difficult to talk about this. As I said earlier, sex is an area in which we often don't have the foundations for talking about constructively, and shame, embarrassment and defensiveness can get in the way very easily. If talking is diffi-cult, congratulations!: you've already identified an area that, if you work on it together, will have huge implications for sexual satisfaction. You'll learn more about how and why later on.

Do you still passionately kiss at times other than when you're having some kind of sex?

A Every chance we get!

B Often

C Hardly ever

D It's extinct!

Does one of you regularly have more pleasure than the other when you have sex?

A No, it's equal

B Sometimes, but it's fine

C More often than not

D Yes, it's totally one-sided

How easy is it to talk about sex together? For example, to ask for what you'd like?

A Really easy

B Mostly easy

C Mostly awkward

D Really hard

Does sex always end in penetrative sex?

A No, we often mix it up

B Some of the time

C More often than not

D Every time, yes

Does one of you feel the responsibility for most of the household tasks/childcare?

A   Shared completely equally

B   One of us does more than our fair share of visible and invisible* household labour, but it's negotiated fairly in relation to our working hours

C   One of us does more than our fair share of the visible and invisible household labour and it doesn't feel negotiated fairly/ feels unequal

Does sex often follow a predictable pattern (e.g. who does what, in what order)

A   Sex is different every time

B   Mostly does

C   Mostly doesn't

D   I can predict what we'll end up doing before we've done it, every time

Do you plan any time in your week/month to nurture your sex life or be physically intimate?

A   Yes, we try and make time for it

B   Yes, but not as much as we'd like

C   We do, but somehow we don't seem to make it happen

D   No, we just hope it will happen

---

* 'Invisible' work for the household includes remembering birthdays, replying to school/ nursery Whatsapp chats etc.

How connected do you feel as sexual partners outside of sex (e.g. flirting, sexts, suggestion, compliments about your appearance)

A Very connected, it defines us
B We have periods like this, then long stretches of not being like this
C Not at all, we feel like flatmates

Do you make time for each other to really connect or to have fun together away from the kids?

A As much as we can, circumstances permitting
B We don't prioritise us, really
C We have good intentions, but it just doesn't happen
D What is 'time' away from the kids??!

If you scored mostly As, your sexual relationship currently includes many of the aspects we know predict a great sex life and will help you maintain sexual satisfaction over the long term. You prioritise your sex life and nurture it through conversation, making time to connect, seeing sex as more than penetration, and making sure sex is working for both of you. Keeping on this track has all the hallmarks of a sex life that can withstand the impact of having children. I recommend you keep doing what you're doing, but use what you learn in this book to take this further, deepening your understanding with some of the intentional check-in conversations here.

If you scored mostly Bs and Cs, perhaps you've been together a little while now and sex has fallen off the agenda a bit? Or perhaps sex has become hard to talk about and things have slid a little from where you want them to be? The destination of this trajectory, if things go unchanged, might not be the one you both would choose, and parenthood will be making things significantly harder (perhaps it would have been mostly As before kids came along?). Have a look at some of the questions you answered. I don't want you to make changes yet, but your answers will give you clues on the types of things that will make a difference. For example, if you find that every time you have sex it looks the same, it would benefit your sex life to make an effort to mix it up a bit, now more than ever. This is because we know that predictability in our sex life makes sex less enticing and rewarding. When something is less enticing and rewarding, we need really high motivation to do it. High motivation to do something with low reward is more challenging for parents, as there are other priorities (sleep, anyone?) that will have a higher reward, which will always supersede sex, at least for one of you.

If you scored mostly Ds, your sex life may be running aground. Perhaps that's why you picked up this book? Do not fear, as there's so much you can do to get things back on track, even with the extra challenge of being parents. You may have fallen into a pattern of privileging one person's pleasure, and not relating to each other sexually unless you're actually having sex, and letting kissing and the like slide off the agenda unless it's part of initiating sex or sex itself. You've probably seen the fallout of this in your sex life in terms of feeling less connected, one or both of you seeing a drop in desire, finding it hard to initiate sex, and perhaps seeing a negative impact on your relationship satisfaction. This is normal, and a real risk for parents, but it doesn't have to be this way. There is so much that can help you get back on track without having to invest lots of time into sex.

I asked you to do the sex-life barometer as I want you to consider what course your sex life is on. Perhaps there are things that you'd already let slip or fallen into habits regarding before your child(ren) came along, and this trajectory has been further set by being parents? Or could things not have been any better in your sex life and having kids has disrupted your course?

The fact is, long-term relationships themselves *can* be challenging for your sex life, especially if you don't understand how to keep sex good (and, let's be honest, *no one* ever tells us how to get this stuff right). Some of you may have read my book, *Mind the Gap: The Truth About Desire and How to Futureproof Your Sex Life* (Headline Home, 2020), and if you have, you'll know there's literally a ton of sex science that tells us how desire and good sex work, and they work very differently to how we've been socialized to expect them to. In the next chapter I'll summarize some of the key aspects of this, as this is vital information to help you navigate your sex lives as parents, as a foundational understanding of how desire works in long-term relationships is crucial to later parts of this book.

Your beliefs about sexual compatibility

How you view your relationship and your compatibility also matters. Research tells us that people who are higher in what we call 'destiny beliefs' view their relationship and sex-life success as the result of having a highly compatible partner with whom they share natural chemistry. People who are higher in 'growth beliefs' believe that relationships and sex lives are maintained through hard work and effort. Research tells us that people with 'growth' relationship beliefs find it easier to cope with challenges around sex and are more likely to try to find solutions. Those with destiny relationship beliefs are more likely to avoid talking about challenges and hope it will just get better.[1]

Although 'destiny beliefs' can make it easier for people to stay committed to relationships than 'growth beliefs', sexual dissatisfaction tends to hit those with 'destiny beliefs' harder and can affect their relationship satisfaction more significantly than those who lean towards ideas of 'growth'. It can be harder for people with 'destiny beliefs' to cope with challenges and hold on to hope that things can improve. This is extremely relevant for parents, as new parents holding 'destiny beliefs' have been shown to be associated with lower relationship satisfaction and poorer sexual wellbeing.[2] There is a risk that those with 'destiny beliefs' will see this as a sign that the relationship is doomed and feel less hopeful about making changes.

How do *you* view relationships? You may, of course, find yourself with someone with a very different set of relationship beliefs to you. For example, they are team 'destiny' and you're team 'growth'. Perhaps you can see a way forward with talking and effort and they don't want to talk about it?

I notice these differences in the couples that I work with, and your perspectives here are worth noticing and making explicit, so that you can find a way around it. What this means is challenging your perception that sexual problems are a sign of incompatibility and instead moving to an understanding that sex lives face challenges, sex lives can be improved, and that this period of your life is one most ripe for challenges. This can itself increase sexual satisfaction and relationship satisfaction, even before you start to make any other changes to your sex life. Moving to this position will also allow you to consider any other small changes you find in this book that can help you grow from where you are now to where you want to be.

TASK: Are you 'team growth' or 'team destiny'?

Make time to talk about your perspectives on relationships and sex. Here are some questions to help your thinking:

Do you think good relationships or sex lives are built on chemistry or effort?

What do you think of the idea of 'soul mates'?

Do you think it's acceptable if a relationship has something to be worked on? Or is it a sign it's not right?

Does it worry you when things aren't going so well (like with sex), as it might mean we're not compatible?

Starting here will allow you to spot the differences between your perspectives before you start to move forward with any other changes suggested in this book. The aim of this discussion isn't to change each other's perspective, however, just to understand where each other is coming from, and why you might feel differently about the status quo as well as your confidence about the potential impact of any changes you make. Notice if one or both of you identity most with team 'destiny'. If so, you may need to work harder on your optimism when things aren't going to plan. If one of you is team 'destiny' and the other connects more to 'growth beliefs', the person who connects more to growth might find it easier to connect with the idea of tasks or making changes, and hold optimism for you both when things are hard.

TASK: What do you miss most?

As a final exercise for this chapter, I'd like you to have a conversation about what you miss about your sex life pre-kids. Again, this is not a blame conversation, so watch out for an urge to make it so and adjust what you say accordingly. My top tip here is avoid black-and-white statements that start with 'You'. This will mean avoiding phrases like *'You never . . .'* and *'You make me feel . . . '*, which will only result in hurt and defensiveness. Instead, positioning it from your own perspective, try *'I feel . . .'* or, from the perspective of the relationship, *'I miss when we used to do . . . '*.

This is an exercise in noticing the real fact of life that *things have changed* since the early days of your relationship, and noting the impact of this change on both of you. It's also an exercise in reminding you that whatever is happening now is less about you two and more about the impact of circumstance. Moving in together, long-term monogamy, having kids: these are life events that typically lower sexual satisfaction. Take a moment to reflect on what you miss about your pre-kids' life. It will give us some clues so we can consider small changes which can, in turn, make a big difference.

TASK: What do you miss about your sex life pre-kids?

Try to describe to each other:

What you enjoyed most about it

What you miss most about it

Anything you wish you'd done more of back then

How your sex life made you feel back then, about yourself, each other and the relationship

Have this conversation together before moving forward.

3

Taking stock of the journey
Your sex life before kids

I n an era where lust and passion dominate our perspective of a
good sexual connection, and are often how a 'good sex life' is represented to us on screen, a sex life where passion can last the
distance of time appears to be one of the holy grails of popular culture. It is *absolutely possible to maintain high levels of sexual satisfaction
and desire while having sex with the same person time and time again*, but
it doesn't happen by accident, just because you have chosen monogamy. It requires investment, nurturing and, for most, some effort.
Perhaps the most crucial aspect it requires is knowledge about what
desire is and how it works. This is the focus of this chapter.

Early learning

We all have our own individual relationship with sex, which is based
on our unique histories, contexts and life experiences up until this
point, and we bring these into our sex lives in long-term relationships. For example, we learn about how much power we have over
our right to bodily autonomy in childhood, by being forced to kiss a
relative goodbye, say, or to finish all the food on our plate. This kind
of learning teaches us that we should privilege social convention,
being polite and meeting other people's needs even at a cost to our

personal, physical or psychological discomfort. In a sex- and body-negative society, we may learn that sex equals shame, that sex is 'wrong' or that our role in sex is to please others, look good, perform, or to manage our inner discomfort silently. The negative impact of this on our future sex lives is sizeable, and this is why a commitment to lifelong communication about sex with the young people in our lives is so crucial. As a parent, being aware of the part you play in this at this stage of your child's life (and beyond) can have hugely beneficial consequences for them in adulthood. But, for yourself, understanding the powerful role of social learning and norms with regards to sex, pleasure, assertiveness, comfort talking about sex, and consent and how this intersects with gender (plus other contexts, such as race or age) is crucial to understanding your relationship with sex and desire in your relationships.

For the purposes of this chapter, let's look at some of the key ways this early learning influences our sex lives in monogamous long-term relationships, which are often the backdrop to our parenting setup. 'Sexual scripts' are blueprints we are socialized into by society, media and language about what sex is and what it looks like. Humans learn by absorbing societal messages, and social learning about sex indicates that we all learn about 'sexual scripts' early in our sexual development.[1] If you've ever heard the 'bases' analogy from baseball – i.e. 'getting to first base' etc – to explain what sexual acts people have done with someone else, you will have heard sexual scripts theory in action. Research tells us that people can describe to you a hierarchy of sexual acts that you can progress through, usually with penetrative sex at the top. It's really common for heterosexual couples, particularly, to fall into a 'set menu' when it comes to sex based on these scripts, and this is largely because we live in a cisheteronormative world, so the scripts we learn about are about the group perceived to be the majority. This generally looks like a starter that's a bit of a quick fumble, or perhaps oral sex, then a main course of penetrative vaginal sex. However, I often say it's better to think of sex as a buffet. You can have whatever you want in any order. It doesn't need to include the same things every time, or end with the same dish. Imagine how much more novel and exciting that would be? There are no sexual scripts for queer couples, which although a by-product of being a marginalized group in many ways is actually a blessing, as this results in much less predictable sexual encounters. If you were to adopt this idea in your own sex life, and subvert these age-old scripts, your sex life might look quite different. Sex could be an intense all-night kissing session. Sex could be oral sex only. Sex could be both of you being sexual together with no penetration and no orgasms, or entirely focused on one of you with no touch at all to the other. Sex can be whatever you want. Later on, we'll understand why introducing novelty in this way can benefit the sex lives of parents especially.

Language is also a key aspect of our social learning that can limit our sex lives. In my opinion, 'sex' is any physical or psychological act that uses your body or mind for sexual pleasure or expression. I never use the word 'foreplay', as, to me, it represents the creation of a hierarchy through language that elevates some types of sex being seen as 'better' or 'more like proper sex'. This is a problem as:

- It marks out one type of sex (penis in vagina) as superior to all others and the 'main event', even though this type of sex brings more pleasure to people with penises than people with vaginas.

- It suggests sex follows a set formula (akin to sexual scripts), but we know that predictability and lack of novelty are generally rubbish for sex for most people.

- It is not LGBTQIA+ (LGBTQIA+ not inclusive), as it suggests that much of the type of sex that LGBTQIA people (*and* non LGBTQIA people!) have is not 'real sex' if there is no penis involved, or if people enjoy sex without penetration.

The use of the word foreplay is in direct opposition to considering ways to diversify your sex life to keep it more interesting and less predictable, as, by its existence, it removes the option of sex that doesn't include penetration.

These are just a few of the ways our early leanings influence how we find ourselves behaving (and understanding) sex in long-term relationships. Let me explain how these learnings can create sexual problems when there aren't any to speak of.

Sexual relationships often begin with an initial phase of high infatuation and passion. This stage is characterized by a desire to be near each other constantly, feelings of lust, and thoughts about that person that can feel bordering on obsession. This period of early infatuation is followed by a stage of greater emotional closeness and companionate love, where distance from the person is more easily tolerated. It's important to note that, typically, people experience higher levels of desire to have sex in the early stages of a relationship. After some time, when they enter more of a companionate love phase (roughly one to two years in), their levels of desire will typically reduce.[2] We also know that, for people who choose to cohabit, living with a partner can lead to more sex in the early stages, then generally declines in frequency.[3] It's extremely common for people to blame these changes in their sex life, particularly in desire, on themselves or name it as a problem in their relationship, when, actually, it is more likely to be a natural phenomenon connected to the stage of their relationship.

There are two important things to consider about this pattern of change over time. The first is that, although a drop in desire from the first few months or year is common for many couples, it is certainly not the case that this drop in desire should lead to sexual or relationship dissatisfaction. The second is that desire declining over the course of a relationship doesn't happen for everyone, and even though it's associated with the length of the relationship, this does not mean that relationship length itself is the key factor that causes the decline. In fact, there are many other relational factors that might pick up speed over the length of a relationship, such as sexual predictability, problems in the equity/division of household labour, living together, the amount of time spent connecting with each other (too much or too little intimacy) and, of course, the impact of having children. Relationship factors such as these have greater influence on our sexual relationships than the length of time we have been together and are the more likely culprits for changes in desire.

This change feels like a problem to people, as this early passion and lust is the type of desire you see most often represented on TV and in books. Because we see this represented most often, we are more familiar with sex that emerges out of this context – we've seen it on screen a thousand times. It's what we often think of when we think of the word 'desire', and we consider this passion and lust as synonymous with *being in love*. Desire, in our minds, therefore equals passion and lust. We imagine it as a feeling that takes over you and must be acted upon. What we have very little representation of, and therefore do not learn about, is how people navigate sex later on in relationships, when love is still there, but desire typically requires more nurturing and encouragement, and where two people might be coming from very different starting points. We very rarely see representations of desire such as this, desire that perhaps isn't there to start with, but builds as we intentionally choose to nurture it.

Our levels of desire for our partners will ebb and flow over time, and at different rates from each other, leading to other differences that will need negotiation. Research tells us that differences in sexual desire within couples are so commonplace that they should be thought of as inevitable rather than possible.[4] The 'what' that people desire will change over the course of a relationship too, and it's common for couples to also have to navigate differences in the things they like sexually, and how often they do them.

What is crucial here is that having a good sex life is not about always needing to be on the same page, or wanting as much sex as your partner, but the success with which you navigate these differences together. Having a good sex life is also about sometimes needing to invest in helping each other get in the zone, and not seeing this as about a lack of love or a problem between you. Both of these become particularly relevant in parenthood, as challenges, differences and stressors relating to our sex lives can be amplified.

But how much desire should I feel?

You might find it interesting to know that 34 per cent of women and 15 per cent of men* in the UK report a lack of interest in sex, lasting three months or more in the past year, according to large-scale research data.[5] Similar findings have been reported in other Western countries. This is a third of women and almost one in five men. Other

---

* In Natsal 3 (the National Survey of Sexual Attitudes and Lifestyles – a vital resource), there was no category for non-binary identities to this data. There are a handful of studies looking at sexual wellbeing in trans and non-binary people, and some emerging differences between definitions of sexual satisfaction or wellbeing in the trans and non-binary community, which make direct comparison with large-scale data from mostly cisgendered populations problematic.

research discovered that a large proportion of women reported feeling like sex either 'never', or 'once or twice a month' in their long-term relationship,[6] telling us that not feeling like sex ever out of the blue should be considered normal in a long-term relationship, but particularly for women. If so many people are reporting a lack of interest in sex, particularly in long-term relationships, can a lack of interest in sex even be considered a 'problem'? How do we know how much interest in sex is normal?

There are several conceptual problems with how we have measured desire in research that make it hard to know for sure what is 'normal'.[7] Many of the old studies of gendered differences in desire included questions like 'how often do you think about/feel like/initiate sex?' to measure desire. What questions such as these are really measuring is what we call 'spontaneous desire' – desire that feels like it comes out of the blue. It took decades of sex science before we realized that there can be gender/sex differences in how people experience desire, and the one way we were privileging and measuring (out of the blue or 'spontaneous' desire) was more often experienced by men.[8] This made it look like men's level of desire was the benchmark and women's experience, by comparison, was lesser and, crucially, problematic. Many people (particularly women) were referred to people like me for problems with desire, as they didn't feel like sex as much as their male partners, or they didn't feel like sex at all. They believed – or were told – they had 'low sex drive' or 'lack of libido', and you can be forgiven for understanding why.

Sex researchers then realized that there's another type of desire, called 'responsive desire', which basically means desire that is triggered by something (a kiss, a sex scene on TV, someone flirting). When sex researchers started to measure *this* type of desire, by showing someone something sexual then seeing if their desire followed, the gender difference was eradicated.[9] People of all genders found that their desire emerged in a sexual context, so once they were shown something erotic and then desire was measured, desire usually followed. This problem of measuring desire by how often people feel like having sex, and our societal idea that desire that feels that it comes out of the blue is superior, explains why we often fall for the myth that men have more desire than women.* We know now that unless we are attempting to trigger desire first, we are only measuring one type of desire. My guess is that when people are reporting their lack of interest in sex, they are actually just reporting on spontaneous desire.

The problem we face is that the societal ideas about what desire is and how it works, which teach us what to expect in our relationships, have not caught up with newer scientific understandings, so people are still sat waiting for their spontaneous desire to hit them, at which point they'll act on it by initiating sex. People not feeling this desire, or not feeling it often, are still feeling like the problem (and sometimes also being seen as/named as the problem by their partner). Partners who do retain high levels of spontaneous desire in long-term relationships are left baffled by their partner's experience of never feeling like sex, but noticing that they really enjoy sex when it happens and saying 'that was so great, why don't we do it more?'. This comes up time and time again in therapy with couples, with partners saying to me: 'I just don't understand it, they really enjoy sex

* Experiences of desire are underpinned by hormones, but not exclusively defined by them. Trans men and non-binary people on testosterone and trans women and non-binary people on oestrogen often have different experiences of desire than they did before starting hormones for this reason. For example, trans men/people on testosterone may start to experience more out-of-the-blue desire. Trans women/people on oestrogen may start to notice their desire needs more nurturing, rather than being so out of the blue. This isn't the case for everybody as psychological processes, such as learning about sex, memories about sex, our relationship contexts and our brains, can also inhibit desire, superseding the impact of hormones.

when we have it, but they never ever want to do it. How is that possible?' Responsive desire is how.

I often explain to people it's a bit like going to the gym. There are some people who want to work out, as it fits their motivations (to be healthy), but they often find themselves not actually feeling like exercising the moment they had planned to go. They have to set the context (put on their gym gear, get their exercise playlist on, travel to the gym), and sometimes that helps get them in the zone. Other times they don't feel like it until they start exercising, and their enjoyment and desire to do it kicks in while they are doing it. The rewards for exercising are large, and they feel good, not just because exercise is enjoyable in its own right (endorphins, sense of accomplishment etc), but also as it met their initial motivations (a commitment to their health). On the way home from the gym, they smile to themselves about the fact that they almost didn't go as they bask in the satisfaction. This example neatly maps onto a similar experience for someone with non-sexual motivations to be sexual (for example, to feel close, express love, please a partner or feel secure in the relationship), who more often experiences responsive desire. Their desire comes later, once they have decided to invest. In contrast, when people experience spontaneous desire, they are motivated by wanting to exercise from the get-go. They can't wait to get on that step machine. They don't have to get in the zone, as they are already there.

A perception of a change in how desire is experienced over time is further amplified by the fact that, at the start of the relationship, people generally did have the experience of desire that felt more spontaneous, and, to them, the comparison of how they now experience desire feels unfavourable and problematic. People have also not been taught anything on how desire might need to be nurtured or triggered, or how to maintain desire in the most challenging of circumstances – long-term monogamy and parenthood. People do not know that they can have desire feature as much as they want in their long-term relationships as long as they know how.

All of this means that there is no norm in sexual medicine for what our levels of sexual desire should be. Amazing, right? Where else in science is there no norm? We have norms for height, norms for intelligence, norms for how long it takes men to come etc, etc. These can all easily be displayed on a bell-shaped curve with an average in the middle and a range that we expect most people to fall within. Not desire. Desire is too dependent on everything else that is going on. It has the potential to vary significantly person to person, relationship to relationship, day to day.

It's extremely common for people (particularly women) to come to see me and blame this change in desire on themselves. My perspective is that, until popular culture catches up with the scientific understanding of desire, the distress they experience in relation to it is entirely driven by unrealistic expectations, not necessarily a problem with their desire itself. I believe that helping people to understand how their desire works, what they can expect of it, and how to maintain desire in their relationships can make a difference to the large numbers of people who are concerned that their desire isn't working the way it should.

What is desire and how does it happen?

The colloquial phrases 'sex drive' and 'libido' to describe desire are misleading, as they imply an internal state or drive that is ever-present regardless of context. 'Drive' suggests sex is something we feel compelled to seek out. If we haven't eaten, we are 'driven' to eat, so hunger definitely does operate as a drive, but desire doesn't work that way. In fact, for some humans, the less sex they have, the less feelings of 'drive' for sex they have.

Let's understand the key processes involved in desire so that we can see it for what it really is. Humans have an automatic and instinctive response of physical arousal (our bodies responding with increased blood flow to the genitals) when we come into contact with things that our brains code as sexual (from now on I'll refer to these things as 'sexual stimuli'), such as the sight of a naked body or a sensation on our skin. Much ground-breaking research has shown us that, instead of being the thing that comes first and launches us into action, desire is actually kick-started by these physical processes of instinctive arousal.[10]

What is crucial, though, is that this arousal can be side-lined or shut down by our brain, as it uses complex cognitive processes like attention, learning and memory to decide how much desire to feel. For example, if sex has been largely unpleasant so far, then our learning might be 'it's not worth it'. If our experience of sex is that it's more about someone else's pleasure than our own, we will not be that motivated to get involved. If our relationship dynamic has an absence of sexual connection, our brains won't necessarily evaluate the stimulus of, say, a partner's kiss as erotic.

This is crucial to your new understanding about desire, as it's likely that, up until now, you've imagined that you should just feel like having sex instinctively (as a drive), and that if you don't, there's a problem with you. What actually needs to happen for you to feel desire is something like this:[11]

HOW DESIRE WORKS

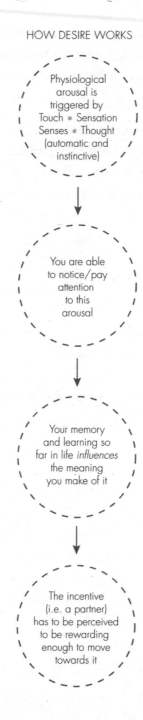

Physiological
arousal is
triggered by
Touch • Sensation
Senses • Thought
(automatic and
instinctive)

You are able
to notice/pay
attention
to this
arousal

Your memory
and learning so
far in life *influences*
the meaning
you make of it

The incentive
(i.e. a partner)
has to be perceived
to be rewarding
enough to move
towards it

Your brain first has to be able to notice this arousal (what's going on in your body or your mind), then make meaning of this, based on a lifetime of learning and experience (is this sexual? If so, is it positive and good for me or not?).

Before moving towards sexual behaviour, our brains will then do a quick calculation of the anticipated rewards of acting on our impulses, as well as the anticipated costs (i.e. 'this will feel great' vs 'this will cut my sleep short by thirty minutes and mean I'm too tired to function tomorrow').

A key factor and the final piece of the jigsaw is how much of a 'pull' the stimulus (a sexual partner) has. New partners are novel and therefore have more of a pull for us, as a rule, which is one of the reasons why people generally have more desire at the start of a relationship, as novelty and unpredictability catch our attention and motivate us to act.

If we can't pay attention to sexual stimuli or our own physiological arousal, as we are too distracted by the demands of parenting, or all the things that could go wrong, desire won't follow. Everything we have learned about sex becomes crucial here. Our past experience, learning from society and memory influences how we expect desire should work, our ideas about what sex looks like and our sense of how obliged we might be to meet another person's needs if we get into a sexual situation then change our minds. This learning influences how we relate to sex in our relationship in many ways. Later on in this chapter we will look at the processes I've just summarized in more detail, so you can establish how they show up for you.

A new understanding of desire

In 2000, Dr Rosemary Basson, a Canadian doctor with an interest in sexual medicine, proposed a new model of sexual response.[12] Until this point, models of desire were based on data that privileged men's experience, and positioned desire as something people should just have. This historical understanding, as with much of science, seeped into our collective psyche and told us what was 'normal'. It's one of the reasons people incorrectly feel they have 'low desire' if they don't feel like sex out of the blue.

Basson's model included many aspects that had been picked up by newer sex research at the time, including the importance of context and that the initial motivation for sex might not be sexual but meeting another need for the person or the relationship. It also contained newer understandings from research that desire might emerge out of arousal rather than just appear out of the blue. It highlighted the impact of psychological and physical wellbeing in potentially disrupting our desire and pleasure and satisfaction as an important reward to maintain it. Basson's model also included the fact that many people in established relationships feel little 'spontaneous' desire. She also questioned whether a lack of understanding about women's desire in particular was largely responsible for the high rates of women reporting concerns about desire in global studies.

The key points of Basson's circular model are that people* in established relationships usually start from a state of sexual neutrality (that is, without desire). However, the model suggests that if they or

---

* Basson's model was largely based on cis women's desire, due to emerging research and the political context of sex science, which had until then been based largely on men's experience. Her work is also applicable to men and, in my experience, many men and non-binary people feel their desire fits this model too.

their partner are motivated to be sexual to gain something for themselves or the relationship (e.g. closeness, feeling attractive) and are willing to seek out or be receptive to sexual stimuli, these are vital foundations to the process. Then, if there are few, or surmountable, psychological or biological barriers (for example, stress, distractions, negative thoughts about their body or tiredness), they may find themselves experiencing sexual arousal in their bodies as a response to this sexual stimuli. Desire is then triggered by this arousal (it can also operate more spontaneously at times and sometimes be the starting point itself as a sexual motivation).

BASSON'S MODEL (2000)

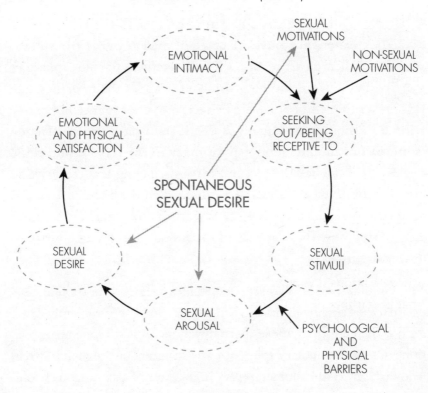

This circular model of desire highlights the part that motivation plays. As we discussed in Chapter 1, this motivation could be sexual (feeling desire out of the blue) or non-sexual (feeling like it's been ages and it would be great to connect). The other person must be able to be receptive to the idea of desire (this is not the same as having desire: it's about not being closed to the idea of sex). Both people will then need something to trigger it, and nothing too distracting in their minds or bodies that gets in the way of it. Once they begin being physically intimate with one another (kissing, being naked, touch etc), bodily changes of arousal (such as increased blood flow) will usually trigger desire (by the process we looked at in the last section). This means that for many people, it is this point that desire (a motivation to be sexual) kicks in, not at the start.

If, after triggering desire (and acting on it with the behaviour of sex), they experience physical or emotional rewards from being sexual together (pleasure, orgasms, satisfaction), people experience increased emotional intimacy directed towards their partner, and this makes them more likely to be receptive to or to seek out sexual stimuli in the future. Equally, a decrease in pleasure, satisfaction from sex or reduced emotional intimacy in the relationship could negatively influence the picture, leave us feeling less receptive to sexual stimuli. Basson's model is often called the circular model of sexual response, as there is no clear start or end point, and it can be easy to spot how the sequence of events can play out in a virtuous *or* vicious circle.

This circular model, as you can see, makes provision for spontaneous desire to be there from time to time. It's important to remember that it's not the case that people (particularly women) in long-term relationships can't or don't experience any spontaneous sexual desire in its own right. Some women report high levels of spontaneous sexual desire, just as some men don't. And some women experience spontaneous sexual desire from time to time, say once per month, which (for women not on hormonal contraception) can be linked to the period around ovulation and just before their period.[13] But it's not the case for all, and desire that needs to be nurtured is the more likely starting point for most. Simply being in a long-term relationship, for women particularly, has been shown by research to be closely associated with a lack of interest in sex.[14]

Basson's model normalized the experience of non-sexual motivations for seeking out or being receptive to sexual stimuli (think of the list you came up with for your own motivations in Chapter 1). It may be these reasons, not feeling desire, which prompt us to have sex. This is especially relevant to parents, as even if one of you *does* experience spontaneous desire frequently, the presence of kids means this is unlikely to happen at a time when sex is possible. It's more likely that you identify the time for sex first, then have to get yourself in a sexual headspace second. The problem with our societal understanding of desire is that, when we see it as a drive, as ever present, as something which should just *be there*, it makes having to get in a sexual headspace seem like a problem, when in fact it is normal some or even most of the time. Many of us also feel deskilled at knowing how to get ourselves, or our partners, in a sexual headspace.

Basson's model is exceptionally useful in helping some people understand how desire features in their life and where they can make changes that will make a difference to their sex lives, particularly in long-term relationships. For this reason, I want to focus on each part of the model in a little more detail, so you can really understand how it applies to your experience.

Being receptive

The seeking out, or being receptive to, has sometimes been called 'willingness', a kind of 'start-and-see-how-you-go' kind of thing – the problem, though, is that, when you're waiting for sexual desire before you engage in *any* type of sexual activity (and we often do this, as we have been led to believe that this is how things should be), we sometimes do the opposite of being receptive, by putting up a virtual stop light to any situation where sex might be expected. We can even become hypervigilant to any subtle cue or initiation from a partner that they might want things to go this way. This stage can, therefore, be the first place our desire is extinguished, even before it's had a chance to catch alight, as in the case of Tori below.

Tori knows that Dan always wants to have sex on a Saturday morning, as it's the first day of the week that both of them don't have to jump out of bed when the alarm goes off. She wakes up before him and heads to the bathroom for a shower to avoid any awkwardness.

In the above example, Tori is hypervigilant to Dan's desire, is not feeling receptive, and, as such, makes decisions to actively avoid any sexual stimuli. This can be a common experience when differences in desire have become a source of conflict. In contrast, in the example below, Meena is more receptive to sexual stimuli and this pays off in the gradual building of arousal, leading to desire once sexual stimuli is involved.

Meena knows that Roxy has sex on her mind when she starts stroking the small of her back with her fingers while they watch TV. Meena

> *doesn't, at that moment, feel like she wants sex, but she is enjoying the touch and is happy to let Roxy keep touching her in this way, as it feels nice. After a while, Meena starts to feel the familiar sensation that her arousal is building and, before she knows it, they are kissing passionately. At some point Meena starts to feel like she would like things to go further.*

One of the biggest barriers to being receptive to sexual stimuli in order to allow desire to emerge, in my clinical experience, is the pressure that comes from sexual scripts – ideas such as 'don't lead people (especially men) on', 'it's impolite to start then stop', and that sex must look a certain way (ending with a penis in a vagina). These scripts stop us at the first hurdle, as how can you enjoy a passionate kiss for a kiss's sake if you feel it will lead to turning a partner on, giving them the idea that you want sex when you (currently) don't, and then ultimately their disappointment when you turn them down? The truth is you can't, and in the playing out of these scripts, opportunities for sexual stimuli (the passionate kiss), which might trigger arousal and desire, are lost. Research tells us that people who approach sexual scripts with more flexibility have higher levels of sexual satisfaction.[15]

In my experience, couples have to really understand the importance of being able to be truly receptive to experience desire by having a culture of high receptivity and low pressure when it comes to how they relate to each other sexually. In reality, the opposite often happens when there is a desire discrepancy. One partner becomes hypervigilant to being disappointed and the other becomes hypervigilant to disappointing. Add this to the experience of less sex in the relationship than (at least) one person might like, or lower sexual satisfaction in parenthood, and every kiss, touch or moment of being naked together can feel that it is loaded with pressure for it to lead to sex. For the person who has been feeling less desire, it can feel easier to avoid this rather than feel immense pressure for more. For the person who has been feeling more desire, the less of these moments there are, the more important it can feel for them to be responded to or go somewhere. Before you know it, you're in a spiral of pressure and disappointment around something as simple as a kiss.

Sexual currency

I coined the term 'sexual currency'[16] as a way to refer to the amount of sexual charge or interaction between us and a sexual partner outside of actual sexual experiences. If 'sex' can be defined as any sexual act involving a body part of yours or your partner's designed to bring pleasure to one or both of you, then sexual currency can be defined as any way of relating to a partner that has the undertones of sex to it but does not necessarily include a sexual act. This could be a brief but suggestive touch as you pass your partner in the kitchen, a seconds-long but passionate kiss before heading off to work, or just spending time naked in bed together not having sex. The litmus test is: would you do it with your aunt? If not, and it doesn't involve a sexual act of some type, it's sexual currency.

In the early stages of a relationship, we typically have extremely high levels of sexual currency. We spend large amounts of time kissing, making intense eye contact, flirting, touching each other's bodies, complimenting, giving affirmations about our desire, being suggestive by looks, comments, texts and emails, and being physically close. If you watch a couple in the early stages of their relationship, you can see the high levels of sexual currency running between them. Their interaction is sexually charged, even when they are not having sex. Their relationship is defined by a sexual connection. The more they act this way towards one another, the more they feel sexual towards each other. It's a virtuous circle that results in more desire and more sex. In fact, we can hypothesize that one of the key features of a new relationship, which brings with it higher levels of spontaneous desire, is higher levels of sexual currency.

As relationships become more established, we generally settle into other, more sustainable ways to co-exist, as well as new habits of physically relating. Continuing to relate to our partners as sexual beings, not just housemates, friends or co-parents, is a way of making our relationship a sexual one, even in the absence of acts of sex. Continuing to share moments like this together reminds us that we are sexual beings, and we are being looked at in this way by the other. Having moments of connecting via sexual currency during a typical day or dotted over the week provides us with natural, frequent opportunities to transition into being more sexual together, should we want to, by providing us with foundational stepping stones to move from a non-sexual interaction (washing up, talking about our day) to more of a sexual zone, naturally and without awkwardness, as, after all, it's *what our relationship is about and the reason we are not just friends*. Considering sexual currency as part of our sex lives rightly situates the performance of our sexuality on a spectrum rather than an on/off switch (i.e. if we're not having sex, then there is no sexual relationship happening). Sexual currency is about the culture of our relationship, and what's good about culture is it's fluid and shifts, depending on how the people act within it.

For some couples, sexual currency is ever present, and though it may have declined since that first heady few months of their relationship, they still feel there is a sexual charge between them that they enjoy indulging and intentionally nurture. For these couples, no matter how often they have sex together, they feel connected sexually, and find the transition from putting the weekly shop away to kissing passionately against the fridge an easy one to make. These couples may find a period of time without having sex makes less difference to their sexual satisfaction, as they are still getting most or all of their motivations for sex met via sexual currency (for example, feeling desired, feeling close, excitement). Couples with high levels of sexual currency feel the presence of their sexual relationship whether they are having sex once a day or once a year.

For others, sexual currency has become increasingly absent since those first heady months together, and this absence makes it hard to see their partner (or relationship) as particularly sexual. Compliments, passionate kissing and suggestive looks are so absent that, even if you wanted to do them, they can feel awkward, and even if they are intended simply to convey attraction, they can feel like a clumsy initiation of sex. There's a vicious circle here, as the less you relate to each other this way, the less your relationship feels defined as a sexual one, and the less sexual it is. The less sexual it is, the harder it is to transition into being sexual together, even if you both want to. It is hard to be receptive in this scenario.

Nico and Jo had this challenge. Jo came out of the shower and walked around while choosing clothes to wear without a towel. Nico, intending to pay Jo a compliment, said, 'You're so beautiful.' Jo responded with anger. 'Why did you have to say that?' she said, while picking up her towel and quickly covering herself up. 'I didn't need to feel scrutinized. I'm already late.' Nico felt confused. He felt he was offering a compliment, something he didn't often do but often wanted to. They had so little sexual connection between them that Jo felt there must have been more to it. Why was he saying this now? Why did he always have to bring up sex at the worst times. She was unreceptive to Nico's compliment, as it felt so out of the blue, and she was hypervigilant to his clumsy initiations of sex. Sadly for Nico and Jo, this communication intended to simply communicate a compliment added to the stress of their day, as they had a low culture of sexual currency in their relationship, so any hint of it felt loaded and pressurized.

If you are reading this and realizing that you and your partner only ever passionately kiss as part of sex, and never at any other time, or some other aspect of relating to each other mainly as flatmates or co-parents rings true, then the important thing is that you can create a change in this culture easily by starting to do something differently. The other thing that I'd like to say here is that, although I've talked about two types of couples here, one with high levels of sexual currency and one where it's virtually non-existent, there's plenty of variation here in the space between these two, even for the same couple throughout the course of a typical month.

Sexual stimuli

Earlier, I defined sexual stimuli as anything our brains code as sexual. This may, of course, include acts of sexual currency between us and a partner, but it also encapsulates our environments, sensations within our own body, and internally generated thoughts as well. Let me explain.

Do you remember Roxy and Meena, with the casual back touching during TV time? The frequency of this type of sexual currency between them acts as sexual stimuli and will have an impact on how often Meena feels desire. Meena won't always feel desire when Roxy touches her back and kisses her in this way – for example, if she's had a stressful day and is preoccupied, if they've just had a row and she's feeling resentful, or if she's feeling tired. However, the more they have these kinds of interactions, the more chance there is that some of the time desire will be triggered. Sexual stimuli is anything that can trigger our arousal, whether we mean it to or not. Intentionally thinking about sex or fantasizing is a sexual stimulus, as might be a partner's attempt at initiation using indirect means. We might interpret something that someone (a partner or someone else) does as a sexual stimulus even if they didn't intend it to be. Also, we can't always adequately guess what kind of sexual stimuli might turn us, or our partners, on, and they will be different for all of us, at different times, in different relationships. Also, sometimes sexual stimuli might be erotic for us on one occasion but completely turn us off the next. Remember Tori from page 72? Let's imagine that Tori was feeling receptive and didn't jump out of bed on that Saturday morning.

> *Tori often experienced Dan's behaviour in bed on Saturday mornings as a sexual stimulus, as he often rolled over to her half asleep, ran his hands over her naked stomach and kissed her neck. She enjoyed the sensation of his hands on her body, and there was something about him doing this in bed when they were sleepy and warm that she found really sexy. Tori had woken up ten minutes earlier than Dan, and in this time had wondered whether they might have sex, given it was Saturday and they had nowhere to be. In those ten minutes before Dan awoke, Tori indulged in sexual thoughts and found herself feeling arousal and some desire before he'd even woken up.*

In this example, Tori has the sexual stimuli of being physically close to Dan and the experience of enjoyable touch from him, as well as her own inner world of sexual thoughts, which has acted as a kick-starter for her desire. Both act as sexual stimuli. In the first example, Tori rarely got to experience these as she had already got out of bed in anticipation, knowing it was coming and second-guessing where Dan wanted it to go – somewhere she didn't, at that moment. In the second example, Tori was feeling receptive and had the opportunity for arousal and desire to be triggered.

What about Dan? There are several things that could have been going on for him. Firstly, he may not have intended this touch and kiss to be any more than that, it might just be his way of connecting and enjoying Tori's body for five minutes before they get out of bed, i.e. sexual currency not sexual initiation. It's also possible that, for Dan, this touch may act as an internal sexual stimuli and might be a way he stimulates his own arousal and desire. Finally (and potentially in combination with the other reasons), it's possible that Dan could have been communicating with Tori, via indirect sexual initiation, that he would like them to be sexual together. Remember also that Dan would have had his own reasons or motivations to be sexual, and it is likely that Tori's reaction of seeming to want to avoid him and jump out of bed or, alternatively, enjoying five minutes of touch or a kiss, might have made an enormous difference to his needs being met, depending on the reasons he was prompted to connect with her that way.

Later on we will look more closely at the role of a particular type of sexual communication, often called 'initiation', and why getting this right is so crucial to parents. Alongside 'accidental' sexual stimuli (for example, seeing a sex scene on TV that you find hot) and increasing sexual currency (an intentional way of relating sexually, such as reinstating passionate kissing, which at times will act as sexual stimuli), 'initiation' is a direct attempt at using sexual currency to communicate something to someone else.

We might want to nurture our responsive desire and be receptive to sexual stimuli so that we can go on to experience sexual arousal and desire, but as well as considering our exposure (and ability to notice or pay attention to) to sexual stimuli on a broader level, it is also worth considering whether we have gotten stuck in a non-sexy rut around initiation, or perhaps it features rarely in our sex life these days at all? We'll cover 'initiation' further in later chapters and I'll be inviting you to reflect on whether how it currently happens works for you.

Sexual stimuli are not just about what a partner does or doesn't do. We know that, for many people, fantasizing or thinking about sex acts as a sexual stimulus, as does watching porn, reading or listening to erotica, or talking about sex with others. Some people report that there may be certain types of touch, smell, music, or memories that act as triggers for them. One of the reasons parenting is more challenging to our sex lives is that we may have less actual time and less psychological headspace to invest in these things, or notice them when they happen.

If one of you has been worried about your seemingly absent desire up until now, it can be a revelation to see what happens if you expose yourself to a sexual stimulus, such as reading or listening to erotica or watching porn, as, in my experience, it helps people in two ways. Firstly, to understand that their responsive desire is working as it should and, therefore, that they are normal. Secondly, to understand that, if this is the case, there is something else with a partner that is getting in the way. This could be the notion of having not previously been receptive due to our old ideas of how desire works. It could be connected to a lack of time, or a lack of sexual stimuli due to having low sexual currency in your relationship. It's also possible that if this part of the model does go to plan, then something else kicks in to interrupt desire.

Physical, psychological and circumstantial barriers

Physical barriers to desire can include medication use (for example, the impact of SSRIs used to treat low mood), hormonal changes, pain and, of course, the big one for parents: tiredness. Many of these things will stop our desire from emerging, even if we want it to. Similarly, the attention we are able to pay to our arousal or our ability to be in the moment, the content of thoughts we have related to our bodies or sex, and the learning or associations we have about sex related to every element of our sex and relationship history can do the same.

What's going through your mind during sex matters. Negative thoughts about ourselves, sex, our bodies, or not being able to pay attention to the good stuff turns down the intensity and even stops sexual arousal (and therefore prevents us from feeling desire). In the example of Andie, below, there were high levels of receptivity, sexual currency and therefore sexual stimuli, but there were psychological barriers too that threatened to dampen her desire.

Andie often felt open to the idea of sex happening, and she and her partner created loads of opportunities for sexual stimuli in their relationship – they often kissed for the sake of kissing and frequently spent lots of time in bed together talking, laughing and with close physical contact. However, as soon as Andie had the thought that she or her partner might want it to go further, she was plagued with a whole host of worries about herself and her body. These were often focused on changes she'd spotted since pregnancy, but she was also plagued with a whole host of others. She worried that she didn't have the right underwear on, that it had been a while since she'd showered, how much body hair she had right now, and what her body would look like in this light. Sometimes she'd notice that she'd almost have to battle through these thoughts until the point came where she noticed that she felt arousal and desire kick in. When this happened, she suddenly had the experience that these thoughts had faded into the background and desire had taken over.

The role of attention

A number of studies have shown the devastating power of distraction on sexual arousal.[17] Our brain has only got so much attention at any one time to devote to something, and as soon as something else competes for attention, it is divided. Not being able to pay attention is one of the key culprits stopping us being in tune. The more out of the moment and in our heads we are, the less arousal (and therefore desire) we will feel.

This means that whatever is going on sexually – for example, watching a sexual partner undress, a sudden intrusive sexual thought or the experience of a kiss – our physical sexual response is affected by how much attention we are able to pay to it in that moment. The kiss could be really hot, but if you are too busy thinking about the fact that you've got to be up in six hours, your body won't respond to it as if it is.

Generally all non-sexual distraction is unhelpful: we want our attention to be focused on positive sexual thoughts and sensations as much as possible. There's almost no limit to the types of thoughts our brains can generate during sex, all of which can distract us or heighten our anxiety. They could be self-critical thoughts like Andie was having, such as 'they are disgusted by my post-baby body'. Our thoughts can be related to how close or far away we are from desire, i.e. 'I'm never going to come'. They could be thoughts about unwanted consequences from sex, such as pain. We could be distracted by thoughts about the environment around us or worries about something non sex-related, such as your toddler walking in or hearing, or that you haven't filled in that school-trip permission slip that needs to be in tomorrow. We might just have a constant parenting to-do list swimming around in our minds (more on inequity in household labour in Chapter 5). Repeatedly switching our attention between tasks (often called 'multitasking') has a higher cognitive load on our brain, which can lead to difficulties paying attention, inefficiency and forgetting.[18] Not only can this further add to our mental to-do list, but it may also be affecting our experience of being mentally present during sex.

Negative thoughts during sex are also often related to many unhelpful ideas around sex found in society at large, rather than reflective of your reality in that moment. This is a real shame, right? You might predict your partner is turned off by your stomach, as you've been sold an idea that only flat stomachs are sexy, and this means you start losing sexual sensation, when, in fact, your partner isn't thinking this at all.

By now you might be starting to get a picture of how complex our brains are when it comes to sex. Yes, our brains do instinctively trigger the physical processes of arousal, but the parts of our brain that allow us to worry about sex, make judgements about sex, or not pay attention to sex can switch off that arousal or pleasure, and get in the way of our sexual functioning. In my clinic, I notice that when people have consistently busy minds, they describe becoming so accustomed to their thoughts racing and pinging back and forward between different upcoming tasks or obligations that this becomes their natural state. Multitasking every minute outside of sex then expecting to feel able to be fully present to bodily sensations and sexual response (which requires our attention to be present, not distracted), may not be possible without first doing some work to counter to the habits of their mind outside of sex.

How can we get our brains working for us, not against us?

Our ability to direct our attention towards or away from negative or distracting thoughts, and to pay attention to sexual sensations or stimuli, makes a difference to what we feel in our bodies. Our brains generate thoughts all the time, but we can be distracted by ones that feel worrying or burdensome and spend time focusing on them. Some of us will have more to distract us than others (again, more on the mental load and parenthood later).

A growing number of studies have shown that mindfulness helps people be more in tune between body and mind, and therefore improves sexual response.[19] Mindfulness is known to increase arousal, pleasure and desire and has been a key revelation in sex therapy over the last decade or so. The more in tune with our body, the more desire, arousal and pleasure we experience; and our attention can be harnessed through mindfulness. Several pivotal studies in the last decade have shown that practising mindfulness can increase physical arousal, pleasure and desire. In fact, research tells us that women who find it easier to have orgasms are typically more 'mindful' in everyday life, and find it easier to be in the moment in sex.[20] I'm sure you can understand how this works by now. Mindfulness has been shown to increase our attention to sex and move us away from thoughts or distractions that are less helpful. It's a way of taking control of our brains and getting them to work for us, not against us. It fits perfectly into our understanding of how desire works, and what can get in the way of it. Mindfulness is a skill that you can develop, and there is strong evidence that it will benefit your sex life. It's also extremely accessible, low-cost and something that you can fit into daily life. What's not to like? There's so much to say about mindfulness that I would suggest that, if your interest has been sparked by this chapter and you'd like to learn more, you get yourself a copy of Dr Lori Brotto's book, *Better Sex Through Mindfulness: How Women can Cultivate Desire* (Greystone Books, 2018). Brotto is a professor, psychologist and researcher based in Vancouver, Canada, and a world leader in this field.

If you are interested in increasing your ability to tune in to your body, and reduce distraction, negative thoughts or pressures, mindfulness is a tool at your disposal and there are multiple apps available to support your developing skill. Download one and listen to a five- to ten-minute session as often as you can, ideally once a day (but hey, parents have little time, so do what you can). Research demonstrates that a regular mindfulness practice such as this improves wellbeing, attention and sexual response.[21] And this can have wider benefits in addition to just your sex life.

A key psychological barrier we haven't discussed so far is expectation and pressure. There's nothing like feeling we have to do something or that something is expected of us to make that thing less enticing, and sex is no different. If we feel every kiss has to lead to sex, and if we feel that every time we have sex it has to lead to a certain type of sex, desire takes a hit. In my experience, expectation and pressure for a foregone conclusion are two of the key ingredients of a less-than-satisfactory sex life. Social learning about 'politeness' and not leading people on is crucial here, as feeling as though 'we've started something, so we have to finish it' (especially if this is privileging one person's needs over another) is just not great for long-term desire. Similarly, wedding nights, date nights, weekends away and nights in hotels can all have a similar effect.

The flip side of this is that anticipation can build desire and shouldn't be underestimated as a tool at your disposal to trigger desire. The key difference here is that pressure and predictability are about a foregone conclusion, while anticipation is building excitement for something that may or may not transpire. Take a minute here to consider how pressure, predictability or anticipation feature in your sex life alongside any other problematic thoughts or distractions you identified in the last chapter. The way to overcome this potential psychological barrier is to create a culture of low pressure between you. This means creating situations of physical or emotional intimacy that trigger desire, but have a solid agreement that this need not lead to a foregone conclusion. I often explain to couples that I'd like them to move towards a 'trivial and often' idea of sexually relating, rather than 'rarely and crucial'. This, I find, can often require a complete shift in understanding for most couples, but once they are able to see the results that this low-pressure/high-frequency way of sexually relating brings, it can often have a remarkable impact on their sex life moving forward.

In my opinion, couples often don't give enough credit to the impact of their individual life circumstances on their sex life and, for parents, challenges such as a lack of free time are one of the most obvious sticking points. Circumstantial barriers such as these are not named explicitly as part of Basson's model, but they would fit under psychological barriers, or as part of the wider context of the relationship. There's nothing more powerful and freeing than a couple who feel that their sex life is doomed due to some kind of incompatible desire problem realizing that they simply don't currently have time for sex, and if they did, it might be different. The information this provides for a significant and meaningful change can be relationship-changing. They may not have come to this understanding before as they believed that desire and sex should just happen spontaneously and 'naturally', without effort.

When there are practical factors, such as time, which get in the way of desire emerging, there are several options available. One option is to choose to prioritize sex in your life and devote regular time to your relationship in a way that works for you both (a compromise might also be required here). Another is to accept that your sex life can't happen the way you'd like it to, as life currently gets in the way, and rest safe in the knowledge that this doesn't mean there is anything wrong with either of you, or that your relationship is doomed. Later on in this book I will be encouraging you to reflect on the realistic time you have available for your stage of parenthood and the most effective way to use it.

Emotional and physical satisfaction

Sex is not all about orgasms, and certainly Basson usefully frames 'emotional and physical satisfaction' as a broader definition of having enjoyed the experience. However, having less pleasure, connection or enjoyment during sex will limit the positive consequences and make it harder to feel motivated to be sexual over time. Pleasure is crucial to desire due to the importance of learning and memory for us to feel incentivized to be sexual. Put simply, our desire flourishes, or is inhibited, by the amount of pleasure or satisfaction we experience.

Making sex mutually satisfying is not a goal that is out of reach for *any* couple, and those who allow their sex lives to move towards something that benefits one person's pleasure often over another's should expect desire to decrease over time.

Other rewarding aspects of sex outside of orgasms could include, for example, feeling attractive, finding it erotic, feeling connected, feeling close, having fun together or feeling free to express your sexuality. The more these things are happening, as you can see from the model, the more likely the experience will be satisfying and reinforce future desire. But if these things aren't happening, if sex is lacking in reward generally, not just in orgasms, then this will need to be addressed.

Emotional intimacy

The circular model suggests that the positive consequence of sexual activity featuring emotional and physical satisfaction is increased emotional intimacy with a partner, leading to a sense of closeness and wellbeing. In contrast, it can be assumed that a lack of emotional and physical satisfaction from sexual activity might result in a lowered sense of sexual intimacy and connection over time.

This is important to the model as the level of emotional intimacy feeds into the likelihood that someone might feel receptive to future sexual stimuli. A less rewarding version of this circular model, however, might lead to a situation where a lack of emotional closeness or, instead, irritation towards our partner may make sexual neutrality more difficult, leading us to feel less receptive to sexual stimuli over time. Consider for a moment when you feel most emotionally intimate with your partner and what it is that facilitates this feeling. For some of you, it will be about time together to really connect, for others it will be about good communication and feeling listened to, for others it will be about having fun together. Maximizing these aspects of your relationship by making time to create opportunities for them, or simply treating them as important and essential to nourish, is key. You will learn how to do this more successfully as parents in the later chapter on communication.

At this stage you can probably see that, over the course of your life, there may have been a range of ways you've experienced desire based on what we know about desire from sex science. The first is frequent thoughts of sex out of the blue, and although this is more common early in relationships (and more common for men), many people of all genders identify with this as a way their desire continues to work in a long-term relationship too. More likely, perhaps, might be a pattern of rarely noticing yourself thinking about sex, or feeling like sex out of the blue, but if you read, watch or think about something erotic, you notice arousal in your body, which you may or may not act upon. Or perhaps you very rarely think about sex but notice that, once you've let yourself be open to it and started some kind of sexual touch, kiss or act with a sexual partner, desire usually, or always, follows. This follows a pattern of more responsive desire. It is completely normal.

For some people there may be a mixture of times when they feel like sex out of the blue, times when you are motivated to have sex for another reason and actively seek out sexual stimuli in the absence of feeling desire, and times when you are receptive to sexual stimuli and happy to see if desire builds. All of these manifestations of desire are normal. How you understand desire, however, is crucial to your ability to find workarounds in your sex life once kids come along. This chapter has hopefully given you the foundation you need to understand why.

Bringing this all together – Amy and Mark

Amy felt that she was someone with a low sex drive. She very rarely thought about having sex with Mark, but when she did, which was about every two months, she acted on it by showing him some kind of signal that she wanted to be sexual (like wearing nothing to bed) and he usually responded. When she did this, and they had satisfying sex, she often thought afterwards: 'That was great – we should do that more.'

The rest of the time, if Mark kissed her, the kind of kiss that's more than a peck on the lips, her immediate thought was: 'Oh no! He wants sex and I'm not feeling like it! I better close it down now so he doesn't get the wrong idea.' She had started to wear more to bed, and avoided any conversations about sex, mostly as she felt awkward, or wanted to sidestep a row.

Because of this, they had far less sexual stimuli in their life than they had before. They had stopped kissing passionately unless it was part of sex, and she didn't let Mark run his hands over her body in bed when they woke up like they'd used to, as she could feel him getting hard and this made her worry. Mark picked up on all of this, and stopped touching Amy in this way, or telling her she looked hot, as it was met with such a reaction.

Amy and Mark had young children and were exhausted pretty much all of the time. By the time they had put the kids to bed, tidied up, cooked dinner, and got everything ready for the next day, they were shattered and keen to go to sleep. If they did try to have sex at these times, Amy found herself distracted by thoughts of 'have I got everything ready for the kids tomorrow?' or 'I have to be up in six hours', which made it hard for her to experience much arousal and desire. Sometimes she'd be happy to have sex anyway, more for Mark's pleasure than hers (and also as she felt it was unkind to turn him down once he'd got turned on), and these more perfunctory sexual experiences were lacking in pleasure for her. Mark would come and then they would go to sleep, without even discussing her pleasure or satisfaction.

Amy noticed that she did feel turned on in her body every once in a while, when there was a sex scene on TV, say, or when she was reading a book with some hot sex in it. The problem, she said, was that it felt difficult to translate this into action with Mark, as she didn't always know what to say, or it would happen at times when the kids were awake, or she was alone. Sometimes she would choose to masturbate instead of approaching Mark, either because it was more convenient, quicker, or because her pleasure was more guaranteed, without any of the pressure of pleasing him.

Over time, sex between them became less and less, and a bit of a sore subject. The less sex they had, the more awkward it felt to get started, and the more pressure there was for it to go well and for it to be more about Mark's pleasure and preferences than Amy's. Amy started to avoid sexual stimuli more, as the longer the gaps between them having sex became, the more pressure there was for a passionate kiss to turn into more.

Amy and Mark are, in many ways, a very typical couple and their experience fits a pattern I hear from clients in sex therapy again and again. At this stage, my hope is that, in this example, you can spot all of the different aspects of the picture that we have discussed so far, and how it is impacting on their sex life.

Which of the following can you spot in the example of Amy and Mark?

- Sex-positive sex education and early learning about sex, gender politics and appeasing others

- The impact of a lack of pleasure on desire

- Social scripts of what sex looks like and expectations around desire

- Their motivations for sex and why this matters

- Myths around the ease of spontaneous sex

- How we'd expect spontaneous desire to be in a long-term relationship

- Relationship dynamics and sex

- The impact of communication about sex or in getting sex started

- Having children

- Their levels of sexual currency

- Available time together and competing priorities

- The role of attention, distraction and negative thoughts

- The unhelpful use of labels

- The role of incentive on sex

- Approach or avoidance motivations for sex

- Predictability, novelty and pressure.

So what can Amy and Mark do about it? Let's use Basson's model as a framework for mapping out where the room for change is in their sex life moving forward.

Amy's new understanding of desire would hopefully mean that she would be feeling more receptive to or willing to seek out sexual stimuli, though it's important to note that she would need to be feeling emotionally close/connected as a foundation (so it would be useful for her to reflect on how their relationship is going generally). She would also need to feel confident that this receptivity wouldn't always be positioned as the green light for sex, but rather a starting point for connection to see if desire can build.

As a couple they would benefit from resurrecting the things she enjoys but doesn't let Mark do for fear of it having to turn into more. This might be about reinstating passionate kissing for kissing's sake, or massage, allowing Mark to touch her in bed in the mornings again, or always wearing little to bed, not just when she feels like sex. This would be a change in the sexual currency between them.

In fact, if I were seeing Amy and Mark for therapy, I'd recommend they have a period of a few weeks where they went to town with sexual currency but banned sex, so that they can see first-hand what difference it makes to desire if they flood their relationship with sexual stimuli, without pressure. An exercise like this gives couples an opportunity to get reacquainted with flirting, reinstating or strengthening the relationship between them as a sexual one, creating more of an association of their partner as a sexual being, and creates many more opportunities to trigger desire. Again, for this to be useful for their sex life, they would both need to commit to these things not needing to lead anywhere, so that there is truly no pressure and that there is no expectation that either of them should feel desire. Many couples find that making this subtle change already starts to improve their sexual satisfaction, even in the absence of sex. For example, one of Mark's reasons for having sex was to feel wanted, and this was why he was so concerned about Amy's avoidance. Imagine the effect it would have on Mark to have Amy sending him suggestive texts or flirting with him throughout the day.

Amy and Mark might want to try making more time together to really connect without the kids, both emotionally and physically. This doesn't need to be outside their home, if a babysitter is out of reach. It could involve an evening of making dinner for each other, for example, talking without the distraction of TV or devices, having a bath together, or going to bed early to chat naked under the covers. Creating space for physical intimacy that might trigger desire is also important if we want to kickstart our responsive desire, so they might want to kiss, lie naked in bed together and talk, or have an evening once a fortnight where they give each other a massage. Remember that arousal and desire might need to be triggered by sexual stimuli. Spending time together might not be enough without more physical/sexual triggers.

Ultimately, Mark and Amy need to decide what priority sex should have and treat it as such, carving out regular time and space between them to have more triggers of desire without pressure for it to be more. Often I get asked what I think about scheduling sex as a strategy for couples in long-term relationships. The answer is that scheduling sex is rarely a good idea, as it creates pressure to have to feel/do something, but scheduling physical intimacy is *always* a good idea, as it is both enjoyable in its own right, keeps this part of a relationship high on the priority list, and provides the perfect environment for responsive desire. It can also meet our motivations for sex even when desire doesn't follow.

Amy and Mark are both exhausted and they may find that, if bedtime is really the only time they can schedule physical intimacy, they might want to move their bedtime thirty minutes earlier, in the hope of reducing their overall tiredness. Even better still, spend this time together once the kids are asleep, rather than last thing at night. Amy struggles with distraction and negative thoughts are a big feature of their current sex life. She would benefit from starting a mindfulness practice outside of sex, with the aim of moving it into sex in time, as well as reducing her general stress levels.

Amy is also carrying all the psychological burden of the household chores and family admin tasks. Mark and Amy need to discuss this and find a way to share this burden so that one of them isn't going to bed worrying about all the tasks that need to be completed for the kids the next day, knowing that, if they don't do it, no one will. It's important for Mark to understand that this is one of her barriers to desire, even if it wouldn't be to him. In some ways, this is where gendered scripts of responsibility might need to be spelled out as operating differently for each of them.

Ideally, Amy and Mark should move towards an understanding of the impact of sex being less rewarding for Amy. They have never created a relationship culture where talking about what they want during sex is acceptable and this limits both of them in their knowledge of the other and the chance to make sex mutually rewarding and interesting. Amy and Mark would benefit from having equal amounts of sex that prioritize Mark's pleasure (like vaginal penetration), and equal amounts of sex that prioritize Amy's (like oral sex), rather than their sex life always following a set and predictable pattern ending in penetrative vaginal sex. It's important that they consider the role of predictability and novelty in their sexual expression, in how their sex looks and the freedom they both have for sexual expression of different types.

Amy is sometimes having sex for avoidance motivations, meaning she is having sex to avoid conflict rather than because she wants to, or even for Mark's pleasure. Amy's long-term desire would benefit from no longer continuing to have sex for these reasons. Mark struggles to be turned down without feeling rejected. If he wants to be sexual, and Amy doesn't feel 'receptive' to seeing if her arousal can be triggered, then they would benefit from talking more about what's behind Mark's motivations for sex on that day and whether there are any other ways it can be met. Amy could use that opportunity to reassure Mark if he's feeling insecure.

We could go on. But hopefully you can see that there are lots of ways Amy and Mark can start to turn this around now that they understand desire better. I've worked with hundreds of couples over the years who have made huge changes to their sex lives by first understanding this, then making practical changes to how they are sexual together. A small change in any area usually has a positive impact, but a handful of changes, like those suggested above, can make a huge impact to a couple's sex life over time.

TASK: What has gotten in the way?

So where are you at in how you understand desire in long-term relationships? Consider the points below.

Prior to reading this book, how much did you subscribe to the belief that you should be feeling spontaneous sexual desire (rate it as a percentage, if you like, with 100 per cent being you completely believed it)?

How did this belief impact on your willingness to be receptive to sexual stimuli?

Has one or both of you found yourself doing/not doing things to not give your partner the 'wrong idea'?

Has one or both of you stopped doing certain things over time as a result?

What would be the effect on your sex life if you started to be more willing to trigger arousal and desire without pressure to feel it?

Desire is a fluid entity that is cultivated or extinguished minute by minute, day by day, between us and a partner, based on how we nurture it. Defining ours and our partner's desire as fixed, static and not amenable to change, based on our past experiences of it, is the first obstacle we create to long-term sexual satisfaction, as it creates a perception that nothing we do or say makes a difference and that it's a problem with *us*. Framing desire in this way not only stops us from making any effort to guide our sex life in the way we want it to go, but it prevents us from being curious to learn anything about how desire actually works.

Generally, with most areas of our life where we want to create change, it can be useful to first understand what's going on and then put a plan in place that we know will undermine what's keeping us stuck. Desire is no different. For some people, simply hearing about how desire works is the quick fix, as knowing they are normal and understanding their body is all they need to take the stress of the situation away or know how to action it. For others, the additional step of making a plan of undermining any previously less helpful patterns is the next step to seeing a more rewarding sex life emerge.

You may be able to identify from reading this, or from the sex-life barometer questionnaire that you completed in Chapter 2, that the level of sexual currency between you is an area of your relationship culture that would benefit from change. In the final chapter, I'll be sharing with you some ideas for tasks you can do to create small changes here that will have big knock-on effects. Increasing sexual currency promotes a culture of enabling receptivity, by virtue of the fact that sexual stimuli are frequent and not in themselves signals of sex. Importantly, to be receptive to situations that might trigger desire, people need to feel able to prioritize their own sexual needs before someone else's, not fear 'letting someone down', and have the sexual agency to feel able to draw the line anywhere they like in the encounter without fear of repercussion.

In this chapter I have outlined some of the key aspects of desire in long-term relationships, as many of you will have this context (having been together for more than a year) as a backdrop to your parenting. We have also touched upon how elements of social learning, such as what sex is and how beliefs about how you 'should' be sexually can hinder this. We have also talked about aspects of our long-term relationship culture, such as sexual currency and how this can help or hinder desire. Much of this has likely influenced your sex life well before kids came along, and although having kids is a significant stressor on sexual satisfaction, how we understand and nurture desire in our relationships is a crucial foundation to this.

4

Action Stations!

The impact of trying to conceive and pregnancy

We all arrive at parenthood in different ways, and the journey itself can bring its own unique challenges, leaving a lasting imprint on our sex lives. This chapter focuses on relationships in which one person was pregnant and includes those who struggled to get pregnant. The following chapter also deals with birth itself and the impact that birth and the first year can have on our future sex lives as parents. If you became a parent through adoption, or surrogacy, you might want to move ahead to the next chapter or go straight to Chapter 6, 'The parenting years', depending on when in your child's life your parenting journey began.

Pregnancy and sexuality

Pregnancy is a profound life event, which brings with it new ways of being seen by others, and new ways of experiencing ourselves. When we are expecting a baby, people want to talk to us about pregnancy all the time, but there is a striking absence of talk about pregnancy sex. It's also rare to see the sexual expression of pregnant people portrayed in film or on TV where the pregnancy itself is incidental to the storyline. Outside of the fetishization of pregnancy in some mainstream porn, being sexual and also happening to be pregnant is just not something that we often see represented in an encouraging way. It's as though as soon as the pregnancy test shows positive, the shutters of societal restrictions come down and displays of sexuality, at least publicly, fade into the distance.

It's possible that this lack of media portrayal and the conversational black hole are two of the reasons for our contradictory views about pregnant people being non-sexual. I say contradictory as the act of sex, for many at least, was probably responsible for the pregnancy in the first place. But given that we know that we learn about what 'normal' sex is from what we see and hear about in the world around us, and that much of this learning comes from the media, we can start to speculate on what effect the absence of sexual images or portrayals of pregnancy sexuality have on our collective psyche. How comfortable can we learn to be about something that is rarely represented to us?

I asked people to share their stories about this with me ahead of writing this book and I was inundated with responses. You can see many of these responses below. There was a strong feeling from people that they wished there was more talk between friends, in antenatal care and in society about the good, the bad and the surprising. They expressed that knowing this would have made them feel 'more normal'. As a clinical psychologist who specialises in sex, I'm not surprised that we struggle to talk openly about pregnancy sex as a society, because we struggle to talk about sex full stop. Furthermore, we place so many restrictions on sexual expression generally that it's no surprise that pregnancy sexuality is even more taboo. It doesn't need to be, of course, but it can be a challenging path to negotiate with no information about what might happen, no reassurance that your sexuality is still valid, or no open talk about what lies ahead.

'I squirted for the first time during pregnancy. It was amazing!'

'I was so horny all the time. My orgasms were so intense and my nipples were so sensitive. Sex was amazing!'

'I found vaginal sex extremely uncomfortable during pregnancy. I had previously tried anal sex and did not enjoy it, however during pregnancy we tried it and I enjoyed it!'

'I was too nervous to have sex with my pregnant partner at all during pregnancy.'

'During my pregnancy, I'm finding it hard to switch from "wholesome mother" to "sexed-up wife", which is pretty confusing for everyone involved.'

'I found my partner incredibly attractive during pregnancy and we enjoyed some of the best sex we'd ever had.'

'I'm at a stage where I'm loving how my body looks, especially the big boobs, and I feel empowered and pretty horny.'

'I feel weird about having sex with my wife; her body is someone else's home.'

I've mentioned already that it is well known in sex science that sexual satisfaction has an impact on psychological wellbeing and relationship satisfaction. Given that we don't talk about sex during pregnancy, myths about pregnancy sex or restrictive attitudes towards it impact on pregnant people and their partners in a way that can create a stifling, guilt-ridden and inflexible sex life. The impact of which can affect a relationship negatively at a time of great transition, a time where sexual satisfaction can be essential for wider relational and personal wellbeing.

What is fascinating to me, as someone who focuses on sexual satisfaction and expression for a living, is that pregnancy is a time of golden opportunity in so many ways. An opportunity to break free of predictable societally-dictated sexual scripts (such as 'sex = penis in vagina') and predictable habits we can easily fall into with the same person over time dictating a set pattern of how sex will happen ('you do A, I do B, then we do C'). The change that pregnancy brings to our bodies, minds and relationships allows us the opportunity to experience new sensations, new ways of being, or to bring new definitions to what sex is. In my opinion, these aspects of pregnancy sexuality don't get the airtime that they should in terms of the potential impact they could have on revitalizing sexual expression and satisfaction – particularly for couples who have been together for some time. These experiences could change the way we relate to sex and benefit our sex lives long after the pregnancy is over. For example, we know from research that if both partners are enjoying sex through pregnancy, they are more likely to report tenderness and positive communication in their relationship four months after delivery.[1]

It isn't all opportunity and pleasure, sadly. Hormonal changes, nausea and fatigue can lead to decreased sexual function, particularly in the first and third trimester. Common sexual problems in pregnancy include pain during penetrative sex, difficulty reaching orgasm, lack of vaginal lubrication and reduction in desire. These kinds of difficulties can be particularly challenging for couples who have never had any problems in their sex life up until this point, or whose sexual repertoire is more fixed and predictable, as they will not have had the opportunity to develop strategies for overcoming obstacles, including talking frankly about sex, or thinking flexibly about their sex life.

Despite how common sexual problems are during pregnancy due to physical changes, there can also be a positive impact on sexual functioning, such as increased sex drive, heightened genital and nipple sensitivity, and more powerful orgasms. These experiences are linked to physical changes in the body (such as increased blood flow) and can provide opportunities for novel experiences of pleasure, expression and desire. For some people, experimentation in pregnancy can lead to the discovery of new sexual preferences that would otherwise have gone unknown. This may have been the case for some of you too.

Think back to the previous chapter and what you now know about the risk of sex becoming predictable, formulaic, and therefore lacking in motivational 'pull' for us in a long-term relationship. Pregnancy has the opportunity to bring the diversity we need, and the impact of this can be longer-lasting than the pregnancy itself.

How much sex we feel like in pregnancy is related to how our bodies are responding but also (and very crucially) what's going on in our minds and relationships too. Sexuality is part of all of us, but the visual cues of a bump or the reminders of pregnancy in other ways can bring this new identity as a parent to the fore, and these two identities – particularly the sexual and the maternal – can feel challenging to integrate. There's a strong idea in our society that parents somehow aren't, or shouldn't, be sexy or sexual and this can bring feelings of guilt or shame in enjoying sex or letting go. Many people report feeling easily distracted during sex by the presence of a bump, or the idea of a baby. This distraction may be experienced by the pregnant person or their partner, but can understandably be amplified for the pregnant person by the sensory cues of feeling the baby move.

Given that body image and sexual satisfaction are strongly linked, it's not surprising that pregnancy body image plays a big part in how pregnant people feel about being sexual. The changes that bodies go through during pregnancy place people at greater risk for body-image concerns, as our society has such narrow and fixed standards of which body sizes represent 'beauty'. Stretchmarks, breast changes or increasing body size might not feel problematic in themselves, but the way people feel about or relate to these changes can impact on their ability to connect with the sexual side of themselves. Trans men or non-binary people who are pregnant have to pause gender affirming hormones and, as a result, may experience changes to their body that trigger dysphoria, potentially reducing their desire to be sexual alone or with a partner.

For some, pregnancy can be a time of really being able to let go of these societal constraints, as having a large abdomen no longer holds an unhelpful negative connotation. The opportunities from this for sexual expression, desire and pleasure are huge, as being less pre-occupied during sex frees us up to focus more of our attention on sensation and arousal. For some, this experience can be empowering and perhaps the first time they've ever felt free of such concerns, opening a new world of psychological investment in sex.

Given that pregnancy is a time of intense physical and psychological transition that can have such a big impact on sex, it's disappointing that we don't talk about it more. How can we prepare people for the opportunities and challenges of changing bodies, changing relationships and new experiences without open and honest discussion about it?

But what if getting pregnant itself was challenging?

Getting pregnant is only one of the 237 documented reasons that humans have sex,[2] but for some people the period of time leading up to a positive pregnancy test might have been heavily focused on getting pregnant as a key non-sexual motivation. For those of you that this applies to, especially if you struggled to conceive or had many miscarriages, sex might have become boring, predictable, associated with stress, not associated with desire, and something that, once you got pregnant, you felt quite happy to take a bit of a break from. Feeling like this after trying to conceive is totally normal. It's also likely to affect one or both of you for some time post-birth. Is this something you've ever talked about? Many people can feel quite ashamed of these feelings, as they feel it takes the shine off the romanticism around conception, or worry that it says something about their sexual relationship. The truth is these are normal feelings to have, and acknowledging them can allow you to open up a conversation about needing to do things differently for a bit.

Rob and Sunita came to see me about the impact of trying to conceive on their sex life. They had conceived without medical intervention, but they had tried every month to get pregnant for almost two-and-a-half years. Sunita told me that, around ovulation, she felt a sense of psyching herself up for having sex and that sex had become going through the motions. She described very little passion or sensuality in the sex that they had, and she couldn't remember the last time she had felt like having sex as opposed to feeling she *had* to. She told me that she felt ashamed to admit that she enjoyed having sex in positions where Rob couldn't see the lack of enthusiasm on her face. I wondered how Rob might feel hearing this in therapy, but he said he felt pleased to hear it wasn't just him. He described feeling dread in the week that followed Sunita's period, as he knew they were going to be trying again soon. Due to the lack of eroticism in the sex that they were having, as well as the pressure for it to happen, he struggled to either stay hard, or to come, and this led to a lot of anxiety for him. He experienced sex like a presentation in work he had to give where all eyes were on him and it had to go well. There wasn't much in the sex itself that was arousing, so he started to try to stay turned on by focusing on things he had seen in porn. This worked for him on a physical level, and they eventually managed to conceive, but what they had been through took its toll. They had both been too ashamed to admit how little they had enjoyed sex for the last few years, as they didn't want to cast any shadows over their sex life, their relationship or their daughter, whom they adored. But they had spent so long finding ways to get through sex by disconnecting with the process and each other that the sex that they had after their daughter was born followed the same pattern. Sunita and Rob needed some help to find new purpose and meaning in sex after being motivated by pregnancy for so long, and to remember how to emotionally connect through sex. But they also needed to acknowledge the impact that trying to conceive had on them, and to be able to talk about this openly, without blame.

How to tackle it

You have a couple of options to be able to redress the impact of trying to conceive. Firstly, it's really okay to have some time off. In fact, one of the best things that you can do is forget about sex for a bit and focus on the sexual currency between you. Another change that will help is to enjoy finally taking the focus away from penis-in-vagina sex for a bit and have a bit more variety in your sex life. For example, sex sessions that are just kissing passionately for fifteen minutes, one of you giving the other oral sex, or making each other come with your hands. All of this is sex and can often be much hotter than the type of sex you had in a formulaic way when trying to get pregnant. Changing up your sex life after trying to conceive can bring with it a novelty-induced spike in desire and allow you both to reset. Societal expectations about what sex looks like (the 'sexual scripts' that we discussed earlier) can make it hard to do this without discussion, hence the need to have an honest conversation about the impact of trying to conceive on both of you, like Sunita and Rob did.

TASK: Our sex life, and getting pregnant

This task is divided into a few parts. Firstly, take a moment to discuss how pregnancy or trying to conceive has had a lasting influence on your sex life now. List three opportunities it brought and three challenges it created. Did it open you both up to new things? Mean you had gotten out of the habit of being sexual by the time the baby was born? Lead to one of you feeling rejected, which continues to affect you now? Take the shine off sex a bit and make it feel like a task on your to-do list?

Reflect on these opportunities and challenges together. Which of the opportunities do you want to make sure you benefit from as you move into your future sex life? For example, if pregnancy was a time during which you had more varied sex in terms of types of sex and positions, and you enjoyed this, make a commitment together to not lose this from your future sex life.

Look at the challenges. Which of those are a sign of something that you might need to work on? For example, if you noticed it was hard for the two of you to talk and overcome issues that were cropping up as bodily changes happened, take this as a sign that it might be helpful to work on better communication about sex, so that you can be better prepared the next time a challenge presents itself.

If there was no impact of pregnancy or trying to conceive, or only a small one, that's okay too. Remember, however, that you may also have had totally different experiences with this.

The final part of this task is to discuss what you need from each other moving forward to counteract or accommodate this. For example, are you nervous to initiate, as you felt so rejected? Do you need more compliments on your appearance to feel sure your partner still finds you attractive? Did you find sex more enjoyable as it was less predictable and want more of this? Did you get so used to not being sexual that you feel you both need to make a real effort to bring your sexuality back together? Do you need a break from sex or at least a break from penis-in-vagina sex to bring back some novelty again?

Ideally share your answers together, and make a commitment to use this information for the good of your sex life moving forward. The real value here is in hearing each other out and going easy on each other. Sometimes challenges around sex can make us feel like we are on different teams, but, remember: you are on the same team, and you both need to hear what the other has felt and what each other needs. If you're struggling to come up with ideas about how to move forward, don't worry – there will be plenty of ideas as you read on in this book.

What if sex has been absent?

It's common during pregnancy for people to either feel worried about having sex, or to feel differently about their changing body, in a way that makes having sex feel less possible or less enticing for a period of time. Interestingly, there are some cultural differences here, with some communities holding stronger beliefs on sex being something they should avoid during pregnancy and being less likely to have sex in this time. In particular, sex research[3] has picked up on trends from Turkey, Thailand, Taiwan, China, Pakistan, Iran, the US and Canada, noting an increased concern around the potential harm to the foetus comparable to other cultures. For some people this may show itself in an adaptation around one's sex life. For example, taking penetrative vaginal sex off the menu and enjoying different types of sex instead, such as using hands, mouths or anal penetration, as I mentioned earlier. But I want to focus specifically here on those couples who don't engage with their sexuality as a couple in any way during pregnancy and the possible impact of this on their sex life.

For some of you, if you had a hard time trying to conceive, having a break from any type of sex for some time may have been a welcome relief for one or both of you, allowing you to 'reset' your interest in sex again without the pressure of an ovulation schedule. This may have been just what your sex life needed and allowed you to start up your sex life again with interest as soon as you were getting some sleep.

For others, a break in being sexual during pregnancy may have established a new status quo of being out of practice relating to each other in a sexual way. It can be a lot to expect, to try to relaunch a sexual relationship that has started to feel distant, awkward or stilted after one of you has given birth, or in the first year of your child's life, when your sex life is up against the biggest challenges possible. The past is the past, and you can't (and may well not wish to) change the decisions you made about your sex life at this time. They were the right decisions for you at the time. But it may be useful for both of you to acknowledge the impact that this may have had on where you are at now, as it contextualizes challenges you may be facing in reinstating your sex life. Not in a way designed to blame, but in a way designed to support understanding and, as a result, support change.

Tilly and Becca were a couple like this. They struggled to conceive via IVF and it was a stressful time for them, with multiple disappointments and heartbreaks, mounting sense of financial pressure, and strain on their relationship. When Tilly finally got pregnant on their sixth round, with only one viable embryo left, she felt an enormous sense of pressure to protect the pregnancy. She had read on various websites and heard from their midwife that sex during pregnancy was safe for them, and they knew this to be the case rationally. But they couldn't shake this idea of the foetus being delicate and vulnerable, and Tilly worried about orgasms shaking the baby out of her womb somehow. They continued to be physically affectionate during pregnancy, with cuddles, brief kisses, holding hands etc, but nothing more sexual than this.

Becca felt less nervous than Tilly, and felt the loss of relating to each other sexually during the pregnancy, but the impact of the previous cycles weighed heavy on her, so she was happy to agree to Tilly's preferences in the hope of a different outcome. It was never really spoken about, but there was a clear underlying communication that sex was off the cards. Their relationship stayed strong, and they were excited about the chapter that was to come. Sex, however, became something that was less and less a part of who they were as a couple. They came to see me when their son was fifteen months old, as they were finally getting some sleep, Tilly was no longer breastfeeding, and they had not had any type of sex together since the IVF days, more than two years previously. They told me that they were feeling distant and 'like

110

sisters' without their sexual connection, that they were both fearful that they were experiencing 'lesbian bed death'* and that they were worried about the impact of this on their relationship.

We worked together to acknowledge that the choice they made was the right choice for them at the time, but to also simultaneously notice the very real changes that this had brought, and how this was showing itself in their current sex life. Not being sexual for some time can push our relationship culture outside of a sexual zone, which can feel hard to come back from. We can address this, but the journey to reinstating being sexual together may require some effort for us to push through habit and awkwardness. When I meet with couples like this (which I do, often), I wonder how they have got the idea that they should be easily able to reverse this pattern, without any professional support, when they are going through potentially the most challenging phase of their personal and relationship life they have ever faced, in a sleep-deprived state. In my opinion, the idea comes from the media's representation of sex and desire as instinctive drives that we all have and should feel directed to a person we love. But as you learned in Chapter 3, this idea of us all having a drive to be sexual regardless of context is just not backed up by science. Absence can make the heart grow fonder, and this can be a boost to sex for some, but an absence of sex can also make us feel like strangers.

For Tilly and Becca, the acknowledgement that came from our conversations in therapy, that the choice they had made to not have sex was simultaneously right for them and had also created a culture that

---

* 'Lesbian bed death' is a term that refers to an idea that gained popularity in the 1980s that women in same-sex relationships were more at risk of their relationship moving to complete sexlessness after a few years of being together. This theory had as its justification the mere fact that they were both women. This urban legend has been discredited by sex science as a myth, but it still impacts on women who have sex with women, as it is still spoken about in the community, and written about often in clickbait internet pieces.

did not support their sex life, was helpful. Agreeing that the expectation of trying to reverse this trend, at a time when they and their relationship had never been more strained, was unrealistic, allowed them to breathe a sigh of relief. In sex therapy, people are hardly ever as concerned about the surface issue they bring (for example, that they have stopped having sex) as the deeper issue they feel it speaks to ('this risks the end of our relationship if we don't fix it'). Tilly and Becca needed to spot and name this awkwardness about reinstating their sexual life together in order to join forces as a team to overcome it. We will talk more about how they did this in Chapter 8.

This chapter is about understanding the impact of your conception and pregnancy journey on the place in which you find your sex life at this stage. The purpose of this is not to reflect negatively on any choices you made. Those choices were right for you at the time. The purpose is to look at the impact of those choices on the sexual trajectory that you started your life as parents with. Were you already on a favourable course, as pregnancy opened up a whole new world of sensation and experience and brought you closer? On the right track, as trying to conceive was some of the most fun sex you have had and reignited your love for sex with each other? Or has pregnancy sex and trying to conceive limited your sex life and created a sense of distance or monotony? How realistic have you each been about getting things back on track, with a new baby and sleep deprivation? Being able to acknowledge the impact of this period together, and make a plan to overcome it, just like Tilly and Becca, can be a crucial part of the picture when it comes to weathering the storm, particularly in the choppy seas of the first few months or years.

5

Batten down the hatches
The first year

Birth is a challenging physical and psychological event that can also be joyous, powerful and spiritual. I want to invite you to take some time to reflect on the impact of the birth of your child, both the physical aspects and the psychological. We'll also look at the first few months to a year after birth as a time of huge upheaval and relationship change and notice which relationship habits support or challenge your sexual and relationship satisfaction at this time. If you don't feel this section is relevant to you, as your child arrived in your life through other means, or after the first year, feel free to skip ahead to the next chapter.

In the last few chapters I have drawn your attention to the fact that our sex lives are formed and moulded by the cumulative effect of patterns to which we have been exposed. For example, within a long-term relationship, while trying to conceive, or perhaps in how our sex lives have been during pregnancy. Research has found that although our sex lives are significantly disrupted by having a new baby, the health of our relationship, ability to communicate and whether we had any sexual difficulties in pregnancy have an important bearing on how likely we are to struggle with our sex lives in this challenging first year.[1] This means that, although having a new baby and the chaos this creates will create a perfect storm for your sex life during this time, how things were *before* your first child arrived will have an impact on how easy it is (or was) for both of you to navigate these choppy waters.

Sex in the first year after having a baby

The more challenging news first. Sexual satisfaction declines in the first twelve months of being a parent for a third to half of all new parents.[2] Sexual difficulties, such as painful sex, arousal, desire and orgasm are common for new parents, particularly in the first year. Around 90 per cent of parents report one or more sexual concerns ,which often resolve by twelve months after birth.[3]

In the first six months to a year of having a new baby, sex often takes a back seat, and this is entirely normal. Just over half of new parents get back to penetrative sex in the first eight weeks and find this is fine for them;[4] by three months this figure has risen to 89 per cent.[5] Despite most couples trying penetrative sex in the first few months, the frequency of penetrative sex for most people doesn't go back to how things were pre-pregnancy until usually after the first year, and for many not for years.

The speed at which people return to having penetrative sex is (unsurprisingly) dependent on how their birth went. Those who had a vaginal birth without the use of instruments (such as forceps), episiotomy, or a second-, third- or fourth-degree tear are more likely to resume sex earlier than those who didn't.[6] In terms of other types of sex, it's interesting to note that, for people who have given birth, solo sex (masturbation) returns to pre-pregnancy levels at around four to six months, much sooner than penetrative sex.[7] Why do you think this is? My guess is that, as with masturbation generally, people feel free to enjoy touch that is right for them (most people with vulvas masturbate with the clitoris at the centre of their focus), at a time which suits them (and by 'time', I'm referring to convenience but also the speed at which it can happen alone, typically within a few minutes) and without feeling scrutiny of their post-birth body. When we think of masturbation this way, we can see how having sex with a partner, especially if there's lower reward in terms of pleasure, and higher perceived effort and self-consciousness, could feel less enticing.

There is some research on the frequency with which people return to partnered sex that isn't penetrative, such as giving oral sex, which is also interesting. For example, one study showing that a third of women had given their male partners oral sex within four weeks of giving birth.[8] We may need to take these figures with a pinch of salt, as this particular study is from 1996, and people's sexual lives, and sense of themselves as having sexual agency has (I hope) shifted since then. I say this as the research tells us that many women don't particularly enjoy giving oral sex to men,[9] so this particular finding, to me, suggests a dynamic that speaks to satisfying partners at a time where the majority of women are not feeling in a sexual headspace at all. I hoped that this may be a 90s trend, but after an hour spent perusing the message board of a popular mums networking site when writing this chapter, I discovered, to my dismay, that the trend of feeling obliged before one is ready (and crucially, feeling resentful about this) is still alive and kicking. There are stories of male partners circling the date six weeks after birth on the calendar as a reminder of what is expected and when. I'm unsure as to whether the multiple stories of women meeting male partners' needs in this early month or two post birth is sexual generosity and a strength to the relationship or a dynamic connected to the (unfounded) patriarchal concept that somehow cishet men will not be able to survive without sex, an assumption that we don't often extend to cishet women in return. I suspect we might find the answer to this if we knew whether this level of sexual giving happened at the same rate in queer relationships too.

One of the things that frustrated me after my own births was that there was no information on what healthcare professionals *actually meant* when they talk about 'having sex' or 'avoiding sex'. I was left with lots of questions about what that looked like and what the risks were. For example, was the issue vaginal penetration, but clitoral stimulation was okay? Was any touch to the vulva not okay if the skin had been damaged? Was it okay to have an orgasm, or might the uterine contractions that happen as part of orgasm be problematic after a caesarean? What if the sex I wanted to have was not about touch to me, but touch to someone else? Was even getting really turned on an issue soon after birth due to increased blood flow?! I believe that we need to be much more specific about what types of sex we might expect someone to avoid, and which are okay. Although most people don't, some people will want to return to having sex in the first few weeks following a baby being born. How do we equip them with the information they need if we can't be specific about what we mean by 'sex'? This, of course, is connected to wider issues with how we use language about sex in society, in that 'sex', particularly in a heteronormative context, is often intended to mean 'penis in vagina', and that this way of seeing sex is linked to a society with a history of associating sexual activity with procreation rather than pleasure.

I spoke with Dr Anita Mitra (aka @gynaegeek), a gynaecologist and author of *The Gynae Geek: Your No-nonsense Guide to 'Down There' Healthcare* (HarperCollins, 2019), about cutting through the nonsense here and getting to the facts. This was her reply:

There aren't any strict rules on when you can start to have sex after birth. It really depends on what kind of birth you had, whether you've had sutures to your perineum, how your bleeding is and how you feel. We also need to take into account what kind of sex you want to have. I'll put my hands up and confess that the medical profession is pretty old-fashioned, so when we refer to 'sex', you can generally assume that the individual is referring to heteronormative penetrative sex.

According to the Royal College of Obstetricians and Gynaecologists, 90 per cent of people having their first vaginal birth will have a graze, tear or episiotomy, and just under 70 per cent following second and subsequent vaginal births. Grazes and small, superficial tears will heal on their own, but sutures are needed for deeper tears, and to close an episiotomy, which is a cut that the midwife or doctor will make, if needed, to give more space for your baby to be born. The sutures used will dissolve in about two weeks, by which time everything should be well knitted together but is still healing inside. I would advise waiting at least until this time to have any kind of vulval touching or penetration to avoid introducing infections or disturbing the healing tissues.

After having a C-section, you won't have sutures in your perineum, but if you laboured beforehand, your vulva may still be quite swollen. There are multiple layers of sutures from the skin down to the wall of the uterus, but you won't be able to disturb any of these if you have any kind of sex.

However, after any kind of birth you will have bleeding (lochia), which can last up to eight weeks. Initially this bleeding is heavy and like a period, and while this is the case I advise against penetrative sex, as the cervix may be slightly more open, increasing the risk of infection of the lining of the womb (endometritis). Over time the bleeding will tail off, becoming pinkish or brown like the end of a period, and at this point resuming penetrative sex is fine, provided you feel comfortable.

Getting turned on, or having an orgasm, isn't going to do any harm at any stage during your recovery.

Urinary incontinence is common after birth, even following a C-section, due to nine months of pressure on your pelvic floor, and it can happen during sex. If this is the case, please be reassured that sex isn't making it worse, but it is a sign that you should see your GP to discuss seeing a pelvic health physiotherapist, who will be able to help you with this. Vulval and vaginal dryness are also common in the months after birth, particularly if you are breastfeeding, and for this reason I highly recommend a good lubricant when you do decide to start having sex. And as always, contraception is still important, as you can get pregnant from about three weeks after birth.

Hopefully, if you are in the birth to a year phase (or might plan to revisit this phase again in the future for another child), Dr Mitra's sound advice will help you make decisions about what types of sex might be okay to return to, should you feel up to it.

So why do our sex lives fall off the agenda?

This will be staggeringly obvious to all of you who have been through early parenthood, but a lack of sex can be due to a combination of factors, including the physical and psychological recovery after birth, sleep deprivation, the stress of having a new baby, the new increase in workload and loss of time, a change in body image, and sometimes the relationship challenges of becoming new parents. Did you know that having a baby takes an estimated extra thirty hours extra time out of our lives a week?[10] (To be honest, when I saw this statistic, I was surprised it wasn't higher – it certainly felt like it was to me.) For those with multiple births or babies with particular health needs, this, of course, would be even higher still.

Sleep

Getting enough sleep has an important relationship with our sex lives. Studies tell us that having even one hour extra sleep a night can increase our chances of having sex the next day by a whopping 14 per cent.[11] We also know that sleeping poorly is associated with reduced sexual satisfaction and reduced frequency of sex.[12] Basically, if you're not getting much sleep, don't expect to want much sex.

I'd like to say that the impact of tiredness on the sex lives of parents is limited to the first six months to a year, but this would not be the truth. Sadly, many people struggle with this until their kids are much older, or at least until they sleep well all night (research suggests that parents' sleep goes back to normal when the youngest child is six years old[13]). Thirty to forty per cent of new parents report being too tired for sex,[14] and the effect of tiredness doesn't just end with sex itself. The same study found that other sensual but non-sexual touch fell of the agenda with tiredness also – for more on this, see p. 74, and the section on 'sexual currency'. Remember that 'sexual currency' connects us as a sexual couple even when we're not having sex, and also acts as stepping stones towards desire. It also helps us to build a foundation of free and easy ways of sexually relating, making it easier to kickstart our desire when it isn't there to begin with. So being tired has a triple-whammy effect on our sex lives by:

- Reducing our motivation to have sex in the first place

- Reducing our motivation to engage in 'sexual currency', behaviours that help us feel connected and satisfied in the relationship when we are *not* having sex

- Reducing 'sexual currency', which has the consequence of reducing opportunities to trigger desire

Tiredness impacts on all of these things, reducing the *frequency* with which sex happens, but interestingly doesn't seem to affect how much we enjoy the sex if, by some miracle, we summon up the energy and enthusiasm to do it.[15]

The outcome of all of this is: if you are getting a full night's sleep, and your partner is awake two to three times through the night, don't expect them to feel as interested in sex as you. The best thing you can do for your sex life in this scenario is share the load. This could look like offering to do the night feed, or taking the baby during the day so that your partner can nap. More on the division of household labour in the next chapter. Sleep deprivation and a good sex life don't go hand in hand, so ease off the pressure around sex and work on sleep. There's a potential impact of economic privilege here also, as those with help from grandparents or paid childcare throughout the night might suffer less, and those with no support suffer more. Where your child sleeps matters too, as you might feel restricted (and/or more disturbed) with your child in your room or your bed. Some couples choose to sleep in separate rooms in the early days, creating not only a separate sleep deprivation experience, but also reducing the opportunity to have sex created by bed sharing with a partner. Sleeping in separate rooms is by no means a bad idea (for any couple, not just new parents), but it's worth considering that it takes away some opportunity to connect physically, which will need to be created another way, and to factor this into any plan you have around your sex life as you move forward.

Research has found a direct correlation between getting up repeatedly to care for your baby/child in the night and lower sexual satisfaction. Researchers looked at several factors related to sexual satisfaction in co-parents of infants (zero to eighteen months) related to sleep, relationship satisfaction, how often the child wakes in the night, and the number of times one of the parents gets up to care for the child in the night.[16]

They found something really interesting – the number of times a parent got up in the night had a significant impact on sexual satisfaction. Basically, the more times you get up to soothe or feed your child, the less likely you are to be content with your sex life. They found that this is most relevant to people who get up twice or more in the night.

But what is the relationship between getting up to see to a child and sexual satisfaction in your relationship? They hypothesized several possible mechanisms which are:

- the negative impact on our mood state of being woken (low mood and stress reduce our interest in sex), particularly if the encounter in the night is emotionally challenging (i.e. a distressed child)

- tiredness (which has been well documented to reduce our interest in sex)

- the impact of hormonal changes on the parent by a process of sleep deprivation

- disruption of parents own sleep patterns resulting in less REM sleep (this stage of sleep is needed for our physical sexual response)

- low energy levels from lack of sleep

If you are the person who has the primary responsibility for night-time caregiving, perhaps as you are breast/chest feeding, or due to the arrangement that you have around responsibilities, then please be aware that you might have very different relationships to sex at this time and this is okay. Remember, it is normal to be woken in the night to care for your child, and meeting their needs and you getting sleep is the most important priority at this time, so give yourself a break if your sex life is struggling in this context.

This research was for parents of children who were less than eighteen months old. Although sleep usually improves for parents as children age, for many parents it stays tough, especially if they add in a second or third child once their first has just started sleeping well. The sleep issue is not going away and all we can do is understand it, and appreciate it will have an impact on sex. The key here is to try not to take it personally, find other ways to feel sexually connected, find other ways to get our motivations for sex met when sex is less available, share night-time waking as best we can, and not expect too much from ourselves.

Whether your child sleeps well or not can feel a bit like a lucky dip, and hanging out with other parents whose babies are sleeping more can also take its toll psychologically, making the challenge of your tiredness even more emotionally salient. Frustrations and arguments between you and your partner about lack of sleep, and perhaps who gets up most or has it worst as a result, can also create emotional distance or resentment between you, making sex with your partner feel less enticing as it lowers our receptivity to being sexual.

Breast and chest* feeding

In this first six months to a year, there can be a strong sense of your body belonging to others and having to adjust to it being touched and consumed all day long. Your breast/chest, as well as being swollen and uncomfortable, may also be painful to the touch, with cracked or painful nipples. It may have also gone from being a part of the body associated with sexuality to feeling like an all-you-can-eat diner with really demanding clientele, which can result in people just feeling like they want ten minutes without someone touching them, not the other way round.

A third to half of mothers who were breastfeeding in one study said it produced erotic feelings for them and a quarter of these said they felt guilt about this.[17] I don't feel this is talked about enough as a potential disincentive to touch from a partner. Some studies have found that breastfeeding doesn't impact on the time to resuming being sexual again post birth, but does seem to impact on the frequency of being sexual post birth.[18] This would make sense, given that the hormones that support milk production can reduce desire and make painful vaginal sex more likely. People who have been pregnant can leak milk when they get turned on and at the point of orgasm, sometimes with quite a forceful squirt. Again, this is something I'm not sure most new parents are warned about, and although this can be laughed at, celebrated or may even be erotic for some, it can be a huge turn-off for others.

The impact of sensory overload, from breast/chestfeeding, or being a primary caregiver more generally, along with breasts/chest feeling like an area with changed meaning, sensitivity or appearance, can be

* Chest feeding is a less gendered term that can be more comfortable for trans and non-binary people who are feeding their child this way.

enough to block any emerging sexual desire. Crucially, if we can't communicate easily about this when we want to be sexual – for example, 'I want to leave my top on' or 'Please don't touch my breasts' – this can impact on our motivation to go there. Instead, we might reduce this discomfort by simply avoiding the whole thing rather than talking about what adjustments might make it do-able. As ever, communication can make the difference here between being a couple who manages to navigate a clear route around the sexual challenges in the first year, and those who do not.

Pelvic floor function and tears

The pelvic floor muscles form a hammock-like structure in the pelvis, running from the pubic bone at the front to the tailbone at the back. In women and people with vulvas, the urethra, vagina and anus pass through, and are supported by, these muscles. The pelvic floor muscles have several important jobs, such as to keep your pelvic organs in place, ensuring continence and supporting the weight of your body, among others. In pregnancy, the pelvic floor muscles support the weight of the pregnancy and can be weakened in this time. They also stretch to allow the baby to be delivered vaginally for those who have a baby this way, and can take some time to heal afterwards.

It is common, but should never be considered to be normal, to have pain, a sensation of heaviness or leaking urine after giving birth. Experiencing these things, and the embarrassment and shame that can be linked with them can understandably have an impact on how people feel about returning to sex. I see plenty of people in my clinic who worry about leaking urine when they are naked, or when they orgasm, who worry about the impact of this on a partner's opinion of them. You will hopefully have received advice pre- and post-natally on looking after your pelvic floor at this time by starting pelvic floor exercises in pregnancy, and getting back to them straight away post birth. There's lots of help on looking after your pelvic floor on apps like Squeezy, registered pelvic health physiotherapists who post tricks, tips and things to look out for on Instagram, and the POGP, a collective group of registered UK pelvic health physiotherapists, who produce factsheets and guides (see the resources section at the end of this book for more information). There's also some great books, such as *Why Did No One Tell Me?* (Vermillion, 2021), by pelvic health physiotherapist Emma Brockwell, which deals, among other things, with pelvic-floor rehab after delivery. If you are worried about your pelvic-floor function, your GP can refer you to a pelvic-health physio for an assessment.

Tears to the vulva are common during delivery, and the majority of people who experience them recover with no lasting impact on their sex lives, particularly with first- and second-degree tears. Damage to the anal sphincter in third- and fourth-degree tears is closely associated with changes in continence and body confidence, however, both of which can affect sexual functioning. Third- or fourth-degree tears can impact on anal continence in a variety of ways (from not being able to hold in passing wind as well as partial or complete anal incontinence). The physical impact of this may even be less impactful than the psychological (i.e. it is far more common to worry about passing wind, or being incontinent of faeces, than it is for this to happen), but the impact of worrying about it (just as with urine leaking, which we talked about earlier) can understandably turn down our sexual desire, or make it hard for us to focus on sexy stuff even if we want to.

Research tells us that people who experience damage to the anal sphincter during childbirth often report concerns with body image related to the effects of this, which can impact on their self-esteem.[19]

Body image and sex do, of course, go hand in hand, especially when we are talking about intimate anatomy and areas of the body that are seen as taboo (like the anus). These concerns about your vulva and vagina don't stop at birth injury either: people can fear that their vagina will be stretched to a point that they or their partner might not enjoy vaginal penetration again (it won't be), or that it might look different in a way that will put their partner off (it might look different, but fears about the impact of this are usually unfounded). These concerns are not just experienced by people who have given birth. Partners who were present at births (or just saw or heard about the discomfort their partner was in afterwards) can also feel worried about what their partner's body (or mind) has gone through and this can impact on their own feelings about sex or motivation to have it.

Something that can really help here is to talk to your partner about how you feel and any fears you have about what you worry might happen, or what you worry they think, as it's likely that it matters less to them than it does to you, and this reassurance can be vital for when you do feel like being sexual again. Talking about such personal fears can be challenging, as many people tell me that they don't want to draw attention to them, in case it turns their partner off. The irony is that sharing these fears can do the opposite – allow you both to relax and enjoy sex without the worry of what they are thinking, or what could go wrong. As you will remember from when we talked about desire earlier, being distracted by non-sexy thoughts or worries is one way our desire can be blocked, so trying to resolve these worries as best we can, by seeking help, or by letting a partner know, can really help your sex life when you return to it. If this is the case for you, please pause here, or bookmark this page, and have a conversation about your biggest fears about this with your partner.

TASK: What can we do about the impact of these physical changes on our sex lives moving forward?

If you gave birth, consider the following questions:

Do you worry your genitals look or might feel different and that your partner may be turned off by them?

Are you worried about passing wind, leaking wee or anal incontinence during sex? What helps you feel more confident here?

Is there something you can both do, to minimize these worries once you feel like being sexual again? (For example, have a towel to hand to put down on the bed, or having sex in the shower)

Do you feel a difference in sensation or pain, which means you want to do things differently for a while? How might you work around this when you get back to sex?

Partners: what worries do you have in relation to your partner's body post birth and what would help you alleviate them?

When you're having this conversation, it's important you try to listen really closely, and reassure each other (if you genuinely can) about your worries. If there's something you're both struggling with here, do seek the advice of a professional to help you move forward. There are some organizations in the resources section at the back of this book that can help.

Also, as you now know, it's good for all couples to try not to fall into a shorthand of penetrative sex being the main focus of sexual activity, and having difficulties following a birth injury can be an opportunity to diversify your sex lives a bit, either while your body recovers, or even for ever, if you want. It's also useful to know that people who've experienced tears often take much longer to start having vaginal sex,[20] so don't feel abnormal if it's the last thing on your mind, even if you're ready to get back to other types of sex (such as mutual masturbation) sooner.

It's important to remember that sex is much more than penetrative vaginal sex, and you really don't have to have vaginal sex ever again, or very often, if you don't want to. That can feel like a huge leap from how the two of you see sex, especially if one of you has a penis, but the truth is, as we covered earlier, vaginal penetration is often the least physically rewarding type of sex for people with vulvas, and you can absolutely have plenty of good sex that meets both of your non-sexual and sexual motivations without it.

Reducing pain during sex

If you do want to experiment with modifying discomfort during vaginal penetration, some positions for penetrative sex will put more pressure on the scar tissue than others, so if you do experience pain at times, you might want to experiment with trying to mix it up in this respect. Lube is everyone's friend (and would be used by everyone during every sexual encounter, if it was up to me). Vaginal penetration is more likely to be painful after a third- or fourth-degree tear, but it can also happen for anyone.

Many people experiencing painful penetrative vaginal sex after birth report that the discomfort diminishes over time, usually between six to twelve months, but it's important not to put up with pain if you're feeling it. Let your partner know, and if you want to have sex, move to a different type of sex which doesn't hurt. Consult with your healthcare provider for support with this at any stage, but especially if it's been twelve months since giving birth and vaginal penetration is still painful.

Please talk to your doctor or relevant healthcare professional about *any* problems or worries you have about your body in this period. Physical problems post birth are common, well researched and often there are solutions. Although you might be feeling embarrassed, the healthcare professional you speak to will have spoken about the problem you are experiencing many times before and will be able to refer you for specialist support. Ideally, this would include a physical examination and an assessment by someone trained to help with these kinds of issues, such as a pelvic health physio. If you'd rather, and have the funds to pay for your care, you can find a qualified pelvic health physio using the POGP website in the resources section at the end of this book.

Mental health post-birth

I mentioned at the start of this chapter that birth can be a joyous and life-changing event. We are all socialized to expect this from our births – to feel in control, for things to go to plan, for us and our partner (if we have one) to be together and feel connected, to be present psychologically when the child enters into the world, to be free from fear or injury. Sadly, it doesn't always happen this way, and some people have experiences that are unexpected, traumatic and difficult to process.

Birth trauma

Having experiences like this – often referred to as 'birth trauma' – can be triggered by the threat of injury or harm to you, your partner or your baby, alongside feeling out of control, scared, not listened to and dehumanized. For some people the psychological impact of birth can stay with them long after the birth itself. Birth trauma can be experienced by the birthing parent *and* the non-birthing parent.

It makes sense, then, that sexual experiences that involve being in the same physical position you were in in birth or the association with the same parts of your body (or your partner's body) can trigger difficult feelings, memories or sensations for people who have experienced birth trauma. When this happens, our brain starts to experience the current situation as a threat, and sends stress hormones circulating around our bodies. Three things happen from here:

- anxiety supresses sexual arousal, so your body will be less receptive to sexual touch and your arousal and desire will drop

- our minds become preoccupied with worries rather than sexual thoughts, and this also turns down our arousal due to a process of distraction

- when we feel anxious, our bodies respond with tension. This includes the pelvic floor muscles, which surround the opening and bottom third of the vagina, which are very responsive to fear. These muscles tense up, making it difficult for penetration to be comfortable.

All of this means that being worried during sex about feeling out of control, sex hurting, or being reminded of past trauma (birth or sexual trauma) can reduce our arousal and our ability to focus on sex, and create tension in our bodies, making us more likely to experience pain, and a vicious circle can be created.

For some people with birth injuries, such as tears, this anxiety (caused by worry about experiencing pain, or triggering birth trauma itself) can be a contributing factor to painful penetrative sex, even if the tear itself isn't causing too much trouble. If you gave birth and you want to feel able to ease yourself back into sex and gain more confidence, a good way to overcome this is to practise penetration yourself with fingers, a sex toy or a set of vaginal trainers, which you can buy online and which come in different sizes, from the size of a little finger upwards. Make sure you are turned on (as being turned on makes penetration more comfortable and possible), so you might do this as part of masturbation, and use touch, fantasy, audio erotica or porn to get yourself in the zone. Use plenty of lube and in a step-wise fashion, start with something small, such as your little finger or a small vaginal trainer, and see how it feels when there's no pressure and when you're in control. When you feel confident with that size, try again at another sitting with the next size up, and so on. Building your confidence with this when you are alone will take the tension, anxiety and distraction out of it. This undermines that vicious circle, giving you more chance of success when you're with a partner. Although waiting until you're ready to try is absolutely the best advice, sometimes putting it off for a long time can add to the fear that it won't go well, and start the cycle mentioned above. So, for some people, having a practise alone sooner rather than later can be helpful.

If you have experienced birth trauma and your experiences from birth are triggered with certain aspects of sex, there are two things that can help. The first is to access support from your GP, or antenatal team, as you may be able to access a birth reflections clinic to review what happened, which can help with getting answers, piecing things together, processing and perhaps access to psychological support. The second thing is to alert your partner to the fact that this is happening, what the likely triggers are (for example, certain positions), how you might look or what you might do when you feel this way so they can easily spot it, and encourage them to use (or to prompt you to use) grounding techniques to help you stay anchored in the present. You can discuss what these might be beforehand but they might be something like:

- an embrace to feel connected and to remind yourself that you are not in a clinical environment and are safe

- a phrase that the two of you agree on that is said out loud

- moving your focus to something that puts you in control and helps you feel relaxed (for example, holding hands and eye gazing until the feeling has passed).

There are organizations to support you with birth trauma in the resources section at the end of this book.

Psychological wellbeing

Many parents experience low mood and depression in the first few weeks of their child's life, and it's important to know that this is common, particularly for the person who has given birth. Talking and sharing how you feel in this period, as well as asking for support from partners, family and friends can help. A smaller (but still very sizeable) number of people will experience more challenging mental health problems, such as post-natal depression, which a recent review of global research suggested is as high as 26 per cent across the globe in the postpartum period for people giving birth.[21] Post-natal depression is strongly associated with a lack of social support, conflict or dissatisfaction in the relationship, and stressful life events. As with most things, there are groups of people who are more at risk of post-natal depression due to having intersecting challenges or past or current experiences of oppression (for example, socioeconomic status, physical health challenges, childhood trauma).[22]

Although post-natal depression and birth trauma are sadly both common, there are other challenges with mental health that new parents (particularly but not exclusively the birthing parent) can face, including anxiety, obsessive compulsive disorder, or post-natal psychosis. If you are in this period and struggling with your mental health, please know that there are people around to help you who will not judge you and will also support you to cope. There are things that can help. Most importantly, if you are struggling with your mood in any of these ways, please forget about sex for now. It will wait, and what is happening with your mood (or the medications you have been given to help your mood) will be one of the factors impacting your desire, and your sexual function (for example, your ability to orgasm). Your feelings about sex are likely to improve once your psychological wellbeing does, and, if they don't, you can address them then when you are feeling better. Talk to your GP, health visitor or postnatal team. Let your partner, family or friends know, if they don't already.

I have put some support organizations in the resources section at the end of this book – they can be a great place to access support from others who have had similar experiences, as well as information about what can help.

How Not to Let Having Kids Ruin Your Sex Life

Forget about frequency

The frequency of sex is often something we use in society as a yard-stick of a 'normal' sex life, but it's important to note that frequency of sex does not correlate that well with sexual satisfaction. We looked at this in Chapter 1 when we considered what we know about sexual satisfaction. I often say that having sex once a year that blows your socks off and leaves you feeling great about yourself and your relationship is better for you than weekly sex that leaves you feeling lacking in pleasure or connection. Sexual satisfaction can also be achieved by not having sex – for example, in how you connect and meet those needs in other ways, in turning each other down grace-fully and in understanding and showing empathy when the other person isn't in a sexual headspace. So let's put frequency and the time it takes people to get back to having (any type of) sex to one side and look at what happens to sexual satisfaction and sexual desire in the first year of being parents.

As we discussed in Chapter 1, sex is often a way to connect, to feel wanted, to create moments of intimacy, and to create a strong emo-tional climate in a relationship, helping us feel like a team. It makes sense, then, that a change in ability to do this could create challenges in relationships. You could be forgiven for thinking that the solution for this is to simply try to make yourself have more sex, even if it is low down your priority list, as sexual satisfaction often leads to rela-tionship satisfaction and 'charges the battery' of the relationship climate. This is *not* the answer, especially not in this first year, when you have other competing priorities for your wellbeing. Later on in this book I will share with you some ideas of how you can improve your sexual satisfaction without necessarily having sex or any more sex than you're having now and when you only have small windows of time available. All of the tips in this book are relevant for birth to

134

a year, as long as you feel you have the headspace. Rest assured, though, that some simple conversations can be enough just now. Let's look at how.

What did you expect for your sex life?

Dr Natalie Rosen is a clinical psychologist and sex researcher based in Nova Scotia, Canada, and a colleague I admire greatly for the contribution she and her team at CaSHLab (Couples and Sexual Health Laboratory) have made to the field of sex research, particularly women who experience sexual pain and new parents' sexual lives. In a 2022 paper by Rosen and colleagues, they proposed a mechanism by which sexual satisfaction is determined for new parents.[23] They looked at data from relationship satisfaction for new parents and discovered that 35 per cent of new mothers reported that their expectations for their relationship as new parents were not met. They outlined that, in this relationship research, if new mothers' expectations for non-sexual aspects of the relationship (such as partner support, childcare and equal division of labour) are not met, it was associated with future predictions of relationship dissatisfaction for them and their partners in the short-term future (three months), and also in their longer-term future (eighteen months). Rosen and colleagues wanted to see whether the same could be true for sexual satisfaction. Could having very high hopes for your sex life remaining unchanged by having a baby, and your hopes being dashed, tell us more about how sexual satisfaction might be for couples in new parenthood, more than what's actually happening in their sex lives?

Rosen and colleagues hypothesized that, as with other aspects of the new experience of parenthood, people would have ideas about what their sex life would be like afterwards (and it turns out people are largely optimistic about their ability to cope with parenthood, relationship changes and how their sex lives will be before they have a baby). They found that the direction of this estimate mattered. New parents who expected their sex lives to be unaffected by new parenthood had lower sexual satisfaction once the baby arrived, and the ones who had low expectations for their sex life reported being more sexually satisfied. This was for the person who had given birth as well as the non-birth parent. It wasn't related to other factors, such as how much sex they were having, the presence of breastfeeding or not, or how long the couple had been together.

This is important research, as it tells us that having conversations with our partner about what we hope/hoped might happen, and how we feel about the reality, might be key to improving our sexual satisfaction (with knock-on effects on relationship satisfaction) as new parents, *not* necessarily by how much sex we are having.

This data becomes especially relevant when we see that less than 20 per cent of new parents get any information on what to expect for their sex lives.[24] Did you have information about sex and what to expect during your antenatal classes or as part of your NCT group? If you are reading this and you are a healthcare professional who works with expecting parents in any way, here is where you come in. The sex lives of (most) new parents take a significant hit and it's important that people are prepared for this. When parents are prepared, they are less likely to feel sex is an issue post birth (even if it is), and they are also less likely to take it personally and blame themselves or their relationship. Both of these things can have a huge impact on sexual and relationship satisfaction. Maintaining sexual satisfaction despite not having a regular sex life can help new parents survive this challenging period without taking its toll on the relationship. There are other strategies, too, which I'll share with you later on.

TASK: What were you expecting?

Reflect on this for yourself for a second. How did you expect things to be in your sex life as a new parent? Did you imagine things would stay the same? Did you expect things would be really tricky? Did you hope the impact on your sex life would be less than it has been? How has it panned out? Matched those expectations? Fallen short of them? Exceeded them? How has the reality, compared to your expectations, left you feeling about your sex life? If you feel able, talk to your partner about their answers to these questions too.

At this stage of your parenting journey, I urge you to give yourselves a break from worrying about your sex life, but do keep talking. Try not to let all sexual currency disappear, but remember: sex does *not* have to include penetrative sex. In fact, there's a whole world of sex available to you without it. If you do manage to find a miraculous window between naps, nappies and feeding and you feel like doing it, use plenty of lube, and if you're not feeling like it, don't worry too much. At some point (although it's hard to feel like this at the time!) you will have the time and inclination to work at it again, and as long as you've kept some element of intimacy, connection and comfort with each other and kept talking, you'll be able to get things back on track. Pay attention to sleep and your psychological wellbeing, as these will be the foundation for returning to a more satisfying sex life when you feel ready.

The key takeaway here is that many new parents aren't back to having any kind of frequency around their sex life until almost the end of the first year of a baby's life, and even then (as you'll find out in the next chapter), sex can feel tricky. I tell you this in an attempt to chill you out about 'getting your sex life back' if you have a child under one. There is still loads you can do to connect and reaffirm yourselves as a sexual couple apart from having sex and, in the later chapters of this book, I'll tell you how.

6

Weather the storm

The parenting years

S exual satisfaction can be at its lowest in a couple's lifetime for the first few years of having small children.[1] Similarly, parents experience more conflict and steeper declines in relationship satisfaction in the eight years following the birth of their first child than couples of the same relationship length without children.[2] All of this points to the fact that being a parent of young children, although a hugely rewarding time for many, is also a challenging time for relationships and sex lives. A decline in sexual and relationship satisfaction in this period is linked to poorer mental health, risk of infidelity in monogamous couples, relationship breakdown and less collaborative or sensitive parenting.[3]

I'm not sharing this with you because I want you to feel hopeless. I'm sharing this with you because I want you to feel hope*ful*. The fact that this is common should give you comfort that this is not about you or your relationship. It's normal, and with that understanding you can work on the ingredients of sexual and relationship satisfaction, ingredients that will allow your sex life to emerge into a new and brighter phase.

Your challenge in this phase is simply to survive until you have the energy, time and headspace to improve things. Parenting is a storm for your sex life. There is no point trying to resist or fight the storm, as the storm is coming and is bigger than you. Instead, secure the boat as best you can. Make it strong and hold tight, until the storm passes. If you do this, you stand more chance of emerging unscathed. There couldn't be a more relevant proverb to describe the impact of having kids between the ages of one and five at home in regards to your sex life.

This is not to say that there aren't plenty of couples who manage to have a great sexual connection through the first five years of their children's lives without too much effort – there are. If this is you, do still read this chapter, as it will help you to nurture this positive trajectory and understand the ingredients that contribute to it. Far more likely, though, is that you are finding this stage tough.

From my experience with clients, a sex life knocked off course in years one to five of a child's life can often have more impact on you as a couple than the adjustment that accompanies birth to the first year. I have a couple of hunches as to why. Firstly, by the time a child is one or over, there is a social pressure to have 'bounced back' in a million different ways, including sex. Secondly, the excitement, adrenaline and newness of having a baby might have worn off, and the exhaustion of a different kind of tiredness may have firmly settled in. Thirdly, one or both of you may have started to run out of patience with your sex life and you may be starting to wonder 'is this just how it's going to be from now on?' Expressions such as 'Don't worry, we'll get back to it when you're ready' might have been replaced with digs and jibes about how long it's been since you had sex, disguised as thinly veiled 'jokes'. I also notice that it can be harder for people to deal with a similar sex life in year three of parenthood as they had in year zero, precisely because it can look like you have fallen into a new trend of sex leaving the relationship, and this can be terrifying for one or both of you. Perhaps, in some ways, you have, and it feels hard to reverse this. One of the aspects of monogamy rarely spoken about is that sex is one of the few needs we might have that we can't meet outside of the relationship when there are challenges within it. Other needs our partners might not be able to meet, such as someone who might provide emotional support or someone who might share similar interests, we can get from family or friends. Sex is the one thing that, in monogamy, relies solely on each other.

But what exactly is it that makes things so hard in this phase? Some of the top reported challenges to our sex life that having children can bring are:[4]

- Tiredness

- Stress

- Being time-poor

- Reduced feelings of closeness

- Feeling a lack of support from a partner

If you are already a parent, there is zero chance these things will come as a surprise to you, and, indeed, we've covered some of them elsewhere in this book. Before you read on, pause for a second and consider how many of these factors affect your sex life. If you are reading this together, pause and have a discussion about the top three things that you both feel are getting in the way for you and whether you both rank them in the same order. You may, of course, have two, or more, children in this age range, and therefore notice a cumulative effect, or have children with additional needs. You may also have your own, additional contexts, which exacerbate the challenges of parenthood, such as difficulties with your psychological or physical health, disability, financial hardship or other caring responsibilities.

> **TASK:** What are the top three things for you? Does your partner have a similar or different view?

Tiredness

This is a biggie. Sex research is awash with studies which show the impact of lack of sleep on our sex lives. It's not just the impact of sheer exhaustion and lack of energy to get it on. It's also the fact that tiredness impacts on our ability to pay attention, and our physical and psychological wellbeing. Parenthood is a demanding task which requires holding multiple things in mind and switching inbetween tasks frequently. You'll remember from Chapter 3 how important attention is for sex. Lack of sleep also affects the body's chemistry, depleting stores of the very hormones we need as a foundation to underpin sexual functioning. We looked at the impact of sleep deprivation in the first year in the last chapter, but we rarely talk about the *long-term* impact of poor sleep and fatigue on parents in toddlerhood and beyond. Staggeringly, research tells us that parents' sleep is still low in quality, even until a child is six years old.[5]

In many ways it's simple – if you're regularly sleep deprived, then don't expect your sex life to be your priority and find other ways to stay connected sexually. More on how to do this later. Those of you getting up often in the night still: please give yourself a break. Parenthood is hard and sleep deprivation is often the toughest part!

Staying connected in other ways during this time is important, though, and will make for a smoother transition back to a good sex life when things have settled.

If you are mostly getting to sleep through the night, and the tiredness is general exhaustion from being a parent rather than sleep deprivation, then I see you – and I know it's tough. But I do want you to take a gentle look at whether tiredness is the absolute barrier you think it is all of the time. For example, often we feel too tired to go to the gym, but when we go it boosts our mental and physical energy. Often we feel we only have the energy to sit on the sofa and watch TV, but doing so can leave us feeling lethargic and low. I've no doubt you are absolutely shattered most of the time, and this is a barrier to even consider thinking about expending any energy having sex, but I wonder whether it's worth considering whether the pay-off from occasionally helping yourself get in the mood and investing in sex (even infrequently) might actually improve your wellbeing in comparison to other ways you might spend your time? We'll come on to this later when we think about small changes that can make a big difference.

Stress

Stress is a natural by-product of not feeling we have the capacity of being able to meet all of the demands being placed on us. Research indicates that, contrary to the idea that parenthood improves psychological wellbeing, the stress that inadequate government childcare policies and low social support place on parents in industrialized countries leads to parents scoring lower on happiness than non-parents.[6] The impact of this is gendered, with women reporting lower life satisfaction after becoming parents than men.[7] LGBTQIA+

(LGBTQIA+) parents have the impact of additional practical and financial stressors in creating their families, institutionalized transphobia, homophobia and cisheteronormativity in maternity services and healthcare, and unwanted and intrusive questions about their family structure, i.e. 'which one of you is the *real* dad?' Queer families may also face stressors with being seen as a valid family by other families at school on top of other parenting stressors.

As well as impacting on our life and relationship satisfaction, which will often impact on our sex lives indirectly, stress can reduce our desire and how well our bodies work sexually.[8] This happens via two main processes. The first is that the system that controls the stress response in the body, the sympathetic nervous system, reduces other bodily responses, such as sexual arousal, when we feel stress. It's not just thinking about sex that gets shut down, there's also an impact on things like cell regeneration, skin repair and fighting infection. If you've ever noticed dull skin, or that you're getting sick more easily and struggling to have an appetite when you've been stressed, this is what's going on. The other way in which stress impacts our sex lives is that it fills our mind with distractions and worrying thoughts. The effort of dealing with these thoughts diverts our attention from being able to focus on anything sexual in our environment, such as our partner's touch, a flirtatious glance or a sexual feeling in our body. This means that any triggers to be sexual in our environment (which you now know we often need to kick-start our desire) simply don't land.

There are a few things you can do here, and as with tiredness, how you manage this may depend on the stage of parenthood you are at. Firstly, simply know the impact that stress can have on sexual response. You are not broken. Batten down the hatches and focus on keeping connected. Secondly, if you have a tiny bit more capacity, accept that you might need to allow yourself a small amount of time a day to help you manage your high levels of stress (five minutes a day of doing something just for you: listening to a mindfulness app, sitting outside listening to the birds, a breathing practice, or sitting still, listening to a piece of music you find calming will do it). Five minutes a day might sound tricky, but you can help each other to find and protect this time. Think of it like charging up your phone battery proactively before it runs low.

Secondly, be realistic about the circumstances you find yourself in right now and what you're dealing with. Do you have other things to worry about, such as ill health, caring for an elderly family member, or having enough money for food? Times have been hard for many recently and research tells us that economic pressure has a negative influence on our sexual satisfaction. If this is the case for you, don't add to this stress by feeling broken sexually. Know that this will all be playing a part in how your sex life is at the moment, talk to each other about it and revisit conversations about sex once other things feel more manageable.

Household labour, childcare and gender inequality

In her 2020 book, *All The Rage: Mothers, Fathers and the Myth of Equal Partnership* (Harper Perennial), journalist-turned-clinical psychologist Darcy Lockman outlines the facts underpinning gender inequality in household labour. She describes swathes of women (as well as herself) who witnessed their mums taking on the lion's share of the household management, as well as going to work in what was the boom in labour for women in the late 1970s and 1980s, but still retaining the responsibility for all of the housework, cooking and childcare at home. She, and the many other women she interviewed, described how they genuinely thought that, after bearing witness to their mothers' struggles and labelling themselves as feminists, they had chosen a relationship defined by equality and would never find themselves in the same position. They described how this equality had shown itself (to an almost equal degree) in the early days of co-habiting with their male partners, only to become gross inequality when their first child arrived. Even worse, with the birth of the second, men were doing less of the household labour and childcare, not more. These patterns were backed up by scholarly research on the division of household labour for parents.[9]

Lockman positioned this against a backdrop of feminist history, presenting research as she lays out the facts. She describes the biological essentialism argument held by many that women are somehow more predisposed to caregiving, or nurturing, or simply better at multi-tasking. This is not backed up by science. Lockman hypothesizes that we adopt this idea, at times, to protect ourselves from the stark truth that our patriarchal society facilitates most men in relationships with women not doing their fair share (as they can get away with it), and women putting up with it (as compared with her dad's contribution, he's great). She argues that, yes, men have stepped up in their role as more active and present fathers than their own fathers were, and that in research men are more likely to report that they are carrying equal responsibility than their female partners for household labour, when, in fact, they are not. The illusion of equality is there, but the mental load still falls unequally.

Lockman lays out the shocking truth that women in the US do twice the unpaid domestic work than men in the home, even if they both work. In fact, women do about six more hours of domestic labour per week than their male partner even if they are the primary earner.[10] She describes the structural systems that keep this pattern in motion, such as legislation around parental leave. For example, the ratio of men to women's free labour around the home is smallest in Scandinavian countries, which have more equality over paid parental leave, such as Norway. In these countries, men and women have more equal levels of household labour, though women *still* do more. The largest unpaid labour gap is in Southeast Asia, where women's rate of unpaid work around the home beats men's at a rate of six hours to one. Depressingly, Lockman shares the statistic that it has been estimated that it will take another seventy-five years before we achieve equity between men and women for unpaid labour within homes.

This pattern of inequity of household labour amplifying after the birth of a couple's first child also extends, of course, to time spent on childcare, where women in relationships with men do more.[11] Lockman describes how the pattern of birth parent as default parent gets set based on maternity leave, then gets stuck this way, with mothers (when in partnerships with men) then remaining the default parent. Lockman describes how mothers spend more overall time with their children, with more multitasking and overall responsibility for timekeeping. The work that men do in their role as fathers is more likely to be based on more fun, engaging or relational childrearing tasks (for example, taking them swimming). In contrast, women are more likely to end up with the more mentally draining, arguably less 'fun' tasks, such as laundry, personal care and mealtimes. This inequality in type of task, combined with inequality in task division, is, of course, likely to cause resentment. Resentment that may seep into sexual relationships, and resentment that may make holding desire for sex (perhaps feeling like another 'job', targeted towards the person one is currently feeling resentment towards) difficult. Inequality in the domestic load of housework and childcare also reduces women's time, headspace and opportunity to explore their own, individual identity outside the home. Together, these concepts of how inequity in household labour impact on women's sex lives are known as the heteronormativity theory of women's low desire.[12] Basically, women in relationships with men are more at risk of their sex life being knocked off course by societal and gendered expectations of their responsibility for domestic labour than any other group, particularly if they are parents.

This same pattern of inequity is, of course, possible, but is not backed up in research as a trend in same gender/sex relationships, where the division of labour is more equal.[13]

How 'dads are so useless' narratives contribute

Recently, I was in A&E with my son after he had an accident. In the many hours we waited, I noticed the signs on the wall stating that, for the sake of space, only one parent was allowed in paediatric A&E. I noticed that all the parents there were women, which I suppose isn't that unusual, as women are often default caregivers. There was some camaraderie and sharing of snacks between some of the parents of babies and toddlers who were getting restless, and one woman said to another: *'Oh my gosh, thanks! I asked his dad to pack a bag and he didn't think to pack any snacks! Useless!'* The other woman replied: *'That will teach you to trust a man to do it!'* People laughed, and although I noticed this was in part a bonding moment between women who were wanting to connect with others in a time of stress, I also noticed how this very discourse of 'Dads are so useless' is a bit of an own goal for women in relationships with men who are feeling overwhelmed. Unless fathers are treated as equal caregivers with equal responsibility, how are they ever able to develop the skills to know what needs packing? Until men take (and

148

are allowed to take) equal responsibility, how will women ever stop being the manager of the house? Until women stop taking on the position of manager of the house, sometimes having to keep track of the needs of three, four or five people, how can they ever have space in their heads for sex?

Jokes are jokes, but they are also sometimes an insight into the position we feel recruited into by society, our relationships and ourselves. Society is geared to assume mothers as primary caregivers, and women are professionally and economically disadvantaged by this (for example, maternity leave affecting women's career progression so that it makes more sense for them to go part-time as their male partner earns more, thus becoming the household manager by default). But does being the one who works fewer paid hours in order to take on childcare also mean you need to take on all the household admin? Does it mean you need to buy your mother-in-law's birthday present and remember to make sure everyone's clothes are washed for the week ahead?

My experience in A&E also shines a light on how the way we perceive and talk about men's capabilities in this regard also corners women into a position of being the only one who can do it right. To lighten the load of the household admin burden, then, women may also need to let go of the idea that no one else can do what they do as well as them and let go of the need for things to be done their way. Partners, and especially dads, need to take a long hard look at how household admin is distributed and notice how, although they personally benefit from the status quo, their sex life (and relationship) suffers.

Inequality here has an enormous impact on sex, due to six main processes:

- Fatigue from working more hours

- Less physical time available for sex, or to think about sex

- The cognitive load required to hold things in mind, and to shift from one task to the next frequently

- Resentment from the inequality, which reduces relationship satisfaction

- Reduced ability to engage in own hobbies and activities, which promote psychological wellbeing and allow space outside of the role of mother and household manager

- Reduced time available for rest, relaxation and sleep, which are essential for desire

- The perception of a male partner as a 'third child' who needs mothering, reducing the sexual motivation towards that partner

If you're reading this, and you're not the one carrying it all, but are wishing your partner had more headspace for sex, or was less stressed, then sharing the load is a very practical and effective change you can make to improve your sex lives as parents.

Sharing the load, however, does not mean 'tell me a job that needs doing and I'll do it'. That still requires the other person to be the 'manager' of the house and be responsible for delegation and keeping track of tasks. This does *not* reduce stress, nor does it reduce the mental load. Being the boss of the house and delegating tasks is labour in itself. An equal division of labour for a two-parent family with two kids might look like this: each parent has responsibility for the admin for each child (this may include being in one WhatsApp parents' group chat for social, nursery, or school class, receiving school newsletters or calls, and organizing clubs). Whoever is responsible for that child responds to the chat about birthday parties, buys gifts for said parties and pays school lunch money. This is different from one person holding both kids' needs, school dates, friends' birthdays and responsibility for WhatsApp chats in their mind, and the other person offering to help from time to time. The particular division of labour needs to be individualized, of course, for that family's circumstances, but this example is to illustrate the need for one person to hold in mind and execute the whole task needed, not to be told to do the task, when to do the task, or what is required to complete it.

The heteronormativity theory of low sexual desire in women also includes speculation about the psychological mechanisms by which this gender inequity in household labour reduces desire. Researchers suggest that this is about having a sense of unfairness about the different loads you both carry, having less time available to you for rest and relaxation, the increase in stress it brings, and seeing your partner as a dependant (essentially, viewing them as another child).[14]

The authors of this study stress that it's not how you have divided the labour, but the fact that it may be experienced by one person as unwanted, undervalued, invisible, unrecognized and, therefore, feels unjust. This means that it may not be considered unfair by a person who may have reduced their working hours to part-time, leaving their partner working full-time, so that they could do a larger share of the household labour. However, it may be considered unfair if both people find themselves equally busy or work similar hours, and one of them holds the lion's share of holding the household together just because they are a woman. The resentment that can build from experiencing this as unjust can eat away at a relationship over time, making it hard to feel desire for a partner (in fact, having sex can feel like another thing on a full to-do list that you must do to look after someone else).

'Like a third child'

I once had a conversation with a mum who had a second baby at roughly the same time as me. Once, over coffee with the kids nearby, she told me that she felt like she had three children that she had to care for. Her partner was very successful, and earned a good salary that meant that she did not have to return to work, which she appreciated. But since she had stopped working and had children, he had become increasingly reliant on her for basic tasks. She told me that she had to buy his clothes, plan his outfits for the week and even buy his shoes. She told me that he didn't know what shoe size he was, and with the long hours he worked, he had no time to shop, so it was up to her to find them, order them, make sure they fitted and go to the post office to send them back if they didn't. She told me: 'It's like he's not capable of doing anything around the house any more, even for himself.'

She was describing an extreme example of inequity in household labour but also describing the dynamic of seeing your partner as another dependent. Mothering, as wonderful as it can be at times, is a relationship that is inherently non-sexual. Mothers can, of course, be sexy, but we know that mothering itself is not, and research shows that our mothering identities can feel in contrast to our sense of ourselves as sexual beings.[15] When we have to place our partner in the same category as our children, it puts them in this non-sexual role, making it hard to maintain desire or sexual interest in them. This dynamic does not have to be exclusive to cis women in relationships with cis men, though. For example, there may be couples for whom this is the other way round and the male partner is doing the lion's share, but this is rare due to gender inequality in society, patriarchy and the assumption of the mother as the default parent in opposite gender/sex relationships. Also, although we know that this trend doesn't show itself so much in same gender/sex couples, this doesn't mean that it can't be a problem for queer couples too.

Given a change in the equal distribution of household labour can result in a change in sexual frequency[16] as well as satisfaction, there is some solid evidence here that looking at how this works in your relationship (both the visible and the hidden labour) and creating a more 'just' (not necessarily 'even') distribution can help your sex life. As a starting point, I recommend you sit together and brainstorm all the tasks that need to be done or held in mind in each of the following categories:

Family management: e.g. managing everyone's schedules, being the default parent called by school/nursery, holding the responsibility for staying one step ahead for the smooth running of the family

Finance: e.g. budgeting, keeping track of finances and spending, researching utility bill deals, pricing up costs for big events such as birthdays

Life and social planning: e.g. setting up playdates, remembering family birthdays, organizing childcare, planning birthdays and parties, buying clothes

Communication on behalf of others: e.g. managing the WhatsApp chats with school, other parents, nursery groups, maintaining child's and family friendships through text communication

Cleaning: e.g. bathrooms, tidying up, hoovering, ensuring there are clean clothes for the week, washing, ironing

---

House and car maintenance: e.g. watering plants, washing the car, sorting the garden, clearing leaves, cleaning windows

Childcare and child development: e.g. sterilizing bottles, considering their nutrition, homework, bath-time, packing nappy/snack/toy bags to leave the house, bedtime, comforting

Food planning and meals: e.g. meal planning, shopping, cooking and preparing snacks

Parenting logistics: e.g. accepting and filling in any forms re the school trip and making sure the child has what they need for it, costumes for World Book Day, taking them to activities or parties

Household administration: e.g. contacting banks, babysitters, tradespeople etc.

Once you have lists under each section, decide how you feel they should be distributed in a just way, taking into account your unique circumstances. Be aware that household labour tasks are also not weighted evenly when it comes to the impact on your sex lives. Research suggests that tasks related to childcare, social life planning (remembering birthdays, organizing things with friends) and parenthood logistics (i.e. keeping on top of school forms/dinner money etc) have a higher cognitive burden and are most associated with negative effects on one's sex life.[17] Pay particular attention, therefore, to how these tasks are divided.

If you'd like more support with this, Eve Rodsky, author of the 2019 *New York Times*-bestselling book, *Fair Play: Share the Mental Load, Rebalance Your Relationship and Transform Your Life* (G. P. Putnam and

Sons), has developed a card game for couples based on rebalancing the division of household labour, including childcare. Rodsky interviewed hundreds of couples to form 102 tasks that are often needed to maintain family life. These 102 cards include things like 'send thank-you cards', 'complete school forms' or 'meal planning'. Couples work together to first select the cards appropriate to their family then divide them, having discussions as they go about what is necessary to know/undertake for each task.

Crucially, whoever takes that task is fully responsible for it, so the other person no longer needs to hold it in mind, or be asked how to do it, or do parts of it. The cards do not need to be divided equally, but the process of making this labour explicit and it being done with a sense of fairness are key. Rodsky also highlights the importance of this task creating space for both people to have their own free time and to indulge in their own interests outside of the family, interests that allow them to feel exhilarated, fulfilled and content. If you are feeling ground down by the mental load of the household labour or childcare, and notice yourself having no time for yourself, or feeling resentful that a partner seems not to notice the washing in the washing basket, or consider packing your child's bag for nursery, looking into establishing equity here may be the best thing you can do for your sex life right now.

Domestic drift

I coined the phrase 'domestic drift' to explain the phenomenon of having the idea that it would be great to have sex earlier in the day, only to have this intention knocked out of you by the housework or bath-/bedtime routine with the kids. I came up with this term as clients were describing this phenomenon so often and were explaining it like it only happened to them. Most commonly (but certainly not exclusively), a male partner would explain his frustration to me that his female partner would float the idea of sex earlier in the day, only to take it away in the evening when domestic drift had settled in. Domestic drift can happen to all of us, but if it happens more to women in relationships with men, perhaps we should ask ourselves about the relationship between inequity of division of childcare and household labour on the likelihood of experiencing it.

Being time-poor

No one prepares you for just how much time and energy little people take up minute to minute, hour to hour. In the last chapter I shared with you that having a child equates to an extra thirty hours a week labour.[18] In those early days and months especially, it can feel as though your entire existence is dedicated to tending to another little human, so tending to yourself, never mind your relationship or sex life, can feel like an impossible task. Reflect on your pre-kids sex life for a second. At what part of the day or week did you enjoy sex most? Were there other factors that supported this time slot suiting you? (For example, you enjoyed sex in the morning, but only if you'd had a good night's sleep the night before.) How possible are these times for sex now?

When there are practical factors, such as time, that get in the way of your sex life, there are two different ways forward. The first is to choose to prioritize sex in your life and devote regular time to your relationship in a way that works for you both (a very small amount of time and a compromise might also be required here). The second is to accept that your sex life can't happen the way you'd like it to, as life gets in the way, and rest safe in the knowledge that this doesn't mean there is anything wrong with either of you, or that your relationship is doomed. If you choose the latter, you can revisit making time for sex when the time feels right. I suggest the former, as there is always some time that can be made to connect as a sexual couple, even if it's not to have sex, and even if it's only five minutes a week. Attempting to reinstate being sexual with each other again after several years' break can feel awkward and jarring, and so might be, for some people, the more challenging option long term. With both options, talking about the decision that feels right for your relationship right now, and your intentions here with one another, is key. Making a shared decision not to worry about sex for a while but a commitment to come back to a conversation about it and get back on track in the future has a different impact to not discussing sex and one or both of you wondering where your sex life has gone and whether it will ever come back. Without a clear communication and shared sense of agreement, stress and resentment can build in that time, making any return to sex high pressure and high consequence.

I'll be addressing how you can make a commitment to prioritize your sexual connection in only a few minutes a day later on, but the key point I'm making here is that, compared to your pre-kids life, there is indeed very little time, and that must be taken into account. Things are not the same and you can't expect your sex life to continue as if they are. It may seem obvious, but one of the problems I notice parents falling into here is an assumption that sex should happen just as easily as before, despite the fact that they have very little time available. Time is not just about the time needed to have sex. It's about the time needed to set the contexts in motion that support desire emerging and sex feeling like an option. Take Mercy and Ben as an example.

Mercy and Ben had three girls under six. Before the kids came along, Mercy was an avid exerciser, and working out was a way that she felt connected to her body. Workouts often put Mercy in the mood for sex and often preceded her coming home and kissing Ben passionately in the hope it would lead to more. Exercise connected Mercy to her body, and her sexuality. Ben felt more connected to his sexuality when he had time with his friends, and space to miss Mercy. Since the girls came along, they both had less time for sex, but they also had less time for the things that connected them to their sexual selves. The impact of this was that, when they did feel like they should have sex, and one of them suggested it, it was especially difficult for either of them to get in the headspace without these other factors, which supported their individual sexuality being as available to them.

When I worked with Mercy and Ben on improving their sex life, we acknowledged we couldn't magic up an extra four hours a week for them to work out and see friends. This was just not an option at this stage in their life. But they did try to find ways to bring in a little more of what each of them needed. Once she had realized how much she missed exercise – not just in connection to her sexuality – Mercy decided to get a running buggy. Ben made a commitment to a weekly Zoom catch-up with his friends, as well as the odd face-to-face meet-up. The most important part of our work was the understanding that, for both of them, it might be harder to get in the zone without these things, and to work on their acceptance of that. For example, Ben realized how important space to be himself allowed him to feel connected to Mercy sexually. Mercy moved to a belief that 'My relationship and sex life are not doomed if I don't immediately respond with arousal when he kisses me', and to finding ways to navigate this lack of initial desire with much more nuanced communication. I'll be sharing with you how to do this in Chapter 7.

Nurturing connection

The nature of parenthood as a time-sapping pursuit means that sharing childcare can be the only way to get anything done. This model of tag-team parenting, although efficient, can leave us feeling like ships in the night – passing each other briefly and without meaningful communication as we hand over kids and the metaphorical baton to each other. Consider this for yourself. What kind of conversations do you have with each other in these moments? Perhaps a quick 'Hi!' as the other arrives home, with a quick peck on the lips? A kiss that is perhaps devoid of any true passion, sincerity or meaning as our partner simultaneously looks behind us to make eye contact with the small child in the high-chair behind us at the same time. Perhaps we might say something like 'She has eaten. He has hardly touched his dinner but keeps asking for snacks. The swimming stuff is in the wash. Remember to pick up milk. Bye!' as we run out of the door they arrived through seconds ago. Not only do we miss out on opportunities for any emotional connection in these frantic yet business-like moments, but we do not have the chance to witness the work that each of us is doing, as we are often doing it alone, out of sight of the other. When we don't witness each other's work, or take the time to really hear what it has been like via true emotional connection, it can be easy to see the struggles of parenthood through our own lens of experience only.

If our contribution feels unseen, unappreciated or unheard, the stress we are under in a couple can start to feel like a competition as to who has it worse. You can start feeling resentful that one of you always gets out of bed first when the kids cry out, or one of you doesn't pull their weight with the washing up. The little things start to matter more, as there's many more of those little things to cope with.

So I want you to reflect here: how are things in the rest of your relationship? Are you connecting and having fun still? Do you respect each other and not take each other for granted? Are there any grumbling resentments that having kids has raised? Do you manage to find any time together, even five minutes a day, to really connect emotionally?

TASK: Plan fifteen minutes of uninterrupted time to talk about how your day has felt and really listen to each other, with no distractions. Don't try to 'fix'. Just listen and empathize (even better if you can make this a daily habit).

One of the best foundations you can put in place for starting to get sex back on track is to address any underlying issues or resentments first, then make time to really connect, as above, but also by considering how you spend the brief time you have together.

How you spend time matters

Research by Dr Amy Muise and colleagues has added to what we know about how we spend time with our partners and the impact of this on sex.[19] We already know that couples who engage in activities that excite and inspire them with a partner revisit some of those much sought-after early relationship feelings towards one another, and the team wanted to look at the impact of these same behaviours on sexual desire. They discovered that couples that spent time on 'self-expansion' activities (as opposed to just time together as usual) were more likely to experience sexual desire, and more likely to have sex. What's important here is that it was not the amount of time couples spent together but how they spent it that resulted in higher reported desire and sexual activity.

Self-expansion activities are ways of spending time that 'excite, inspire and connect'. They are activities that create space to learn new things about ourselves or each other, and/or create conditions of novelty, distance and newness, akin to those early months and years together, fanning the flames of desire. There's no prescriptive activity here, as these feelings might be sparked by different things by different people, but it may be as simple as playing a board game together, baking an elaborate cake together, planning your dream home or dream holiday, doing a new sport together, or volunteering for a charity that connects you politically.

A crucial finding of this study was that the longer sexual partners had been together, or the more pressed for time they were (think: parents), the more impact self-expansion activities such as these had on their sex lives. Time to sit and plan that campervan tour of northern Europe you plan to do once the kids are older?

TASK: Self-expansion activities

Brainstorm a list of activities that fit the brief of being exciting, inspiring, new or fun and which you could do together. If you pick an activity, avoid things one of you already does or is good at, as this is about connecting over new experiences together. Don't feel this has to be a big time commitment. It could look a bit like this:

- Spend one evening a week/month making future plans for days out/holidays/ projects you'd like to do around the home. Having a shared project can be exciting and make you feel like a team.

• Spend one evening a month doing something new together that's fun. It could be an hour of trying to cook something elaborate together, playing a board game, making something, or trying to sketch each other. Doing new fun things together counts as 'self-expanding' activities and connects us to the feelings we had at the start of the relationship when we were getting to know each other and the time we spent together felt invigorating. Depending on whether you have access to or can afford a babysitter, this may need to be things you can do at home for now, but this is okay. Don't feel not being able to go out of the house means you can't have quality time having fun together. If you do get an opportunity to get out without the kids at any point, your sex life will thank you for spending those few hours trying a new activity together, rather than going for dinner/drinks every time. It doesn't matter what. It can be pottery, climbing, a dance class or tennis. As long as it's new to both of you, and pushes your limits of competence or confidence, it's good for your relationship, and the science says it's good for your sex life too.

This is a relatively easy experiment to try with little consequence if it ends up not being your thing. It could have huge benefits, either for your relationship, your psychological wellbeing, or your sex life. Worth giving a go?

Teenagers in the house

Whenever I do an Instagram poll on the impact of kids on people's sex lives, I am inundated with people struggling with the first five to ten years particularly. There is, however, another less obvious time of parenthood that people also report impacts significantly on their sexual satisfaction: having teenagers at home.

There are a couple of reasons for this. The first is that having sex first requires private time, for the two of you to connect. As much as you might be time-poor in this regard in the first five years (because, let's face it, by the time the kids are asleep you will be utterly exhausted too), there will be a different challenge to your time when they are older. Yes, you are now getting enough sleep, so could make use of the evenings that you are both at home together. Sadly, your teenagers are likely to go to bed at the same time or later than you, meaning the only private time you can get is in bed. Have a think about when you prefer to have sex. If you are a morning person, this might be easier to manage with a teenager at home. If you are an afternoon or early evening person, you might be faced with a teenager awake in the house, which for some people is a paralyzing prospect. There are several aspects of having teenagers at home that people feel can get in the way of their sex life. The first is that sexual currency might be muted or absent for fear of embarrassing your teen or embarrassing yourself. The second is that you have further restricted places or times to have sex easily, unlike when they were younger and you could be sure they wouldn't come downstairs after a certain time. The last is that you might be worried about them overhearing, or guessing you are having sex if you say you are going to your bedroom at 8 p.m., for example.

It's understandable. None of us want our family members to think about us as sexual beings, do we?

163

That's our default position as a society, but I'd like you to question this concept. Some of you were probably raised with no sense of your parents as sexual, and sex was likely something that wasn't talked about at home, but that doesn't mean that this strategy is best or, indeed, helpful. Being mortified as a teen if you did over-hear or walk in on your parents having sex does not mean this was bad for you, it means you were a teenager and everyone else seemed non-sexual and past it.

As well as allowing you to actually have a sex life, there are a couple of messages that being able to communicate to your older child or teenager that you enjoy private, intimate time together undisturbed sends them. Firstly, everyone has a right to privacy. This should be an important family rule. Do beware of double standards here if you regularly walk into their room unannounced. If you expect them to respect your privacy, they need to feel this from you also.

Secondly, sex is not something shameful, furtive or to be kept a secret. It's something fun, pleasurable and, for most people, part of a good relationship. The communication that you are happy to (even subtly) let them know that you enjoy each other in this way will allow them to communicate with you about their sex life in return. It will also act as sex education as a strong communication of the mes-sage 'sex is not a dirty secret or something we think people shouldn't do'. Parents who give this message clearly are giving their child a real gift that will benefit them in so many ways in years to come.

Lastly, it allows you to place boundaries around your relationship and prioritize it at times over parenthood. The message you are commu-nicating to them is 'we exist as a couple outside of being your parents. This is important to us and we want to nurture it'. Isn't this a message you want them to take into their own relationships as adults?

Privacy is a concept teenagers should understand, and it should be absolutely acceptable for you to say 'me and your mum are going to hang out/relax/hang out together upstairs. We want privacy, so please don't disturb us – thanks!'. It's okay if they know or guess you are hoping to have sex. Sex is not something to be ashamed of, and this is a message that they will benefit from hearing loud and clear.

Parenthood, identity and sexuality

I often describe sexuality to my clients as an aspect of our personality that we can flex. It can be compared in some ways to creativity in that regard. Creativity is part of human nature, just like sexuality. Some people are defined by their creativity. They live their life in a way that connects to it, and it shows itself in their work, their home, their dress, their hobbies. They feel bereft without access to it, and not being able to express it has a detrimental impact on their sense of self. Other people enjoy it, but can dip in and out of engaging with their creativity, and cope with large periods of time without being able to express it. A third group don't connect to it hugely at all and are quite happy not prioritizing it as a way to spend their time. All are normal. All can fluctuate. Similar can also be said for how people connect with their sexuality. Read this paragraph again, thinking about connecting with your sexual identity as the focus. Which of these categories do you fall into? Are you and your partner similar or different in this regard?

When we become a parent, this new role dominates our sense of self and, for a period of time, out of a combination of necessity and lack of time for anything else, can become the defining aspect of our identity. This is important; after all, it's a big task to hand and one that requires losing ourselves in it for the sake of other people, at least temporarily. This may affect how we relate to other parts of our identities as we lose time to invest in them and evaluate them through new-parent tinted glasses. How does a mum dress? How does a dad dance? Are parents sexual beings? The answer should, of course, be that we can be whatever we want to be when we are parents, but as with many aspects of our lives, we often live out the scripts available to us within society. For example, the very fact there is a word for the way mums dress, i.e. 'mumsy', which implies unsexy and unfashionable, and kind of 'past it', means there are social forces at play, which then affect our sense of self in parenthood if we identify as mothers. 'I can't be sexy' or 'I am past it'. Changing body shape post birth can contribute to this feeling of shifting identity and less sense of one's value as a sexual object in society as well.

Let's consider what messages are out there for parents about sexuality split by gender. If you are a cis woman, you will have absorbed a social script of good mothers not being inherently sexual. You have probably heard about the 'Madonna/whore' dichotomy,[20] as a theory to explain this. You may well reject such ideas outright as old-fashioned, but as with all societal stories, it can be hard for us not to be affected by them, or allow them to shape our behaviour, even if we don't believe them to be true.

As a group of people who are socialized from very early on to put other people's needs before their own, women are up against it to then feel able to prioritize sexuality over tasks of parenthood with a backdrop of such cultural narratives. I specify cis women in this example as trans women and femmes, trans men and trans masc people and non-binary/gender queer people have no social scripts available to them in terms of parenthood and sexuality. In fact, they have very few scripts about parenthood full stop, apart from the fact that parenthood is not for them, and that having a trans parent will be difficult for their children, neither of which are true. So if trans and non-binary people manage to overcome the hurdles in front of them and become parents, there is likely to be a complete absence of scripts around what sexuality as a new parent should look like for them. This could be both liberating, as well as create a sense of invisibility when needing support around one's sex life.

Cis men seem to fare better than any other group here, *quelle surprise*. There aren't so many widely-held stories in society about how dads should dress, or that sex is not becoming of their new role. In fact, 'hot dads' are a thing, and having a baby can add to a father's sex appeal. Are you old enough to remember that Athena poster everyone had in their bedroom of the gorgeous, half-naked man cradling the baby? Can you imagine a similar poster showing a mother holding a baby as an object of teenage lust in the same way?

Just as with ageing ('silver fox'), cis men's status seems to benefit from something that is devaluing to cis women. This does not mean that there isn't interpersonal conflict in roles for fathers, as there may well be. Just that this conflict isn't further exaggerated by restricting societal scripts. For example, what does a dad do if sex is a crucial part of his identity and it is suddenly missing? Is he able to verbalize it? Get his needs met in other ways? Recognize the impact of this on his psychological wellbeing and his relationship? How does he do this without being tarred by the other social script that 'men are just always up for sex', which risks minimizing or trivializing the devastating impact of this change on him? Cis men are not immune from clashes of identity with sexuality and parenthood, and neither are trans men, trans women and non-binary people. But the scripts around parenthood and sexuality for these groups are different to those of cis women. It is important you understand the impact of these scripts on yourself, and your partner, no matter whether you have similar, or different gender identities.

TASK: Has your changing identity affected your sexual identity?

Talk with each other about how the identity of mother/father/ parent/*insert own preferred term here has affected your sense of sexual identity. Do you feel a clash that you didn't feel before? When does it feel more or less jarring (for example, 'I feel least connected to my sexuality when I've just done bedtime stories' or 'I feel most connected to my sexuality when I'm at work/have had a mental or physical break from the kids/feel like we are doing something just us as a couple'). Discuss how easy or difficult you find mentally switching roles between nurturing parent and sexy partner. What do you need to help you make that transition more smoothly?

Reflect on the role of gender in this process and notice where there are clashes and similarities. Give each other a break here to have different experiences. Notice the impact of the desexualization of motherhood on women, and if you are a man, or your partner is one, don't fall for the reduction of father's sexuality to scratching a biological itch.

Finally, consider how easy or difficult you are finding this phase of your life as a couple as a consequence. It's okay to have differences here, but the key is really listening and understanding the impact on the other. One of you might be coping fine with no or little sex, as sex is not crucial to your psychological wellbeing or sense of self. The other might be struggling quite a bit, and might be finding that a way they used to use to feel connected, alive or to experience joy is absent. Neither is right nor wrong, neither version of this invalidates the other. But it's likely that before now you haven't given much thought for how important sexuality is to both of you, and how the current situation may be impacting on you both differently.

I want to suggest that, at this point, it is important to make a distinction between one person's sadness about the current status quo with regards to sex from another person's obligation to relive that sadness. It is the relationship here that is in focus (and aspects of it that have changed, such as having been together a long time, habits/culture that have become less helpful, having kids, tiredness), not *you* as an individual partner, which has led to this change. This means it is *the relationship* that you should both be turning to and hoping to create change in, *not* each other. Creating change in the relationship will create new possibilities for each of you individually, supporting a more sexual relationship. Hoping that your partner will just say yes to sex more when you tell them how much you miss sex is not an effective strategy. It will lead to pressure, guilt and sex out of obligation, which will reduce desire in the long term. Instead I'm asking you both to play the long game by understanding what changes the relationship needs to support the sex life that you want.

In this chapter we have looked at the idea that having kids under five might be the most challenging time of parents' sex lives, despite the high levels of reported sexual problems and stress of the trying to conceive, pregnancy or the birth-to-a-year phase. The reason for this, I would argue, is that psychological allowances can be more easily made for these more unusual, transient times of our parenting journey. They also appear as phases, to have a distinct start and end point, which are fairly self-contained, even if they last for a few years. After the first year, however, people often feel a pressure to 'bounce back' in all kinds of ways, including sex, and this can be exceptionally hard to do following the disruption to our sex lives of the stages that precede it.

In this phase of having small children, there is often no distinct end point in the near future, especially if more children are planned, or the couple have multiple kids under five and see a long trajectory of having small kids at home. This, plus the impact of high levels of household and childcare labour, having to return to work for those on parental leave, and the settling in of a new norm in terms of a sex life that may have already been derailed from the few years that proceeded it can paint a fairly bleak picture in most people's minds. Resentment, fatigue and new ways of relating that are low in sexual currency and high in stress can be understandable reactions to new demands and pressures. Less time for connection, fostering our identities away from parenthood and sex than ever before coupled with a risk of escalating resentment due to inequality of domestic labour, particularly between men and women parenting children together, can be further dangers.

It may feel like your sex life is on the brink of catastrophe in the first five years of having kids, but despite this bleak picture, I'm here to tell you that it is all salvageable, and how. Your sex life can come out the other side unscathed as long as you both understand what's happening and why, and as long as you work as a team to address what you can and let go of what you can't. The challenges that you are facing are not unique to you, but common to all long-term relationships and all parents. You just happen to be the ones learning how to navigate them.

7

Navigating together
Skills to set you on course

O ur relationship with sex, our partners, our sexuality and our bodies is in constant flux. Think back across the last few years and decades. Your preferences for how much sex, types of sex, how you like to be seen sexually, who you're attracted to, and the way you like to feel or express yourself during sex will have changed – subtly, or perhaps even dramatically.

Imagine a sixteen-year-old you. You may not have been sexually active with another person yet, or perhaps you were. How confident was that person to know what felt good? Ask another person for what they wanted? Feel proud about their body? Talk about something that worried them around sex? Express what they thought sex should look like? Know what really did it for them?

Now do this again for you at twenty-five, and then again at thirty-five for those of you old enough to remember life before WhatsApp. Now throw a kid or two into the mix.

It's all change, right? The old saying is that 'change is the only constant in life', and it's true for sex as well as parenthood. I bet when you reflect on your pre-parenthood self, there is a lot about your relationship with sex, your confidence and your body that is unrecognizable from sixteen-year-old you. There certainly is for me.

Have a think about the following areas and notice the change there has been, both from your 'sexual debut'* to pre-kids, and then again, since kids have come along.

Body image / Body confidence / Assertiveness / Preferences for touch / Available time / Worries / Priorities / Knowledge of own body and likes/dislikes/Living circumstances/Confidence

Whatever your age at this point in time, think forward to the next few decades. What are the chances that your relationship with your body, how your body works, how much the kids need you and in what way, who you are and how this affects how you like to be sexually, the things that you're into, will change again? I can guarantee to you that they will.

Consider yourself, then, at key ages in the future, from wherever you are now. For example, if you are mid-thirties, consider yourself at forty-five, fifty-five, sixty-five and seventy-five. Think about people you know at those ages. Big life changes, like kids leaving home, stopping work, grief, or a physical health change are likely for all of us, and these can throw our sex lives into a place of uncertainty and flux. Change, however, no matter what our age, can also be a huge opportunity. For example, as hard as the menopause can be for some people's sex lives, it can be a positive change for others, when the threat of accidental pregnancy or the disruption or pain of periods goes away for the first time ever. Societal ideas about age will have you believing your sex life is on a downward

---

*'Sexual debut' is a sex positive term for celebrating your emerging sexuality and the expression of this with others. Unlike the sex negative term 'virginity', it does not pedestal certain types of sex as more important in this process than others, and does not imply something was 'lost' or 'taken' from you.

trajectory from your thirties onwards, but this couldn't be less the case. For example, women are known to gain more sexual confidence as they age, as they throw off the shackles of the patriarchal male gaze and become more sexually assertive. Not having kids at home can give people sexual freedom they haven't felt in years. Let me give you an example of a frequent situation that I see in my sex therapy clinic.

> *Joan, who is fifty-three, has been in a monogamous relationship with Bob for thirty years. They have four adult children, the youngest of whom has finally just left home, so they now have their small home all to themselves. Joan and Bob have always worried about money, and Joan worried about getting pregnant again, as they didn't have the space or finances to have more children. Now it's just the two of them, they are getting on better than ever, Joan is feeling more confident in her body, they don't have to worry about being overheard, and Joan knows she is postmenopausal and getting pregnant is no longer a concern. Joan tells me that she feels a renewed sense of her sexuality and wants to feel alive, and develop this side of her life again. She wants to try things she's never tried and find out who she really is sexually, now she has time, space and privacy. BUT there's a problem. Sexual exploration can be a solo pursuit, but, in this instance, what she wants involves Bob. She tells me they have never, in thirty years, had a direct conversation about sex, and she can't even imagine where to start.*

The context of Joan's sexuality has shifted her into a new phase of comfort, confidence and a desire to explore. For once their life circumstances (privacy, no risk of pregnancy) allow their sexual relationship to blossom into something they have never had together The only thing stopping Joan from accessing the sex life she wants is the ability to discuss this easily with Bob. Their culture of not talking about sex is stifling their growth as a sexual couple.

Sex is communication

We can be sure that our own relationship with sex will change, as it has already throughout our lives, and we can also be sure that having kids can be one of the biggest changes to which our sex lives may need to adapt.

Now let's consider what sex *actually* is. Yes, sex is something we often do with our bodies, and often with another person. But the physical act of sex is only one part of it. I want to propose to you that sex is, in essence, communication.

From moment to moment during sex, each touch or movement is a communication – 'I want to do that, do you?'

From day to day, each spoken phrase or nonverbal signal is a communication: 'I'd like to have sex, would you?'

From year to year, communication allows us to futureproof our sex life and allows it to not only stay fresh and boredom-free, but also to adapt to our changing lives and bodies: 'I'd like our sex life to be like this, would you?'

It's a communication that can be explicitly verbal ('Please kiss me here'), subtly verbal ('That's so nice'), indirect or passive-aggressive using jokes or digs, or non-verbal using all kinds of direct and indirect clues. As with all communication, there's a constant risk for our intention to be missed, hurtful, off the mark, or misinterpreted.

There's also a risk we just stop doing it altogether, as communicating about sex can be so hard.

Have a look at the examples above and reflect on how you and your partner currently communicate about sex. Is it direct? Verbal? Non-verbal? Passive-aggressive? Hurtful? Subtle? Are there things you don't communicate but wish you could? Do you think your partner feels the same way? Are there things that you know are intended as communication in your sex life that you actually don't like? You might think you don't communicate at all about sex, but not talking about sex, or just talking in jokes or digs, is still a communication. It's a communication that *we don't talk about this* or *this is not part of our relationship culture*. It may also communicate: *I don't feel safe or comfortable discussing this with you* or *I'm angry or hurt by this*.

There's a risk that we can miscommunicate about all sorts of things in relationships. But talking about sex is harder than talking about most things in life, so there's more chance that, if we don't perfect how we do it in sexual relationships, we run the risk of not being able to navigate the sex life that we want.

Let's talk about why.

Communication = good sex

We've established that our sexuality (our wants, needs and preferences) change over our lifetime, and that we and our partners need to be able to know about and talk about this, so that we can adapt to this change in a way that keeps our sex life interesting and satisfying. For example, 'Since I've been pregnant, I actually really like penetrative vaginal sex in a way I wasn't that fussed about before – can we start doing more of it?'

We've also established that the very nature of sex is negotiation. On a broad level, this might be 'what kind of sex life do we want to have as a couple?'; week by week it might be: 'I want sex now, do you?'; and, in the moment, negotiations like: 'I want to do X to you but I'm not sure if you want that or not'. Negotiation is exceptionally difficult without communication. Imagine trying to get anything else in life done in partnership with someone else without being able to talk about it.

Talking is essential for negotiation, and negotiation is crucial to good sex. At the start of a relationship, or when things are going well, it may appear that sex just happens and doesn't need any negotiation. This is not strictly true, but it can be more easily masked during this early stage, when spontaneous desire, lust and forgiveness are high. But the challenge comes when we want something different, when problems crop up or when life gets in the way. By then, we can be out of practice with negotiating about sex, or we have started to interpret having to talk about it as a sign that there is a problem, which makes one or both of us feel defensive from the outset, and jeopardizes a successful outcome.

Lastly, communication about sex is essential to a good sex life because we and our sex lives are *heavily influenced by the world we live in.* Unless we are able to explicitly state otherwise, we risk being shoe-horned into a model of what society tells us sex *should* look like. This can be what we think we should be doing based on sexual scripts (see pages 56–7), rather than what we actually want. For example, a partner in a heterosexual couple might need to proactively voice: 'I actually could take or leave penis-in-vagina sex, to be honest. Can we not always do it? In fact, I'd be happy if only 10 per cent of our sex ended this way', or else penetrative sex will be automatically assumed to be the 'main event' based on dominant sexual scripts of heterosexual sex always including penis-in-vagina sex. Frequently going along with sex that's not doing much for us will affect our satisfaction and desire in the long term. For parents who are already up against it with challenges to their sex lives, it's crucial that, when sex does happen, it's high in enjoyment and satisfaction.

I could share a million examples of these things with you in terms of the couples I've worked with. Everything from difficulty asking to use lube ('they'll see it as a sign that I'm not turned on enough'), to asking for oral sex ('I'm pretty sure he doesn't like it as he doesn't often do it') to how sex is initiated ('she thinks I like it when she bites my ear but I find it cringey') to how much sex people are having ('she's constantly making "jokes" about how little sex we have com-pared to other people'). Quite often one of the key turning points in therapy comes when something that has never previously been spoken about is talked about in detail, and we discover that neither person was right about what they thought the other person thought about it. In therapy, sometimes we call this new information 'the dif-ference which makes a difference' (a term coined by systemic therapist Gregory Bateson). Seeing things from a different perspective changes the story we had become attached to in our head. It is powerful, but requires communication to unlock it. Without even accessing sex therapy, you have this tool at your fingertips to make a dramatic change, just by improving your communication about sex.

Turning points like this in therapy, which come from speaking the things we are thinking or assuming out loud, and having them con-firmed or rejected by another person, demonstrate the power that *not* talking has in keeping us stuck in old unhelpful patterns. Sex, in my opinion, is the area of our lives and relationships that is most ripe for miscommunication. To keep sex good, and to benefit our desire in the long term, being able to talk to each other about sex is crucial.

Research into the importance of communication for our sex lives tells us this also. Being able to talk about sex has been shown time and time again to highly correlate with a good sex life that stands the test of time.[1] We also know from research that people who are more able to talk about sex with partners enjoy their sex lives more, and that communicating about sex acts as a buffer to a drop in desire.[2] Research into talking about sex for new parents tells us that, for parents, communication about sex is even more important still, as there are unique challenges, and frequent changes in our sex lives, which need adaptation.

Why it's hard to talk about sex

Talking about sex includes being able to talk about what you like, don't like, your fantasies and desires, and your evolving wants, needs and preferences. Sounds simple, right? Well, it might be if we hadn't been strongly socialized *not* to talk about it from an early age. Being out of practice, not having the right words, feeling embarrassed or being raised with the belief that talking about sex is crass, or having sex is dirty or shameful, can all get in the way. Getting the words out can make us feel incredibly vulnerable and anxious – I see this all the time in sex therapy, even in the most confident and outspoken of people. No matter how good we are at talking generally, we're all still up against it, as we live in a world where it's not okay to talk about sex.

Recently, I asked my followers on Instagram to tell me what gets in the way of talking about sex with their partner. This was the list of categories I compiled from their responses:

- Embarrassment

- Worry about being judged

- Shame about their own desires/wants

- Worry about hurting their partner's feelings

- Fear their partner won't take it on board

- Awkwardness/not having the words

- Not being sure about what they even want

- Worry about being perceived as demanding

- Not wanting to rock the boat/cause an argument

Most of you reading this will not have been raised in sex-positive households, where sex was celebrated as something for young people to look forward to, something where pleasure was centred and sex positioned as something that can bring joy rather than risk. It's more likely that sex wasn't talked about, discussions of body parts designed solely to give pleasure (such as the clitoris) weren't named, and you weren't given comfortable language to even refer to your genitals confidently ('front-bottom' is unlikely to feature as appropriate or sexy vocab later on in life). Put simply, we are strongly socialized not to talk about sex, not given the skills or language we need to talk effectively and, as a result of this, many people find themselves having to battle through their own shame and fear, cringing uncomfortably as they form each sex-related word in their mouths.

This sets us up with a challenge in long-term relationships, where talking about sex is crucial to sexual satisfaction. As parents, we need these skills more than ever, given the challenges parenthood brings for our sex lives.

A communication MOT

Getting (back) into practice talking about sex can be especially hard if we find talking and listening to each other generally challenging, even outside of sex. It can also be difficult if we generally find it hard to assert our wants and needs or have both grown a little defensive about our sexual relationship. This is common if sex has started to become the source of conflict or felt like an issue for a while.

Ask yourself how easy or difficult you find talking about any kind of tricky subject in your relationship, and this might be a good barometer for considering how your general communication style might be helping or hindering your sexual communication, given sex is usually harder to discuss than most things. How well do you feel you and your partner currently communicate? Has this been easier or harder since having kids?

Do you feel listened to? Taken seriously? Are difficult topics easy or hard to bring up? Do they get quickly side-lined when they get tough, or can you both stick with it and find a way to delve in even if it's uncomfortable? Does one of you use humour in a way that the other finds dismissive? Does one of you wish the other would use humour a bit more to lighten the tone? Does one (or both) of you interpret any difficult conversation as criticism, or feel frightened and get defensive? Do you feel able to take responsibility for whatever you are talking about in equal measure, or does one of you always seem to bear the brunt of the blame? Do you struggle not to be 'right'? Are you both able to really, intently listen and hear not just the words, but the feelings behind them? Are you able to admit you were wrong and say sorry?

TASK: How we communicate

Consider the following questions about your general communication skills outside of sex and discuss them together:

In what circumstances do we communicate about things best?
e.g. when we have time, when it's just us, when it's a subject we feel aligned on, when it's not emotionally charged, etc

In what circumstances do we struggle the most? e.g. when one or both of us are stressed and pushed for time, when it's a long-standing bugbear between us, etc

Take a moment to consider how you might try to improve this between you. For example, if communication is hardest at moments of pressure, can you both agree to take a second to think before you speak in case your words come out particularly harshly. If one of you feels the other isn't really listening when you talk about how hard your day has been, can you agree to have fifteen minutes where you sit down without distraction, to really listen to each other's highs and lows?

There's another benefit to this improvement in general communication in your relationship, alongside laying the foundations for increased ease in talking about sex. Feeling emotionally close is often an important foundation for feeling like sex with a partner, and many of us can find we just co-exist with the person we are in a long-term relationship with, spending very little (or zero) time together nurturing our emotional connection. Parents are, of course, especially time-poor, so can be really vulnerable to a drop in this form of intimacy or connection, even if they feel they spend lots of time together. Having these types of conversations, where we talk about our hopes, dreams, fears and plans, and being able to *really listen* to each other for just five to ten minutes, are worth weeks' worth of ordinary conversation, when we talk about what's for dinner, who has bought nappies or paid school dinner money, and how the kids have been.

There's plenty of help out there for improving your communication as a couple generally, and if reading this section has got you thinking that you could do with making some changes in this regard, I'd recommend you start here before you do anything else. Finding a way to work on communication outside of sex will be a necessary foundation to benefit your communication within it as well. Shortly we'll revisit the idea of how to talk about making changes in your sex life in a way that works, and I'll be recommending some strategies regarding how to do this. These strategies will be useful only if there aren't fundamental issues in your communication already that could do with addressing, however, so take action now if needed.

TASK: Daily check-ins to feel connected

To work on improving your communication outside of sex, try a daily check-in task, asking about each other's day, really listening, and asking curious questions, not solution giving.

If you would like more support with this, I recommend following the Gottman Institute on social media, who have lots of practical tips on how to avoid falling into common traps of poor communication. They have great books and online courses too, which can really help with getting the foundations of communication right.

How do we communicate about sex?

In sex therapy sessions, it's common for people to tell me that there are many things that they would like to communicate to their part-ner about sex that they feel unable to. It's clear to them (and to me) how feeling unable to talk about sex affects their sexual satisfaction, pleasure, desire and psychological wellbeing.

For example, some people tell me they wish they could communi-cate that there are things they miss, or long for as part of sex, which seem to have fallen by the wayside, such as passion, novelty, or spe-cific sexual acts. Others tell me that the way in which their partner lets them know they want sex leaves them cold. Many tell me that there are growing aspects of their sexual selves or sexual interests that they feel they want to explore, but feel unable to in this rela-tionship as they are not able to communicate it, and they feel too self-conscious asking for this. Communicating during sex, by expressing pleasure, excitement, attraction or compliments, and this being welcomed by a partner, is associated with better sex,[3] but as with much sexual communication, this can often feel challen-ging. Finding the words is further hampered by us being out of practice *saying* the words, or even worse: not having any words we feel comfortable saying out loud.

We could be forgiven for thinking that communication about sex is mainly about talking. In fact, there is a whole host of complex non-verbal or indirect communications that we use to communicate in the absence of, or in addition to, words, and these can be just as useful and just as problematic. Take Andie and Jonas as an example.

Andie had been thinking about Jonas during the day, and was gen-erally feeling content and lucky to be in a relationship with him. The kids had been easy at bedtime and she was feeling unusually well-rested. She decided it would be great to have sex tonight, mainly as she wanted to demonstrate her love to him, but also as it made her feel on cloud nine to connect with him that way (notice here her lack of spontaneous desire, but the presence of the non-sexual motivations 'to demonstrate love' and 'to feel close').

Andie sends a text to Jonas, saying: 'Kids are asleep. Let's have a cosy night in tonight ☺', hoping that Jonas will understand what she means. Before he arrives home, Andie dresses in an outfit she knows Jonas likes, and puts some music on that she finds sensual (note: this is also Andie taking steps to intentionally trigger/nurture her desire). Jonas comes in and is clearly pleased to see her, but seems distracted about his day and the relentless sound of an album he finds annoying. They sit on the sofa together, and Andie asks about his day, all the while stroking the back of his neck with her fingers and looking him in the eye. She kisses him, and he kisses her back but pulls away to tell her about another thing that his colleague did that really irritated him that he forgot to mention. Andie asks him if he wants dinner, or to take a bath together. He replies that he's quite hungry, so dinner would be good. When it's time for bed, Andie takes off her clothes in front of Jonas, looks him straight in the eye and places his hand on her naked body. She sees the glimmer of recognition in his face.

How many indirect or non-verbal communications did you notice Andie doing before Jonas understood what she was getting at? A common word for this is 'initiation'. Initiation of sex (and by 'sex', I, of course, mean being together in any sexual way, not a specific sexual act) is simply a communication that says 'shall we . . .?' It can be tricky, particularly as it can be both direct ('I'm horny and I'd like to have sex? Can we?') or indirect, such as the strategies Andie tries above. Initiation is a crucial part of sex with someone else, but it also depends, rather crucially, on communication. As with any communication, it's ripe for misunderstanding and misinterpretation. This is something that many couples struggle with, but it's even more crucial for couples with kids, who are time-poor, and are less likely to be on the same page sexually, as a misunderstanding here is a missed opportunity. It also gets harder to do the less comfortable we feel with communicating about sex. In my clinical experience, the problem with people's sexual dissatisfaction is often a problem with initiation, even if at first glance it looks like something else.

In my clinical work with couples, I notice patterns that people fall into again and again around this type of miscommunication. Here are some of the common culprits:

- One person has the thought or motivation to be sexual, but the communication is so subtle the other doesn't notice it at all

- The communication is noticed, but not interpreted as sexual

- The communication comes at a time when their partner is too mentally absorbed in something else

- The communication is noticed, is correctly received as sexual, but is a form of sexual communication that turns their partner off, not on (either as they find it unsexy, or just too much pressure)

In the example above, it was the first three of these things for Jonas. In other scenarios, one person's sexual communication can feel overtly sexual or blunt and too much for a partner, who then experiences huge pressure to feel something that they currently don't (desire). I see both of these patterns often, but I see them amplified in parents, for the reasons we have already outlined in other chapters.

What do we know from sex research about this behaviour we often call 'initiation'? Firstly, we know that it's heavily linked with 'sexual scripts' (socially determined ways of acting that we all learn from society and find ourselves acting into), but research over the last few decades has shown that cis women in relationships with cis men are initiating sex more than they used to, reflecting a change in the (outdated but still somewhat influential) sexual scripts that 'men should initiate sex more than women' and 'men are the drivers and women are the gatekeepers of sex'. This is a positive change for women's sexuality, as we know that being the person who initiates sex is also associated with higher levels of sexual satisfaction in the sexual encounter that follows.

Although women in relationships with men initiate sex roughly equally as often as men, research tells us that they tend to initiate sex more directly than men. This means that women in relationships with men are more likely to say 'Let's have sex' than start kissing a partner gently and hoping they get the gist of what this means. There have been some ideas put forward as to why this is the case, especially given that we know women who have sex with women (who, incidentally, report initiating sex more than women in relationships with men) tend to use more subtle or indirect strategies. Sex researchers suggest that the sexual script that 'men are always up for sex' (which, as you now know, is also not true) is still very much alive and kicking, and responsible for women who have sex with men feeling more able to take a risk with direct communication. In contrast, women who have sex with other women, and men having sex with women, might do the opposite and assume that women are more likely to not feel like sex, and so 'test the waters' of initiation more gently.

In my sex therapy work, I see a pattern of direct communication a lot with time-poor couples, particularly straight cis couples with kids. When I ask about initiation in these couples, women will often report very direct initiation, such as *'do you want a shag then?'* It's often news to these women that their male partners may say yes to this, but find it an unsexy or uninspiring start to a sexual encounter. It makes sense why people use it, as when sex becomes yet another thing requiring ticking off on the to-do list, this kind of direct verbal initiation might follow. It may also be very effective for some people and be exactly the type of initiation that does it for them – different strokes for different folks, after all. In my experience, though, it's a sign that a change is needed in communication that may benefit a parent's sex life greatly.

A final word on initiation. It's common, and to be expected, that you might not feel like sex at the same time as someone else, but how we convey that to a partner can have an important consequence on our sexual satisfaction long term. For example, research tells us that 'rejecting' a partner in a reassuring way when they ask for sex (*'I'd really like to and I am really attracted to you but I just have all this work to do'*) leads to higher levels of couple satisfaction long term, rather than if it is done in a critical way (*'Why are you so sex mad all the time? I wish you'd stop nagging me about it, I've got enough on my plate'*).[4] Couples who have good communication about sex also practise letting each other down gently, and this is something you can also take on board as a practical stepping stone to improving your sexual satisfaction.

Is the problem desire, or initiation?

It's obvious when you think about it, but how much sex we want and how much sex we have are often quite different. Feeling like sex (desire) or being open to the idea of sex or nurturing desire (willingness) are about what is going on in our heads. Think about what you have learned so far about the factors that go into these psychological states of 'desire' or 'willingness' to allow them to occur. Everything from how sleep deprived we are, to how connected we feel, to where sex is on our mental to-do list, to how much sexual currency is between us and our ability to pay attention to it. But once these states occur in our minds, what next? 'Sex' is a behaviour, one we might do alone and one we might do with others. The former requires no communication, the latter demands advanced communication skills. Consider the factors that go into acting on your desire, or willingness to begin the behaviour of 'sex'. What needs to happen? You might need to read subtle cues around a partner's emotional state and pick a moment. You will absolutely need to find some way to communicate your ideas to them (verbally or non-verbally). This will feel more or less easy depending on your levels of sexual currency and how your sex life has been feeling recently. A complex dance begins, where you might try to read whether they have picked up on your invitation, and if not, ramp up your communication, and read them again. You may also need to ramp down this communication and change tack depending on their response. Not to mention 'sex' itself isn't one thing. You need to be able to communicate *what kind of sex* you want to have too.

The upshot of all this is that it's really common for couples to come and see me for therapy naming problems with desire* when the problem they are facing often turns out to not be about desire at all, but a problem of initiation. Take Tessa as an example. She came to see me for a lack of desire, but on further questioning she fed back that actually she has desire on her own a few times a month, and also once or twice a month with her long-term partner, George. The issue is not

---

* This is also usually named as one person's problem and 'within' that person, rather than within their relationship or between their relationship and societal understandings of desire, which is the real explanation.

her sexual thoughts or motivation to action them, but that she is not confident in how to translate this into action, and, crucially, not confident in her ability to steer the sex towards something she would find motivating (i.e. sometimes she just wants George to go down on her and then roll over and go to sleep). Tessa struggles to communicate her desire, or what it is she actually desires, verbally or non-verbally. After all, you will remember from Chapter 3 that the behaviour of sex has to feel like it will be rewarding for us to be motivated to move towards it.

So many of us can feel deskilled here, just like Tessa, and it's part of being socialized not to talk about sex, but it's also partly how good our communication about sex is as a couple, and partly how we are socialized to be sexually. (Consider the gendered messages also at play here: for Tessa to initiate in this instance, she has to reject societal ideas that women shouldn't be too overtly sexual, and also societal ideas that women shouldn't put their own needs before others. She also has to be comfortable with receiving oral sex without self-consciousness and not feel a need to reciprocate. These are big hurdles.)

What if the tables were reversed and it was George who wanted to communicate a similar desire? George would need to feel comfortable that Tessa would not interpret his initiation as being selfish behaviour and using women for his own gratification without thought to their pleasure. I must stress here that both of them may worry about this initiation for different reasons, connected to restrictive societal ideas about gender and sexuality (we covered these differences in gendered expectations in Chapter 6). Both of them may be wrong about how the other may see or feel about this initiation, but they will never get the chance to find out as it's not communicated. They also restrict the chances of their desires (in this case receiving oral sex) being met. This diminishes their experience of sex being an extremely rewarding activity, and therefore the motivation to do it again.

For people struggling with initiation, there can be a game of mental pinball. They might think 'What do I do? I want sex but don't want to come on too strong/put myself out there for rejection/offend them. The thing I want to initiate feels too hard to ask for. Perhaps they might be up for it? I am scared to be rejected as sex has become too loaded. Someone has to get it started. I *think* I want to initiate something, but even I don't feel sure that I can get in the zone. What if I start it then I don't want it either? What if they say yes, but don't really want to be doing it?' These split-second musings are all a product of struggling to test the waters with another person due to difficulties communicating about sex.

Words matter

What does the word 'initiation' conjure up for you? For me, someone who initiates is someone who starts something, whether that is by words or actions. To me, the use of the word initiation also says something about the role of the other person involved. After all, if someone 'starts something', *they* have started it. Your choice, as the receiver, is to either go along with it, or end it. In my experience of working with people on their sex lives over the last few decades, people often don't feel that either of these are attractive options when a partner initiates sex. They often feel that not going along with it makes too much of a statement, or will feel too much of a rejection. Going along with it (if they don't feel the same way) might leave them feeling too much pressure ('I need to somehow feel sexy now'), resentful or angry. It will certainly make the sex less satisfying for both people. Sex research tells us that going along with something you are not enjoying, or feeling resentful about, risks diminishing your desire over time.

As a psychologist, I believe that the language we choose shapes our reality. I like to use the word *invitation* rather than initiation with clients when talking about sex for the following reasons.

Invitation implies the offer must be alluring, whereas initiation implies someone has already started the car and you either need to stay put and accompany them for a drive you don't want to go on or open the door and hurl yourself out of the passenger seat to devastating effect.

'Do you want a shag?', spoken in a matter-of-fact way can be the sex equivalent of 'I'm having party for my birthday. It will probably be rubbish. Come if you want?' (We'll talk about how common the invitation of 'shall we have sex?' or 'fancy a shag?' is later on in this chapter, as well as how challenging it can be as a way to get sex started.)

Invitation implies you get to think about it.

Invitations are usually alluring or tempting.

Invitation implies an acceptance that you might say yes, but you might also say no.

Invitation is not a fait accompli, and the person inviting does not automatically feel rejected if the other says no (they might, if this is a long-term pattern, but more on this later).

What my clients often feel would be a marker of a good sex life, they tell me, is that when they invite their partner to be sexual, their partner accepts. *I'd like to suggest to you that a better marker of a good sex life is that they each feel free to invite, and they each feel free to frequently, but graciously, decline.* Let me explain why.

When sex feels like an issue, there can be a lot riding on an invitation. This is amplified if we hold a belief that a marker of a good sex life is that a partner accepts our invitations for sex. For this reason, the person inviting does so sparingly. Perhaps at a time they feel their partner is most likely to accept. Underneath the lack of invitation may be a bubbling resentment about the frequency of sex, a sense of anxiety about inviting or a feeling of disconnection. There may have been ten times before this invitation that they wanted to and didn't, but they chose this time, and so this time really matters to them. Perhaps they feel really strong desire at this moment, or perhaps there is something about the location or day that makes it feel more wanted (a weekend away, or a birthday, for example).

When an invitation is infrequent, and when there is a sense of high pressure around it, the person receiving the invitation can feel more pressure. Pressure to accept, pressure to feel like it, an awareness that there is a lot riding on it for the other person and the relationship. Pressure is, as we have already mentioned, generally bad for our sex lives and can inhibit desire. Infrequency in invitations like this can also take us by surprise and mean we are not at all in that headspace. When a high-stakes invitation such as this one is declined, it can reaffirm the person inviting's sense of rejection, anxiety or resentment, and make them less likely to feel confident to invite again in the future. Both people are then confronted starkly with a reminder of the ongoing issues around sex.

On the other hand, if an invitation can be shared easily and comfortably turned down, both people can feel free to take a risk with it. This allows them to do it more often, which statistically means there will be more times that it will be accepted. It also allows them both to not feel any pressure with having to accept it. Think for a second about the long-term consequences of this. What would be the impact of being able to comfortably invite each other to be sexual more than now? What would be the consequence of being able to turn it down without a risk of conflict or negative emotion? The consequences are: easier communication about desire and wants for sex, more invitation, some of which will happen at times that are right for both to accept, less pressure and an easier, more relaxed sex life.

When an invitation is unsexy

Not all invitations are created equal, and it can be easy to forget that. If you start from a position that at least one of you might not be feeling any desire at the moment of the invitation (possibly both of you), and you remember that desire is more of a motivation than it is a drive, then the invitation needs to be motivating to encourage us to move from what we had planned to spend that time doing – let's say catching up with that week's episode of the latest drama you're into on TV – to something more sexual.

Parenthood to-do lists are infinite. So we also need to feel motivated to spend that chunk of time having sex, rather than doing something else we know is needed or wanted with the same unit of time. For this reason an invitation might work best if it's a) low pressure, i.e. 'do you fancy having a bath together?', and b) attractive, i.e. the bath sounds relaxing and luxurious in its own right. Of course, it may just end up being a bath, but the couple in question know each other, and a bath can often be a precursor to sex. So the person inviting gets to communicate they want to spend time connecting, and there's a hint they might have sex on their mind. The person being invited gets to occupy that space in-between willingness and desire comfortably, and see whether their desire can build. The low pressure allows this invitation to be accepted without needing desire. Even if it doesn't go anywhere, it's pleasurable, connecting and enjoyable.

The alternative to this is an invitation that's high pressure and potentially unalluring to us at the moment in time that it is asked. A direct invitation, such as 'Do you want to have sex?' is a common invitation to sex for parents (not just parents!) that I hear a lot from my clients, as a way of getting sex started. If this is an invitation you use often, it's likely that you've never before considered why such an invitation might not work for either of you. I'd like to suggest that this may be a bigger hurdle in your sex life than you have considered so far. In my clinical work, I recognize that this invitation often comes either from feeling deskilled at knowing how else to communicate it, or from a place of assuming the other person is starting from the same place as you (that is, with desire). Don't give yourself a hard time if you recognize yourself or your relationship in this initiation style, as it's super common, for all the reasons I have outlined. But let's look a little more closely at why it might not support us in the goal we are wanting to move towards: our partner's interest in having sex.

In my experience in this field, 'fancy a shag?' is rarely effective unless you are on the edge of your seat with desire at the point it's asked (possible but unlikely), or it's said in a super-sexy way, accompanied by something else like seductive touch (infrequent, in my experience). It's also extremely high pressure. There's an end goal stated and not much about the journey. It's not particularly sexy, so it is also unlikely to trigger desire in its own right, in the way being physically and emotionally intimate might do (think of the bath example earlier). Despite all this, it is common, and in my clinical experience more common for women to use than men (due to that trend we mentioned earlier of direct communication based on a false assumption that men are always up for it).

Researchers have worked to understand invitation strategies even further, looking at ways of grouping preferred invitations that people reported wanting from their partners.[5] I've described examples of each to give you an idea of what these might look like, but these are not exhaustive. You might find it helpful to reflect on which feel most enticing to you, so your partner knows. You may both find different types of invitation work for you, and it's common to choose to do the one that *we* might like best, which might not necessarily be the one that might work for a partner.

Emotion-Sentimental: arrange a romantic dinner, make me laugh, really listen and show interest in what I say, clear space for us and show thoughtfulness.

Seductive-Exotic: send me sexy pictures, describe something you'd like us to do sexually, show more skin than usual, tease me with seductive language.

Surrender: push me against a wall, kiss me passionately, undress me, take charge of the situation.

Sensation: touch my body (including nonsexual parts), press yourself against me without saying anything, wake me up with sexual touch, kiss me.

Consider how invitations show up in your relationship. Are they high stakes? Do they feel loaded with pressure? Are they unsexy? Do they include a yes/no answer that allows no space for desire to build? Is there an absence of anything that might trigger desire? Do you feel declining them risks negative consequence to the emotional climate of the relationship? If you answered yes to any of the above, you may benefit from working on invitation. For many of you, unlocking easier invitation will be the key to a better sex life as parents, as, after all, invitation is the gateway to the behaviour of sex. How we approach invitation makes the difference to whether the gate feels half open, or firmly shut.

TASK: Understanding invitation strategies in your relationship

For those of you wanting to investigate invitation further in your sex life as parents, here's a task to do with your partner. Hopefully by now you can see that how you communicate with each other about an invitation to physical or sexual intimacy matters to the outcome. It's likely that you've never had this conversation before, but this is exactly the type of communication that your sex life might benefit from at this time in your life as parents.

Answer these questions together from each of your individual perspectives. You will have different answers. This is normal, and one of the reasons why understanding each other's feelings about invitation is essential.

What kind of invitation creates a feeling of interest and low pressure for you?

What kind of invitation brings with it a sense of pressure and leaves you cold?

What kind of invitation do you not yet have as part of your sex life but wish you did?

What would be the effect on you personally if you felt freer to invite your partner in to physical and sexual intimacy?

What would be the effect on you personally if you felt freer to decline graciously without worrying about the fallout on the emotional climate of the relationship?

What do you guess would be the long-term effect on your sex life, if invitation was easy to bring in, and decline freely?

Remember: an invitation can be verbal or non-verbal. It can also be explicitly sexual, or more ambiguous.

Go gently on each other during this conversation. Talking about sex is hard, and you've both been doing the best you can. This might not have been perfect, or what each other needed, but you've been doing your best.

Which approach has featured most in your sex life in the past? Which turn you on most/do you prefer? Which don't feature as much as you'd like in your sex life? Which would you like to try?

Take some time to discuss the above. Don't blame each other for getting into predictable habits or being nervous to try something new. This stuff can be hard and you are not mind readers. Make a commitment to experiment with trying invitation types your partner would like if they feel doable to you.

What if one of us doesn't feel like it?

As well as it being unlikely that you're going to feel like sex at the same time as someone else, there is another important factor that I'd like you to consider. Namely that *the space in between invitation and desire can be hard to inhabit and requires work from both people to nurture.* If someone asks 'Would you like to have sex?', they are directly inviting you to a sexual event and communicating their needs. Wonderful! But there is little chance you will have access to desire at that point in time, so what will your answer be? Your instinctive answer, based on the ideas that we've already discussed, may be 'no', as you are not in that headspace. But a more effective strategy, based on the idea of an invitation rather than an initiation (should you feel open to seeing if desire can be triggered at that moment in time) is: *'Maybe, I'm not sure . . . Can we fool around a bit and see?'*

Being able to tolerate that middle-ground feeling – where you are waiting to see if desire can build – can be anxiety provoking. 'What if I'm not feeling it and have to ask them to stop?' or 'Why do they seem so much more into it than me?' or even 'What if they take this faster than what I need?'

In my experience, it is sometimes harder for people who are used to doing the lion's share of the inviting to have the tables turned and be invited. They are not used to having to manage that uncertainty at the start when the experience is at first driven by someone else's agenda. They are more used to entering into it already in an erotic headspace.

I often talk with clients in therapy about how to help each other through this process of comfortably occupying the space in between invitation and desire. Here are my top tips:

- Know that you, and they, won't always feel like it and it's not a reflection of anything else if your body or mind don't respond to their advances.

- Don't put pressure on every invitation to lead anywhere. Lots of sexual currency (explained on page 74, for those of you wanting a reminder) with no pressure for it to lead anywhere is better for your sex life than low levels of sexual currency and high stakes. The same goes for invitations

- Give it time – someone might *want* their head to follow but it just hasn't *yet* and slowing things right down gives them a chance to catch up. To do this you absolutely both have to sign up to the idea that getting a bit sexual together is not like getting on a water slide at the top and not being able to get off until you've splashed in the pool at the end. It's more like a flight of stairs where you can exit on any floor you like, or choose to keep walking up each flight, a floor at a time, seeing if you want to go further, or deciding that this is a good place to stop.

- Get comfortable with yourself, and your partner(s) being in that in-between place. As long as there's consent to be there, don't put pressure on themselves or yourself to be really horny when you're not yet feeling that way. It's okay to take your time to feel really in it.

- Desire is triggered by arousal, and our minds and bodies instinctively respond to sexual stimuli, as you learned in Chapter 3. This means that we can use our senses to trigger our arousal (touch, seeing someone's naked body etc). Although psychological processes, such as distraction, and physical processes, such as tiredness, can interfere with this automatic arousal, most of the time you would do yourselves a favour by including sexual stimuli into this time where you are exploring whether an invite can lead to desire.

- If you're just too tired to feel anything, your brain gets in the way, or the pressure of your mental to-do list feels too great, it's also okay for either of you to stop and say: '*Mmmm, that was really nice. I'd like to feel more in the zone but I'm just too tired/stressed/over-whelmed, I think – can we revisit this same place again tomorrow/later this week?*' Remember how essential attention is to your sexual response from Chapter 3? If your mind is full, it can really get in the way of your body responding, even if you feel receptive.

- Take a risk. How many times do you stop a partner's invitation as soon as you sense it, as you're aware you are not there *yet*? And even though you want to be? Fear of letting a partner down and being uncomfortable in that sexual limbo can lead us to back away prematurely, meaning we miss out on the opportunity to let our minds and bodies follow. This is important for parents, where invitations and opportunities may be fewer than before.

Take a second to reflect on how comfortable you are occupying the space between invitation and desire. What are your experiences with this? Are you a person who initiates more and struggles when some-one else does as you find this in-between space hard? Do you sometimes think you could feel like moving towards sex if you felt able to take or be given time to see if your desire could build without pressure? Do you feel able to give your partner this space without feeling frustrated or take it personally if they don't respond quickly with desire? If you answered yes to the latter, you may be inadvert-ently contributing to them backing away from your invitations without taking the time to see if desire can build, which may be counterproductive to your sex life.

With my sex therapy clients, I often know it's time for us to end our work when a couple who has come to see me for concerns about desire discrepancies between them can invite each other in, and graciously decline an invitation comfortably and easily. Bonus points here for the couples who are comfortable to allow each other to occupy the space in between invitation and desire to see if they can feel like it, and appreciate that some invitations may be received, and be more effective, than others. When this happens, I know my work is done.

How to change your relationship culture

Our relationship culture is present in the way in which we do things, which is either bedded in, or gradually shifting over time by the repetition of the daily habits we fall into. Our relationship cultures in relation to sex, like all culture, can start to feel ingrained and restrictive of our behaviour. For example, 'we've never talked about our sex life, so now it's hard to'. Culture can gradually emerge over time and move in a way that we might not have chosen. For example, 'we've started to kiss less and less the longer we've been together and now it feels weird'. It can also be dramatic and sudden, in the case of adaptation to a big life change: 'we stopped having sex when I got pregnant and since then sex has fallen off the agenda completely'.

The good news is that a big life change, such as having kids, might be the source of a culture shock or a change in culture for the worse, but it can also provide an opportunity to stop, reflect and create a culture shift in the direction you would like. When you can't continue things as they were, you have an opportunity to redefine how things are, without as much at stake. An overhaul of your sex life allows you to look at everything and have conversations about making changes that couples without a dramatic culture shock don't. For example, consider the case of Nate and Rory, who adopted their two boys at aged eighteen months and four years.

Nate and Rory met in their twenties and instantly had a great sexual connection. In the first few years of their relationship, they enjoyed a free-and-easy sex life, and the spontaneity that having their own separate homes and independent lives brought to it. They often spent time apart, allowing them to miss each other, and focus on themselves, and when they came together for dates, they were both excited to see each other, and also had the build-up to the date to get excited about the sex they might have. Dates also allowed them to spend time getting ready to impress the other, as well as ensure that the two of them had bookmarked that time only as time for them, not to be interrupted by work, family, friends or their phones.

In the five years that followed, they bought a place together and led more of a settled life. Their sex life became more formulaic than either of them would have liked. As they spent more time together, they had less defined time to devote to the other, and it was easy for one of them to feel frustrated when they tried to connect over conversation, and the other was wanting to go to sleep, or was on their phone. They no longer dressed up for each other, and the lack of organized dates meant there was no hint of sex to allow each of them to get in the mood.

They had both always wanted to be dads, and the process of adopting the kids was a long and emotionally draining process. With the extra stress, sex became harder to get started, less satisfying and less passionate than it had been. They were overjoyed with the arrival of their two boys, but things with their sex life got worse still. For a while this culture change went unchecked, as they were too busy learning how to be dads and caring for their new sons as best as they could. Sex became infrequent and neither of them addressed it. At some point, when the boys had been with them a year, Nate made a sarcastic comment, which became a huge row. It forced them to talk about what they might do to get their sex life back on track. The new situation they found themselves in, of being dads of two, of being a family of four, required a complete overhaul of how they were going to maintain a sex life moving forward. For example, in the past when their sex life worked better, sex often happened in the morning. Their youngest was up at 5.30 a.m. every day, however, so that was now impossible.

Nate and Rory are an example of a couple whose sex life was at breaking point since parenthood, but the trajectory for less satisfying sex had actually been set when they moved in together. You might be interested to hear that one of the factors associated with less desire in a long-term relationship is moving in together. This period of time is often correlated with less sexual satisfaction.[6] This is partly as sex is always available and, unlike dating, there are suddenly no triggers for when it might happen. It can always happen the next night, and so it can be got out of, or be hard to start. Moving in together (like co-parenting) also sees a shift of roles from romantic/sexual partner only when you are dating to housemate or co-parent later on. This shift in roles can make it harder for us to hold onto an idea of our partner as sexual, especially if we have low sexual currency or difficulty talking easily about sex. In sitting together and navigating this culture change and what they were going to do to make things better, Nate and Rory were also able to address the more insidious changes that had actually started before the boys arrived.

Parenthood allowed them to come together and make changes under the frame of 'now the boys are here, we need to find a new way', which felt positive and less personal than 'We don't have a good sex life'. Prior to the kids arriving, this conversation may have felt more challenging, but now it was less about them, and more about their new lives. It can be easier to communicate well under the former than the latter.

TASK: Kickstarting culture change

Have a conversation about whether you both want a culture change, and what you feel the positive effects will be. Frame this conversation not about a problem/deficit within your relationship (it's not), but rather an intention you both have to protect the relationship. State the effects of this culture change on your sex life, and, in consequence, if your sex life improved as a result, on you as individual people, and on your relationship satisfaction outside of sex.

Here are some prompts to help your conversation:

What aspects of our sex life or physical intimacy have drifted from how we used to be?

What has been the impact of this drifting off course on our sex life? On our relationship?

What impact would it make if we felt more comfortable talking about sex?

Do we feel it would be useful if we could make changes to our sex life to help us adapt to how parenthood affects it?

What difference would it make to you personally?

What difference do you feel it would make to the
  relationship?

After you have reflected on the above, see if you can use what you
have learned from each other and your own reflection to complete the following statements as a team:

What would you both agree that a change in relationship
  culture around physical or sexual intimacy, or talking
  about sex could have?

We would feel _____

We would be _____

It would mean that _____

Maintaining a culture of easy communication over time

Building a culture of communication through practice and intention,
with the aim of having better sex, allows our sex life to happen more
easily at a time of our lives that is most pressured, and creates space
for our sex lives (and us individually) to grow over time.

Keep this culture alive by nurturing it regularly. Once you get prac-
tised, this won't take intentional effort, exercises like I've set you
already or reminders. It will just become part of what you do and
your sex life will thank you for it.

Although you need to start any new change in culture with a clear
sense of why you're doing it, including the benefits it will bring, and

then making purposeful intention actions, such as some of the exercises I have set you so far, over time this culture will become the new normal, and will only need regular nourishing to keep it alive. In the next chapter, I have included a communication map for you to use to guide yourselves towards a communication that is more favourable for your sex life. Use this map to identify where you are now, and to see a sample journey to move forward comfortably.

For example, there was a time when none of us recycled. Our culture of removing used paper or glass from our house was to put it in the bin. Feels hard to imagine now, doesn't it? We were educated on the benefits of why recycling mattered, and the difference it would make. We then had to create new practices and habits to change our culture, so that recycling became second nature. It would have been hard at first. We would forget, put glass in the bin, feel confused about what could be recycled and what couldn't, not have a dedicated place for it etc. But over time, no effort is needed. In fact, it just feels plain wrong not to do it. You have the power to make this exact same culture change around talking about sex in your relationship.

In this chapter we have examined the huge role that being able to communicate about sex has on our sexual satisfaction, but crucially why this can be so hard for so many of us. We have reviewed how our sexual needs, wants and challenges are in constant flux, and how this is especially evident in the sex lives of parents, as our bodies, relationships and lives adapt to the pressures exerted upon them. We have looked at how crucial being able to talk easily about sex is for getting the sex that we want, which then has a direct impact on our motivation to be sexual as parents, as sex that is enticing is easier for us to prioritize in our time-pressured lives. We have reviewed how frequently communication as an invitation to sex can be misinterpreted, avoided, or steeped in pressure, and how this can undermine the success of this invitation. We have looked at the importance of invitations being alluring, with space for people to be comfortable occupying the space in between willingness and desire to see if desire can build. Lastly, we have reviewed how long-term relationships can easily fall off course, and onto a trajectory that is less than favourable for our sex lives. We have considered how taking a bearing on this relationship culture, and making small changes to our trajectory, might be the intentional action our relationships really need at this moment in time. Parenthood, in many ways, might be the storm that encourages you to review the course you are on, a course on which your relationship was already casually drifting, but now calls for a concerted effort and all hands on deck.

8

Plain sailing

Make small changes with big results

I t can be easy to feel like your sex life needs a drastic overhaul when things aren't going to plan, but this is not only not needed, but simply not viable for most parents. Instead, I want to drive home the idea that small changes can have big results – perhaps even larger in this period than at any other time in your life. The reason such changes can be so impactful is precisely because this period is such a vulnerable time for sexual satisfaction. The impact of slight adjustments of course will allow you not only to weather the storm, but over the long-term trajectory of this parenting chapter of your life lead you to a much sunnier final destination. It may be hard to imagine, but tweaks to your sex life now, at this tricky stage, might lead to a sex life even better than you can imagine when your kids are that bit older.

In this chapter, I will outline a range of small changes you have the power to make. These are based on my decades of clinical experience, sex research, and what we know about how parents maintain sexual satisfaction despite the storm of parenthood. You might choose to do one, a few, or all of these things. You might choose one or two for now but make a commitment to review things in a few months and add in more as the culture of your relationship shifts to make further changes feel more possible. There are no right or wrongs. You may even find that you don't need to do anything at all, as the problem was that your sex life felt unusual, or broken in some way, and you now know this not to be so. A change of perspective such as this will be the small change needed for many of you. So let's start there.

You are not unusual

One of the things that can be hardest for us in our sex lives is not having a clear idea about what everyone else is up to. Inevitably we end up feeling like we are outside of the norm, as our imagination pits us unfavourably in comparison to other people we know. Studies tell us that people overestimate and overreport the amount of sex they have,[1] and our latest large-scale data from the Natsal team (the world's biggest and most rigorous sex survey, which happens in the UK) tells us that the average UK adult aged thirty-five to forty-four (the group most likely to have kids) has sex about twice a month, with a third of people under forty-four not having any sex at all in the last month.[2] I've already introduced the idea that frequency of sex is a poor indicator of a good sex life, and that sexual satisfaction is more about the quality of that sex, how connected you feel and how your motivations for sex are met. Saying that, I know from clinical experience that most people think that everyone is having sex more than they are, and that there is such a thing as a 'normal frequency'. I hope data such as the Natsal stats above reassures many of you who look at other parents on the school run and think 'I bet they have loads of sex'. Most likely not, and even if this is the case, there's also no guarantee that frequency translates to satisfaction.

Knowing we're normal can often change our relationship with a problem we are worried about, even before making a change to the thing itself. So, before we move to other more tangible changes, I just want to say again that experiencing sexual dissatisfaction at this time in your life is normal and can change. It is likely *not* about you having a problem with sex, it is also likely *not* a sign that your relationship is doomed. It is a time to batten down the hatches and get through as unscathed as you can, ready for the next phase in your life.

Small changes

The problems come when we fall off course, and our final destination becomes, subtly, further and further away from what we initially hoped it might be. The effect of this unwanted drift on future trajectory can be more pronounced for parents versus non-parents due to the relative impact of the 'weather' exerted upon us in the storm of parenthood. Long-term partnerships without children still see a drift off course, but generally experience less choppy seas. Experiencing challenges in your sex life at this time is not the issue, it's the fact that we struggle to get it back on track. The real problem for couples comes when they understand this shift to be an inevitable part of being a parent, perhaps the new normal, and as a result, let go of the wheel. I see many of these couples in therapy, and the longer things have been allowed to drift, the longer it can take to get back on course.

When I meet with couples who are parents for sex therapy, I work with them to understand which areas of their relationship are likely culprits for 'stuckness', and therefore opportunities for change. Using the sex life barometer and all you have learned so far, my hope is that you have already started to understand some of this for yourself and your own situation. As there is no one-size-fits-all direction for change, this final chapter is broken down into sections, pulling together four themes that have featured across this book, weaving through each chapter. Each section outlining one of these four themes begins with a list of questions, designed to help you identify the best starting point for you. You may choose to address just one theme at a time, or all of them, in an order to be defined by you.

You may well have already started to implement changes, or have ideas for where to start based on tasks from other chapters. In this chapter I will be recapping and extending some of these ideas, as well as introducing some new ones. My decades of clinical work to help parents get their sex life back on track no matter what their stage of parenthood can be summarized by these four themes: *expanding your sexual perspective, harnessing motivation, tackling competing priorities and optimising your relationship climate.*

My advice to you is to read this chapter in full, then start by choosing either the theme that feels most needed, or the theme that feels easiest to implement to begin with.

Expanding your sexual perspective

REFLECTION: Is this us?

Does one of us frequently feel sad, frustrated or disappointed with the amount of sex that we have?

Do I see my partner as a sexual person, and do I feel they see me in this way?

Do we find any sexual interactions a bit stilted and a stressful signal of pressure and expectation? Or do we enjoy fleeting moments of flirting or passion as just that?

Can we be sexual without it having to lead to sex?

Do we ever passionately kiss when it's not a precursor to sex?

Would we see a positive change in our sexual relationship if we had more sexual currency but the same amount of sex?

Do I/we feel pressure around sex?

Needs and understanding

If you remember in Chapter 1, Ben wants affirmation from Jo and this is connected to a need to feel relationship security for him. There were particular reasons why Ben was struggling at this stage of family life and he was hypervigilant for any signs that Jo was losing interest in him. Jo is exhausted and wants less pressure on sex and to not have to take care of another person's needs. At this moment in time, Jo's motivation to have sex is low. This is normal, as a) she has a baby under one and other competing priorities, and b) her usual motivations for sex were 'fun' (she did not currently feel she had time to invest in fun), 'obligation' (her focus of obligation and care was currently directed to the baby, not Ben) and 'to feel close' (she had never felt closer to Ben since becoming parents; this need was fully met). It is therefore understandable that, for Jo, sex had become a bit take it or leave it, with other things taking priority, but, for Ben, it felt like make or break. As they didn't understand each other's position, the issue seemed to get bigger over time.

If you remember, once they had understood these needs or motivations for themselves and each other, they were in a position to try out alternative ways of meeting them. After some discussion about what else brought a similar form of connection for Ben other than sex, both of them realized that moments of sexual connection or expressions of attraction that didn't lead to sex were just as effective (if not more so), easy to fit into their busy lives, and enjoyable and connecting for both of them.

Sexual currency

What I'm suggesting here is that a good sexual connection does not have to equal sex. Not only does having sexual currency like this running between you meet sexual needs at a time when sex may be less frequent (or off the agenda completely), it also provides a way to continue to affirm your connection with each other as a sexual one, staving off awkwardness and allowing an easy foundation to move from the non-sexual to the sexual when life starts to settle slightly. It helps us continue to see our partner as a sexual being, even when we might not be having much sex. It's a tool to help us stay on course. Sexual currency, whether it's passionately kissing for a few seconds, flirting, suggestive comments, or texts which spell out exactly what you'd like to do (if only you weren't sleep deprived) are the fuel of long-term desire. The irony here is that, just like Jo and Ben, couples who start to have worries about sex are often worried about relating to each other in this way. The higher-desire partner worries that it will prompt rejection, so stops. The lower-desire partner worries it will 'give the wrong message', so stops. Sexual currency *is* our sexual relationship. Since I introduced the idea of sexual currency in my first book, *Mind The Gap* (Headline Home, 2020), I get a stream of steady feedback from couples informing me that this concept, plus a new understanding of desire, has changed their sex life completely.

The principle of sexual currency, as you now know, is that having a sex life is not an on/off switch where having sex is the 'on' and the rest of the time it's off. Our sexual relationship is in the way we relate to each other throughout the day, week or month. Having sex is just one of the ways our sex life together might be visible to a fly on the wall, but there are many others that are much more easily accessible, lower effort and less time-consuming. As Ben found out with the kiss in the lift from Jo, sexual currency may also meet our needs for sex much more effectively than sex itself. Without sexual currency, our sex life relies on actually having sex to feel its existence. Ironically, having sex is much harder to initiate when we don't have much sexual currency between us acting as a foundation, so, without it, having sex gets harder and harder over time.

All of this means that it's likely not about the amount of sex you're having that may be the issue to focus on, but, rather, understanding what needs sex meets for each of you that you're struggling to meet another way when sex is less easily available (read: exhaustion). Understanding this about each other is crucial to moving forward to navigate a better sex life, even if you don't plan to make any changes to how much actual sex you're having. Revisit the reasons each of you wrote down at the end of Chapter 1 now in the same way that Ben and Jo did.

If you are finding this hard to work out about yourself, keep track of it over the next few days, weeks or months. Every time you find yourself thinking of sex, ask yourself: *what is it that I'm actually wanting right now?* It could be excitement, pleasure, fun, escapism, security, affirmation, a sense of nurturing the relationship or a whole host of other things. After you've kept a log of this for a period of time, you may start to see a pattern emerging. This provides a clue as to the needs that sex meets for you, and what you might be missing when it doesn't happen. If you find you don't notice any desire for sex in this time period, then think back to times when you have in the past. What came before your desire?

The small change of understanding each other's motivations for sex and finding other ways to meet them when sex feels out of reach or unwanted can be helpful. Below are some prompt questions to help you figure out whether this is a useful way forward for you at this stage. I've included the questions from Chapter 1, as a reminder, as well as some additional more advanced questions. If you haven't both read Chapter 1 before having this conversation about making changes, it may be useful to read it first. You'll have much more chance of finding this useful if you both understand its full purpose and rationale.

Questions to help you with this small change:

In an ideal world, how would you like your sex life to be?

What would be the impact of this change on you personally?

What would be the impact of this change on your relationship?

How can you adapt both of your ideal sex life answers into a merged relationship goal?

What needs does sex meet for each of you and how could you try to meet these in other ways?*

---

* Note: these ways do not have to be as effective or perfect to be useful things to try.

What needs does sex meet for the relationship and how can you meet those needs in other ways?

What would an increase in sexual currency but no increase in sex do for your sexual satisfaction?

What would be the impact of an increase in sexual satisfaction on your relationship satisfaction?

What would happen if you agreed to take risks in expressing more desire, attraction, or sexual currency in small ways but agree for this not to be a signal that you want sex?*

Make time to think this through and discuss. What will you agree to try together as an experiment? What will you do? When? For how long? What do you need to agree before starting? For example, 'We will agree to turn the peck on the lips we usually do when one of us leaves or returns to the house into more of a lingering/longer kiss. We will do this every time we kiss. We will do this for a month to see what difference it makes. We will agree to both be really focused on each other in this moment. We will make this brief kiss sensual and connecting rather than just going through the motions.'

Increasing the sexual currency between you automatically reduces pressure, as when grabbing your partner and initiating a passionate kiss happens regularly, and not always as a precursor to sex, the kiss becomes a communication rather than an invitation. It says '*I'm attracted to you. I am thinking of you in a sexual way. I want a brief moment with you*'. There is no pressure to feel anything, which often allows the person on the receiving end to lean into it (unless it's at a bad time, of course, such as if

---

* If you have never tried this, try to resist the urge to say 'it won't help' before trying it. In my clinical experience these two small changes often have monumental effects, much to clients' surprise.

one of the kids is crying). As you will now know, being able to lean into it without pressure is much more likely to trigger desire.

Sometimes this kiss might be an invitation to more, or a hopeful route to starting something, and this is okay, as when there is high sexual currency there will be a precedent between you that sometimes it is, and it goes that way, and other times it's not and that's okay too (as it meets other needs anyway without going further and continues to confirm you as a sexual couple). In the communications chapter, we talked about sexy and non-sexy invitations. A low-pressure kiss that might turn into more and sometimes might not is a much more effective invitation than 'fancy a shag', when there has been no sexual currency between you for weeks. A kiss is, of course, much easier to initiate when there is a culture of kissing for the sake of kissing between you. It's a win-win.

TASK: Sexual currency overload

This is an experiment for 'going to town', as it were, on increasing your sexual currency, to kickstart a change in how you relate to each other sexually. For this task to be most effective, you need to make a commitment to each other that the efforts you make to increase sexual currency won't lead to any type of sex together (in terms of any sexual acts). Taking sex off the agenda in this way allows you both to be free to take risks to create and be receptive to each other without expectation or pressure.

You will have an idea from this chapter what this could look like for your relationship, and it may be connected to things you did more of in your early days together. Do as much as you can of the things you know you both like but also throw in anything else you can think of to try. This might be reinstating passionate kissing or doing it more often, being flirtier, sending sex texts, complimenting each other's appearance, touching each other suggestively, flirting with other people, sharing sexual thoughts, fantasies or memories, touching each other in a more sexual way while watching TV or talking – anything you can think of. Aim to 'try on' a more sexual 'couple identity' by doing as much of this as you can throughout the day, week or month. After a week or two, sit down together to discuss:

How easy or difficult was it? Did it get easier as you got more used to it?

How did it make you feel about yourself? Your relationship? Each other?

What impact did it have on your intimacy or closeness?

What impact did it have on your perception of yourselves as a sexual couple?

Did it make sex or desire feel closer or further away?

What else did you notice?

If it's been positive for you, make a commitment to intentionally nurture sexual currency in your sexual relationship from now on. Remember that life (and kids) will get in the way from time to time and that this is normal, but a change in this way allows you to feel sexually connected even when sex feels unachievable. Keep a check on the course of your sexual currency throughout the journey of parenthood. At times you will fall off course a little. This is fine. Notice it, make a shared commitment to get back on track, and correct your trajectory by intentional effort to reinstate it.

Harnessing motivation

REFLECTION: Is this us?

Do you wish you felt like sex more than you do?

Does sex feel like it doesn't have as much to offer you as other activities you could be spending your time on?

Does solo sex produce more pleasure in less time?

Does sex often look the same?

Is sex often associated with negative feelings like awkwardness or worry rather than pleasure and fun?

Do you feel limited in who you are sexually, as your partner expects you to be a certain way sexually?

Sex that is rewarding

If you didn't know about it before you read Chapter 3, you will definitely know by now that feeling like sex in a long-term relationship is not as easy as we are often told it should be. You will understand by now that we might consider ourselves to be without desire as a starting point, but able to trigger desire in the right circumstances. The problem with parenthood is that it is rarely the right circumstances. This doesn't mean that we can't have desire feature in this stage of a relationship, as we can. It means that, to beat other priorities on our mental to-do list as parents, *sex has to be high enough in reward for us to move towards it*. Reward in sex means sex that is high in pleasure, unpredictability, connection and positive emotions.

Awkwardness, lack of pleasure and a sex life that is monotonous or predictable is the *least* rewarding sex we can have. The journey we may have been on in a long-term relationship, trying to conceive or pregnancy may have contributed to sex being less motivating. Let's look at this in more detail.

In Chapter 4 we started to think about the impact of pregnancy and trying to conceive on your sex life. We considered how pregnancy presented you with changes – both opportunities and challenges – and I encouraged you to reflect together on how you could use those as an advantage moving forward. Both trying to conceive and a period of not having sex for some time can create a situation like Tilly and Becca were facing, where awkwardness starts to creep in. I see this most with couples in therapy when they have had long periods of time without being sexual. What can happen is that sex starts to feel like something that you don't do together. Talking about it starts to feel more and more off limits and it can feel easier to see your partner as a friend, flatmate or sibling than a sexual object. For Tilly and Becca, their choice to not have sex for some time (it had been over two years since they had been sexual together) was right for them, but had created much sexual distance between them. Awkwardness is just a shift of culture, and as we know, culture can change by us actively shaping it. This change can be hard initially, as we might not be having sexual thoughts or feelings directed towards our partner, we might even be doubting that we have that attraction any more.* To make this change easier to navigate, it is important that we shape and encourage the culture shift in small and incremental ways. If you remember back to Basson's model in Chapter 3, we spoke of the importance of ensuring a foundation of emotional intimacy and connection first, to allow us to be receptive to the idea of sex with a partner. After this, small steps towards physical intimacy act as a trigger for our arousal, then desire. Pressure to feel desire will act as a psychological barrier and stifle this, so it's important that you give yourself space to rebuild this connection without expectation to feel sexual towards your partner at all for a while.

Let's take a look at how Tilly and Becca did this.

Tilly and Becca decided to start with emotional intimacy and connection, as they identified that, since they have had kids, they still get on great, but mostly have functional or surface-level conversations about parenting or household tasks, with very little time to *really connect*, have fun together, go out on dates, or talk about anything other than the kids. They made a plan to designate one night a fortnight to focusing on each other and their relationship. They don't have the money for a babysitter, so they ask Tilly's mum if she can babysit once a month for them to go out, and they plan to make the other date something they can do in the house once the kids have gone to bed.

---

* It is possible, of course, that we no longer feel attraction to our partner, as making a decision to be monogamous and making a commitment to someone doesn't guarantee our future feelings towards them. Sadly, no amount of sex therapy can fix a lack of attraction or a change of feelings for a partner as we discussed in Chapter 1. BUT awkwardness and not relating to our partner as a sexual being can also look and feel like a lack of attraction, and, in my experience, can often resolve itself once the culture changes to include more sexual ways of relating.

They decide to take it in turns planning the dates and make a deal that, even if it's a date at home, they will make an effort for each other by getting ready in the way they would if they were going out. They brainstormed a list of things they could do at home together that might be fun, different or just a break from the norm (if you plan to do this and are stuck for ideas, google 'date night ideas at home'). Tilly and Becca noticed a return in their connection as partners rather than parents after a few weeks of these dates, and this built the foundations for them to consider bringing back physical intimacy. The at-home date nights became the perfect opportunity to make some of the activities more physical. For example, massages and spa nights. Even some of the non-physical intimacy dates they had on their list (for example, writing a bucket list for the next ten years) were things they could bring physical intimacy to, by doing it in the bath, or while naked/semi-naked in bed.

It didn't take long for Tilly and Becca to start to feel like they wanted to be sexual together, and to notice the awkwardness subsiding. They decided to treat their return to physical intimacy and sex like when they were dating, adding an extra element of excitement to it ('will she kiss me after this date?' or 'when will we take it further?'). Slowing down physical intimacy in this way and making it something to anticipate can be the perfect antidote to those having felt pressure to feel something after a period of time of no sex, but also for those for whom sex felt like it has to happen on demand while, for example, trying to conceive.

A sex life that always starts in the same way, and has the same middle and ending, is not very enticing or motivating for any of us, as our brains are generally into novelty. As I said in my first TED Talk,[3] if every time you go to the same restaurant you have the same meal, in the same order, it gets less exciting. Soon you might find yourself less enthusiastic about visiting that restaurant at all. This can be one of

223

the reasons that sex while trying to conceive can lose its shine. Remember when we talked about the danger of predefined sexual scripts, particularly for men and women having sex together? You *have* to do it, you *have* to do it *that day*, you *have* to do it *that way*. Who wouldn't get bored with that?

Predictability in sex within long-term relationships shows up in a variety of ways, not just in those who struggled to conceive. If you have chosen to be monogamous, then by its very definition your partner will remain the same, and that brings some level of predictability. If not *who* you're having sex with, then there have to be other variables that bring change from time to time, or else you risk boredom and challenges with desire settling in. This is perhaps even more important for parents, for the reasons we've already outlined – sex has to have enough of a pull for us to outweigh the other competing priorities that are stacked high. The antithesis to predictability is novelty, but novelty when it comes to sex has a somewhat cheesy reputation. When you hear 'novelty', it's easy for your mind to go to maids' outfits and edible underwear (this is fine if it's your bag, but novelty can be *so* much more than this). Novelty can be in what you do (have a different type of sex), how you do it (in another room, a different time of day, while remaining clothed) or the feel of it (unusually slow/passionate/frenzied/sensual). It can also be novelty in who you are and the role you take (dominant, playful, sensual, serious).

While we're on the subject, novelty and unpredictability don't just need to be centred in the type of sex you have: they are about every aspect of your sex life together. Here's a few ideas to get you started:

novelty in sexual currency: for example, send a text about your favourite sexual memory together, if you have never done this before

novelty in how you invite each other into sex: for example, if you usually ask directly, try a slower, less obvious seduction

novelty by talking about sex and bringing in new ideas/ perspectives on it: for example, talk about things you have read, and share your ideas about it.

If you have noticed that your current sex life has been affected by awkwardness or distance, perhaps after trying to conceive or the impact of long periods of time not having sex, make a plan, like Tilly and Becca, to gradually take steps to shifting your relationship culture back into a dating and physical intimacy space. This does not need to take a lot of time and money. If you can only find two hours a month at home to do this, this is fine. Set a date to review it every six months or so as your parenting demands change. When you review, try to avoid the question of 'has this change revolutionized our sex life?' as the criteria you judge it against, but rather 'is this slight change of course more favourable to our long-term trajectory?'

TASK:

In my professional experience, there are very few couples in long-term relationships who nurture novelty intentionally. Being cognisant to the role of predictability in making your sex life hold your attention is not just useful for parents, but also for maintaining desire in a monogamous relationship long term. Re-read the section above and, on a piece of paper, write down all the ways you could bring novelty into your sex life using these prompts.

Maximizing pleasure

If you follow me on Instagram, have read my first book or watched my second TED Talk[4] on orgasm inequality, you will know already that there is a gender gap in the amount of pleasure cis women receive from sex when they have sex with cis men compared to any other group. What this means is that when women masturbate, or have sex with other women, they are more likely to orgasm than when they have sex with men. This is not an anatomical issue; it's not that women's bodies are more complex. Women can orgasm at roughly the same rate as men when they masturbate and, if it was about anatomy, there wouldn't be a difference between rates of orgasm from masturbation, having sex with women and having sex with men.

The real reason there is a pleasure gap with sex between men and women (with men orgasming reliably 95 per cent of the time and women 65 per cent of the time[5]) is due to the impact of the patriarchy on what we see as sex, and how entitled women feel to pleasure. Men who are reading this, I just want to state that *you are not the patriarchy*, so please don't take this as a personal attack. The patriarchy is a societal system that privileges and gives power to men over women, not men in general.

Basically, the very act we consider to be 'sex' in our society (a penis in a vagina) is considered to be the pinnacle of sex (and essential for heterosexual people particularly), as evidenced by our sexual scripts and our use of language ('we did everything *but*'). The clitoris and the penis are equivocal structures, so they started off the same in the womb and then developed based on the hormones we were exposed to. For example, the tip of the penis is equivocal to the tip of the clitoris in sensitivity. Penetrative sex stimulates the tip of the penis, and so there's a high rate of orgasm for men when having sex this way. The vagina is quite far from the clitoris, and so most women (about

226

80 per cent) can't orgasm this way, unless the clitoris is stimulated directly (with one of your hands, by a sex toy, or by the rubbing of your bodies in some sexual positions).* Our view of what sex is, therefore, has been influenced over the years by what works for men's bodies over women's. Other types of sex, such as oral sex, are much more likely to result in pleasure for women, but these types of sex have been relegated to not-quite-as-important, by the use of the belittling word 'foreplay'. Don't let this word influence how you see what is and isn't sex (in fact, please ditch it: all sex is sex!). Cast your mind back to the motivations for having sex you both outlined for yourself in Chapter 1. How many of them can only be met by penetrative sex? The answer is only one: getting pregnant. Unless this is your motivation, why would you restrict your sex life in this way when it is such a risk to pleasure equality and novelty in sex?

The other reason that penetrative sex has been pedestalled as the most important sexual act and a marker of things like 'virginity'† is due to the historical relationship between sex and religion. Conservativism in (Western) Christianity, which was once hugely influential in Western culture, marked having sex for pleasure, or anything else apart from procreation, a sin. Colonialism then carried many of these views to other parts of the world, that, until then, had held largely sex-positive and expansive views of sex.

---

* Roughly 20 per cent of women can orgasm this way from the indirect stimulation of the internal clitoris through the vaginal wall, but this is still about the clitoris, just accessed another way. Lloyd, E. A. (2006). *The case of the female orgasm: Bias in the science of evolution.* Harvard University Press.

† 'Virginity': an outdated word historically used to describe the first time someone has penetrative sex. As we touched on in Chapter 7, phrases such as 'sexual debut' place less emphasis on one sexual act, which may or may not have meaning to the person experiencing it and may or may not include pleasure. Sexual debut is also inclusive to those who choose not to, can't or don't want to have penetrative sex in their sex life. It also allows for personal meaning to define importance rather than a sexual act. For example, a person might choose their first orgasm in the presence of another person as being a meaningful moment rather than a penis in a vagina.

The pleasure gap is hugely relevant to your sex life. Let me tell you how. Before you learned more about desire, you would have been forgiven for imagining there was such a thing as 'sex drive', an innate pull towards sex that we all have, perhaps governed by biology, such as our hormones. Now you know desire is more of a motivation towards the behaviour of sex, and that something needs to pull us towards acting on this motivation.[6] As we've already mentioned, when you're a parent with competing priorities, *the reward of sex has to be worth sacrificing the time for other activities (such as sleep) for it to pull us towards it*. Being time-poor makes rewarding sex even more important, as there is more pressure to spend each moment you have to yourself wisely. Low reward in terms of unreliable pleasure will mean the behaviour of sex has very little pull.

The upshot is that if one of you frequently has more pleasure than the other as part of your sex life, this needs addressing. Orgasm inequality affects cis women having sex with cis men most, so if the two of you find yourself fitting these demographics, have a conversation about it, let each other off the hook for having faked it from time to time (it's really common, and is a mixture of playing into the patriarchy's hands and feeling abnormal, as many women don't know it's unusual to not come from vaginal penetration), and most importantly, address it. Improving your ability to talk about sex more comfortably is associated with having more orgasms, so work on communication as well.[7] Having more orgasms is strongly associated with two key consequences:

- greater sexual satisfaction in your relationship[8]

- maintaining desire for sex with your partner[9]

The simplest way to do this is to have other types of sex than penetrative sex, so your sex life has variety and equal pleasure. You could have oral sex, or make each other come just with your hands. Use sex toys like vibrators without worry, fear or judgement. They will not damage your body, they are not a replacement for a partner and they are not a sign of anyone's sexual 'skill'. They are simply a tool at your disposal to make sex quicker,* more pleasurable, and more diverse/novel. Why wouldn't you use this? Sex with variety, lack of predictability and reward is the type of sex we are most inclined to make time for. Remember the effect of novelty we talked about earlier? Mixing up your sex life to have more equal pleasure won't just make sex more rewarding physically, it will also create novelty and difference, which will make sex an activity that your brain sees as more worthwhile, allowing it to rise up the priority list at times. It's the equivalent of going to the same restaurant, but, every time you go, there is a different (and expansive) menu to choose from. You are never exactly sure how it's going to go or where you'll end up. This is a restaurant you'll be more inclined to visit.

TASK: Solo sex as a blueprint

If your partner is a cis woman, ask her how she masturbates. It's likely to be touch to the clitoris only, or touch to the clitoris predominantly, with a side helping of vaginal penetration to add to the sensation. Notice if this is different to the majority of the sex you have together. Communicating your intention to take your time over sex and prioritize your partner's pleasure has been shown to increase cis women's sense of actively pursuing their own orgasm in partnered sex.[10]

---

* My aim isn't to suggest that quick sex equals good sex, BUT being able to speed sex up at times is an efficient way to have sex for time-poor parents, and can therefore make the time investment, or time taken away from other things, such as sleep, feel more worthwhile.

TOP TIP

If you are queer, you may find it useful to view novelty in another way. For example, men having sex with other men have less penetrative sex than any other group,[11] so the novelty around types of sex (and it not always being penetration) may already be there. Novelty, here, may be about how sex happens, how you invite, where it happens, how you play with power. Women having sex with other women already have novelty in types of sex, but typically have longer sex sessions than any other group.[12] Women having sex with other women have sex sessions that last fifty-seven minutes, on average, compared to the eighteen minutes average when women and men have sex together.[13] Novelty here might be seeing if quickies can work (see the next section for a discussion of quickies and novelty). This is particularly relevant for women in relationships together with kids, where long sex sessions can be hard to fit in. For trans or non-binary people, the tips for men having sex with men or women having sex with women above may, of course, be just as relevant. If you are trans and straight, you may also feel pigeonholed into sexual scripts that might make sex predictable, particularly if any of your partner(s) are cis gendered.

Tackling competing priorities

REFLECTION: Is this us?

Do you genuinely have no idea when sex would happen in your life currently?

Are you always exhausted?

Is your child not sleeping through the night yet?

Are you struggling to feel good about yourself or your life?

Time, possibilities and choices

Parenthood is a complete and utter time sapper. Earlier on in the book I mentioned that having a child is an extra thirty hours of work a week, and that doesn't take into account having more than one child, or children with additional needs. Basically, parents are the group of people most time-poor compared to all other groups of sexually active people. If we can't find time to respond to WhatsApp group chats, how can we find time for sex? A lack of time, along with a large helping of tiredness, may be some of the biggest challenges you might feel you are facing, so let's look at them realistically. We'll address tiredness shortly, but let's focus on time first. I want you to notice myths that we are all exposed to around sex that make us feel especially stuck when we are time-poor:

- a good sex life where everyone feels happy is about frequency

- sex has to look a certain way to 'count' as sex and meet our needs

- you should wait until you feel desire and then find the time

- spontaneous sex is better than scheduling time to triggering desire.

These myths (which you now understand better and, hopefully, now know not to be true) can work in cahoots with being time-poor to

231

make our sex lives as parents feel impossible. For example, if you believe that you have to be having sex a few times a week (or even a month) to have a good sex life, this might feel completely unavailable to you, so instead you just give up. If you feel that physical sexual acts are the only way to be sexual with each other, or that you should be waiting to feel desire first, this also limits your sex life significantly. If you feel like spontaneous sex is the marker of true desire and a good sex life, what happens when your circumstances prohibit spontaneity?

Time does not have to be the barrier it has felt like up until now. But it is still a major challenge, so let's take a practical look at it, so that we can a) let ourselves off the hook about a lack of time for sex and b) see if there is any time that we want to use differently.

It can be useful to sit down and write out a typical week in terms of how you both spend your time. Include things like nap times for the kids, school drop offs, work commitments, and time spent doing household chores/watching TV. Make sure it is clear when you are both at home together.

By doing this you can reflect on the moments of your day or week where you can make time for any of the small changes that can make a big difference that I have spoken about in this book. This might include emotional and physical intimacy of any type, or to connect over doing a self-expanding activity together. These might include:

- turning perfunctory kisses into more passionate kisses

- being naked together and running your hands over each other's body for ten minutes

- one of you giving the other a whole body massage

- having a bath together and washing each other's bodies

- ten minutes to have a conversation where you really listen and understand how each other is feeling about work/parenthood/life

- doing something new and fun together for one hour a month

My bet is that, in your current week, there is simply no time set aside for any of this currently, and maybe it even feels that this time is not possible to schedule in. For those of you earlier on in your parenting journey, this may feel most likely.

For those of you who are out of those crazy times of the first couple of months, where you get in the shower fully clothed and need seven coffees to function, my guess is that some of that time *is* achievable, but you are currently, when you have it, spending ten to thirty minutes scrolling Instagram or watching Netflix instead. I'm not trying to shame you here – we all do it! And it can be a great way to relax and get time that's just for you. I'm not asking you to drastically change what your week looks like, just to create a very small change in prioritizing your sexual relationship within a fraction of that time. This small change is also going to have a big change in culture, as it's marking your relationship out as a primary, important one, and one that is sexual via an increase in sexual currency. This culture shift will make it easier for you to manage periods of time with no sex and get back on track with sex more easily when the time comes, and it will also help each of you meet the needs that sex serves for you in the first place, like feeling desired and connected. Lastly, and importantly, making time for each other in this way will, at times, result in responsive desire. The more time you make to connect in this way, the more desire is likely to feature in your relationship.

Discuss what time you can make for each other in this way, and what that time could look like. My top tips for this are: pick something that's super easy to achieve and focus on sexual currency, emotional connection and self-expanding activities, not sex. Try to create new habits around these that don't require either of you to 'initiate' but just become something that you do.

Let's look at Jo and Sam, who did exactly this. Together they have a one-year-old and a three-year-old and both work full-time. They barely have time to do the food shopping, keep on top of the washing and remember to make time to text their friends back. At 8 p.m., when the kids are in bed, they first clean up the mess that the house is in from stray toys and dinner time, then flop in front of the TV for an hour and a half. They go to bed at ten, as both kids wake up at least once a night.

Jo and Sam decide to make the moment they say goodbye each day a five-second passionate kiss instead of a half-second peck on the lips.* They also make sure that every first Friday evening of the month they go to bed at 8 p.m. also, and prioritize being physically intimate and really catching up. These nights sometimes lead to sex, and sometimes don't, but they give their sexual relationship a chance to thrive in this time and they are marking themselves out as a sexual couple by their habit of the kiss and the first Friday time. Knowing the first Friday is coming allows both of them to look forward to that evening and to think about it, as they might if it were a date, and this anticipation in itself can be a trigger for desire. They might each also prepare themselves for going to bed early by taking a shower or a

---

* If a kiss when you leave the house doesn't work, as it's too stressful getting the kids out and everyone ready on time, obviously you can easily change this to when you reunite at the end of the day. The key thing is to make the new habit of doing this every time you see each other so it becomes instinctive, and this change brings a shift in the culture of your relationship towards a more sexual one.

bath, and setting the scene in a way that makes them feel more connected to their sexuality (for example, music, lighting, a glass of wine). They also decide on one Saturday night a month as a night where they try to do something new and fun together, to have a laugh and really connect. For the first one they are planning to look at design inspo and plan a mood board/sketch out their hopes for when they can afford an extension to the kitchen/diner. The one after that they plan to do an online drawing class together from home, as they've always fancied giving this a go.

Jo and Sam have only made a total of two hours once a month for physical intimacy, two hours a month for a night of connection, plus two and a half minutes a month for the kissing spaced over five seconds per day. This is not a huge time commitment in comparison to the twenty-eight hours of watching Netflix they rack up in a month, and they still get to watch twenty-three hours of Netflix! But those small changes will make a *big* difference. Their relationship becomes defined by their sexual connection, and they are making time to be a sexual couple together and to allow desire to be triggered on some of those occasions.

TOP TIP

Avoid making plans to do anything at bedtime. You'll be shattered by then and won't feel like it! If it's an evening chilling in bed or a massage with a glass of wine and music, do it as soon as the kids are asleep, and then you can either get up afterwards and relax or have an early night. Don't be tempted to leave it until 10 p.m. to get started.

TOP TIP

Physical affection alone is *not* enough to trigger desire. Your rule of thumb should be: if I do it with one of the kids then it's not sexual (for example, cuddling on the sofa, a quick kiss on the cheek/lips, holding hands). These things are all nice and great to do with your sexual partner, but they are not inherently sexual, and are unlikely to be enough to trigger desire. Emotional intimacy is also crucial, and self-expanding activities, such as having fun doing something new together, will make your relationship stronger and make desire easier to come by, but please don't neglect physical intimacy, like kissing, being naked together, touching each other's bodies. Most of us need this type of sexual stimuli to trigger responsive desire.

TASK: How can we find time?

Discuss together what amount of time, realistically, you can devote to sexual currency per day (so small units of time) and larger chunks of time (twenty minutes to one to two hours) to physical and emotional intimacy. What will it replace? Where will it fit? Can you make any of it linked to another routine?

Once you have settled on this time, halve it. This will make it feel achievable.

Decide how to spend this time. Forget about sex. Desire will follow when you make time for physical intimacy. You just need to make the time. You don't need to feel anything in particular to make this time happen. It may also take a period of time of reconnecting this way before the relationship culture allows desire to emerge more easily. Don't be disheartened if it doesn't feel like things are changing straight away.

Make this time unavoidable. Put it in a shared family diary. Make sure it happens at the same point or time every day (such as when you say goodbye, or, like Jo and Sam did, the first Friday of every month). Don't fall into a habit of quickly cancelling it if you don't feel in the mood when the day comes. It can take time to get into the right headspace and you might thank yourselves afterwards.

Set a date night to really talk once a month and review this plan. Can you tweak it? Do a bit more? Change what you do or where you do it? Try something new? Discuss its effects on you individually, and on the relationship. Start a new habit of always checking in on your sex life this way and making small changes. It will be good for you in the long term, even when the kids have grown up! Ask yourselves, what are we pleased about that we want to continue? What do we want to do less/more of moving forward? This is about intentionally taking stock of your course and long-term trajectory.

Scheduling

Everything we see on TV pedestals spontaneous sex as best, and TV is one of the ways we learn about sex in society. TV rarely shows representations of how a good sex life is negotiated in this kind of way. We rarely see it modelled to us how setting a context for desire or sex to emerge or taking steps to make sex possible are frequent behaviours people in high-satisfaction long-term sexual relationships do.[14] Sometimes we see spontaneous sex as best as we see it as being linked to sexual compatibility, chemistry or the presence of high desire for each other.[15] When we are believers that spontaneous sex is best, challenges to this, such as becoming a parent, can significantly affect our sexual satisfaction and stop us looking for solutions. This also means we are less intentional about nurturing our sex life, which, as you now know, will have us sailing off course. Moving towards an awareness that spontaneous sex might be impossible or unrealistic in your current circumstances and trying out the belief that scheduling time where desire can emerge is just as good (sex research says it is[16]) could therefore really help your sexual satisfaction.

I feel what people are really referring to when they recoil at the concept of scheduling is the idea that 'sex' being expected is off-putting, and in some ways this can certainly be true, as pressure and expectation can be real desire killers. But there is a difference between carving out time for physical connection and pre-emptively consenting to sex you aren't even sure you want or will feel like, and it's a crucial one. Knowing that there is a no-pressure enjoyment-filled intimacy-fuelled fest planned that evening, which may lead to wanting more but also might not, can be really sexy. Also, knowing that this time is planned not only allows both of you to anticipate and fantasize about it (which are both important triggers for arousal and desire), but also allows you to put things in place that help with the practicalities of making it happen. This might be making sure you switch your phone off or resist checking your stressful work emails, making an effort to be home from work on time, or not answering that call from your aunt, which might take an hour. It might also lead you to take steps to connect with your own sexuality and do what you need to do to feel confident in your body. This might be having a shower, wearing something that makes you feel confident or creating the right environment using music or temperature.

Think back to Jo and Sam, who negotiate the first Friday of the month for physical intimacy. Knowing this night is approaching allows them both to anticipate potential sexual connection. This is similar to the start of a relationship, in the early dating phase, when they might have looked forward to the promise of what might transpire in the build up to it. Most people look back at this phase of their sex life with fondness and romanticism, remembering what it was like to have 'butterflies' and imagine what might happen later on. When you live with someone, this anticipation can be hard to recreate. Why wouldn't you use scheduling to your advantage to help you do this?

The value of quick connection

Although many of my clients tell me the reason they choose masturbation over partnered sex is about guaranteed pleasure and opportunity, a significant proportion tell me that they opt for masturbation due to the fact that it takes up less time in their day (most people can orgasm alone in less than five minutes[17]). There is something in this which is important to note for those who are time-poor, such as parents. Time to orgasm can be the same with partnered sex as masturbation, but it can often take longer due to:

• not getting the stimulation that might work best for your body

• anxiety and distraction interfering with sexual response

• turn taking in sex adding more time to the experience overall

239

- heteronormative scripts about what sex looks like (A, then B, then C, needing to always end in penis-in-vagina sex etc), making it hard to suggest something different that might get you there quicker

- not being able to communicate easily about what you want (not feeling able to say 'I'm ready for you to touch me hard and fast now', for example. This is related to the above point).

It doesn't have to be this way, and I have seen many breakthroughs in therapy when people have told their partner that, actually, they want sex to be fast from time to time and that this lower time investment would make it easier for them to engage in their sex life more.

It makes sense when you think about our desire for sex being more like motivation than a drive. As we know, the behaviour of 'sex' is competing with other priorities in our life (sleep, TV, housework – *so* rock 'n' roll!), and the time taken having sex takes time away from another activity that is also important to us. Add in the extra thirty hours a week that having even just one child brings to our life and things get squeezed considerably. Being able to name a desire for sex to be quick from time to time and the benefit that this might bring can be a useful strategy for some couples and increase our motivation to engage with it as a behaviour. On balance, then, the cost of sex (time) is outweighed by the benefits (closeness/connection/pleasure/fun/escapism). When we are time-poor, the benefits have to feel very tangible for us to even contemplate taking time away from another activity that also feels like a priority. Spending less time on sex, on some occasions, can be the answer.

Quickies aren't for everyone, of course, and you might need to find a way to make them work for you. A cautionary note here for cis men and cis women having sex together: research tells us that longer sexual encounters are most likely to result in orgasm for cis women,[18] and that cis women give up their orgasm goals when they know there is a time pressure to sex.[19] This is not due to a gender difference in time taken to orgasm, as I've already mentioned. It is due to the fact that when cis men and cis women have sex together that is conceptualized as a 'quickie', sexual acts that are less satisfying for cis women are often side-lined in favour of penetrative sex. This is okay if your motivations for sex as a cis woman on this occasion aren't your own pleasure, but for something else you hope to gain, such as connection. This may also be detrimental if there is already an orgasm gap between you. Beware the quickie as a solution for being time-poor if it further highlights one person's pleasure over another's and continues to reinforce the idea of sex as an act with low reward for one person.

To combat this, your quickie might need to be one-sided – sex that's just focused on one of your bodies so this person can get the touch they need. You might need to spend some time ahead of a quickie getting yourself in the mood so you already feel turned on. For example, by fantasizing on the way home from work or listening to audio erotica in the bath. You might need to practise communicating exactly what you want and when to make it super pleasurable and time efficient ('touch me like this, harder, now move this way'). You might want to use sex toys to add to the speed of the encounter. You will need to communicate your desire for it to be quick, as otherwise how will your partner know?

The benefit of quickies aren't just limited to time, as they also bring an injection of fun and novelty. Quickies can connect you sexually without much time investment. Try as best you can to separate sex from orgasms here also. Orgasms add to sexual satisfaction, but they are not essential for good sex. You might enjoy a quickie but not be able to come with a partner in that time frame. Does that matter?

What might be the benefit of more sexual connection, even if fewer orgasms? After all, most people can easily orgasm alone, and we are often motivated to have sex with our partners for other reasons, as you have already discovered. Understanding your motivations for sex will be vital here. You might want to cross-check your common motivations for sex with the potential outcomes of quickies. You could, of course, negotiate giving quicker sex a go and seeing what impact it has for you both, positive *and* negative.

Sleep and chronic tiredness

In Chapter 5 we reflected on the very real fact that feeling too tired for sex is a common reason people give for not feeling able to engage with their sex lives and, as I'm sure you are way too familiar, this is a *very* real challenge for parents. As we have discussed, a good night's sleep is useful for so many aspects of wellbeing and being able to connect with sexual thoughts, feelings and bodily responses is one of them. Earlier, we spoke of how reducing any inequality around sleep might be an important first goal, so if one of you is getting up several times a night, and the other doesn't get up at all, there is an obvious compromise that can be made to lessen the sleep burden. This may be more challenging if one of you is breast/chestfeeding, but, even in this scenario, the other may be able to help in other ways (for example, Rosey Davidson, sleep consultant and author of *The Just Chill Baby Sleep Book* (Vermillion, 2023), suggests that the partner who isn't feeding can do the winding or nappy change afterwards, allowing the person feeding to get back to sleep quicker). If compromise isn't possible, or wanted, then you might need to accept that your sex life may be less satisfactory than you would like it to be until things improve. It's not about you, or your relationship.

When it comes to sleep, one of the biggest mistakes I see couples making is waiting until bedtime to think about having sex. When you are sleep deprived, opportunities for making time for your sexual connection are best found at times when you aren't also beside yourself with exhaustion, like bedtime. For example, perhaps you can switch one weekend nap time a month to a time to connect sexually instead of doing housework or catching up on sleep? (Sadly, this may become impossible when you have more than one child!) If this isn't possible for you, you might find the best time to try to connect sexually is just after the kids have gone to bed. A solution such as this, as effective as it can be, can be tricky to instigate as, unlike bedtime (when you might already be physically close and semi-naked), daytime or early evening sex requires really clear sexual communication. Something like: 'I was thinking – it's been ages since we've had chance to connect physically. Can we go to bed for a bit while Benji naps later?' Unlike bedtime, when you can rely on non-verbal communication, such as reaching over to touch or kiss without saying anything out loud, it won't just happen otherwise. For this strategy to be successful, it also requires a foundational understanding of desire as something to be triggered, rather than something ever present with no effort. Lastly, you have to be comfortable with allowing each other (and yourself) to occupy the space in between willingness and desire, as these days your sex life has to run on opportunity, not when you feel like it. What are the chances that both people will feel desire simultaneously later during naptime? I can tell you: it's close to zero. But what are the chances that, if one of you plants the seed by communicating intent, as long as you are physically close and have no pressure, desire might follow? Quite high, as desire is often triggered in these circumstances. If you do go to bed, then end up napping anyway, there's nothing lost!

TASK: A tired(ness) conversation

Talk together about tiredness and how it interferes with your sex life in a blame-free way. Discuss whether there are any opportunities to share the load of night-time wakings more than you do. If there are, action them. If there are not, then look for other opportunities to connect sexually. Depending on what stage of parenthood you are at, your options could be a) agreeing to do nothing for now, b) agreeing sexual currency in small amounts but no sex, and c) looking for other opportunities for sex (early evening, nap times) that do not need to be frequent, and agreeing to try this out together to see how it feels. If you do the latter, it is essential that the invitation does not have pressure to have sex. Create physical intimacy (such as being in bed together naked, or semi-naked, and talking while touching each other's bodies) and see this as useful for your relationship in its own right, even if it doesn't lead to desire for one or both of you.

Lastly, but importantly in this section: if you are significantly sleep deprived or experiencing another challenge affecting your wellbeing, such as feeling low or feeling anxious in a way that affects your day-to-day life, then addressing these things where you can and seeking help is the work to be done here, not focusing on sex. There are good reasons why sex isn't a priority, and your wellbeing is more important. Sleep deprivation and low mood will affect your sex life and sex will take its place again when things start to improve. Go easy on yourself and work on perfecting the relationship climate to support your emotional intimacy, psychological wellbeing and connection in the meantime.

Perfecting the relationship climate

REFLECTION: Is this us?

Would I feel able to send an explicit text to them if I wanted to?

Could we watch a sex scene on TV and talk about what was hot about it?

Do we feel comfortable sometimes sharing sexual thoughts, fantasies or memories?

Can and do we talk about our hopes, fears, moments of joy and despair and really feel listened to and understood?

Can we turn each other down for sex without it feeling like a problem?

Do we spend any time together laughing and having fun?

Can we ask for exactly what we want sexually, even if it's something we haven't done before?

Is there inequity in the division of childcare or household labour causing resentment?

Does one of us feel like the other doesn't see how much we actually do, and feel constantly distracted by the to-do list of managing a home and family?

In the previous chapter, we reviewed the importance of communication for a relationship climate that promotes good sex. We considered the fact that our sexual selves and sexual wants are never static throughout our lives, and that being able to communicate well about sex is the crucial factor that allows our sexual relationships to navigate these changes and differences successfully, keeping our sexual interest and sexual satisfaction.

I asked you to consider the communication about sex in your relationship currently. This included methods of communication you currently use or feel comfortable with, and how you might like (or might benefit) from expanding these. It also includes aspects of your sex life that you'd like to be different, but not feeling able to talk about sex comfortably prevents. I asked you to consider how easy you find it to communicate generally. By this I mean really feel heard, understood, of interest and supported. For some of you starting here is important, as the emotional closeness that this brings lays the foundations both for being able to talk about sex but also sexual satisfaction. Setting aside a ten-minute check-in at the end of the day where you each really listen to the other's day, to how they are thinking and feeling, without offering solutions or advice might be the starting point for some of you.

As you may well have spotted as we've delved into these topics, there is a relationship between sexual communication, the culture of your sexual relationship and the triggering of desire. Just in case this point hasn't fully formed in your mind yet, here's an example of two couples with opposite patterns in communication and relationship culture.

Alvin and Kyle struggle to talk about anything to do with sex. They have been together thirteen years and have had twins with the help of a surrogate. Their relationship culture supports them greatly as co-parents and friends. They can talk easily about household admin, how to parent and make plans for their family life together. They are supportive of each other emotionally. Their sexual communication is non-verbal and indirect. They don't discuss their sex life and they have very little sexual currency between them. Sex has become less and less frequent in the last five years and is usually initiated by Kyle, who will press his body up against Alvin in the weekend mornings when they are half asleep. This communication is read by both of them as an invitation to have sex. It feels out of context to Alvin, as they haven't had sex for months and it feels a little awkward to know where to start. He hasn't really been feeling that way about Kyle, and knowing that this is where Kyle wants this to go feels high pressure to Alvin. The combination of pressure, awkwardness and the fact that the sex they have had for the last few years always follows this same pattern and hasn't been that rewarding for Alvin (not unpleasurable, just quite samey) means it's hard for Alvin to feel desire. Kyle senses this and feels hurt and rejected. It was a big deal for Kyle to take the risk to let Alvin know, even indirectly, that he would like to have sex, and he wonders why he has bothered. He feels hurt and distances himself emotionally. Months go by before this cycle is repeated.

For Leon and Dionne things are slightly different. They are solid co-parents and friends, but their relationship also connects them as sexual people by the compliments, flirting, brief moments of talking or thinking about sex, or physical sexual currency such as kissing. The communication that they have cultivated over time about sex, both verbal and non-verbal, allows them to modify, adapt, get their sexual needs met, and maintain a sexual connection even when sex isn't an option. Because of this, they have been able to keep their sex life interesting and to meet both of their needs. When Dionne presses her body against Leon's on a Sunday morning, Leon reads this as a demonstration of love, desire, attraction that may indicate that

Dionne wants more, or may just be a feeling in its own right. Leon finds it easy to say 'That feels nice. I wish I had time to stay here with you, but I have to get up for the kids' swimming lessons.' Dionne doesn't feel rejected for several reasons. The first is that she didn't actually feel strongly about it needing to go anywhere – her actions were meeting a need of expressing attraction and feeling close to Leon. The second is that Leon is communicating 'how frustrating that life gets in the way of our sex life – I wish we could indulge in this moment', which is a communication that she is valued, desired and seen by him sexually, and explains his withdrawal as not personal, but about a lack of time. Leon doesn't feel pressure to feel anything, or to accept the invitation, as this kind of communication is not scarce between them. The lack of pressure and the variety in these types of communication that they have between them allows bountiful opportunities for sparking desire and getting their sexual needs met in other ways. They stay connected as a sexual couple.

Predictability in invitations

In the previous chapter, we talked about 'initiation' as sexual communication, and that it might be helpful to consider thinking of this as an 'invitation' – something that we want to feel free to make, which would benefit from being both enticing and not a fait accompli and for a partner to feel free to decline. A lifetime of sex negativity and not being socialized to talk about sex can make this kind of communication hard for many of us. Many of the people I see for sex therapy say: 'I felt like it, but I didn't let my partner know, and I didn't do anything about that feeling.'

We looked at the differences in how people invite each other into sex, with each of us falling into tried-and-tested habits, not all of them effective. As we outlined in the previous chapter, some people invite their partner in by asking directly. Some invite their partner with a physical non-verbal communication, like a gentle kiss to the back of the neck. Some do a mix of both and some don't invite their partner at all.

Asking directly for sex is great if it gets your partner in the zone, but what if there are other things that might be more effective? It's so easy to be shooting off-target here and, as parents, shots off-target are missed opportunities in an otherwise challenging landscape. As well as invitations doing what we want them to do, considering our invitations also allows us to consider whether our invitations might be suffering from predictability. As I mentioned earlier, novelty is not just how you have sex, but also how you invite. As you now understand, predictability and sex don't make great long-term partners. Your predictable invitations might work in months one to three, but the same signal over and over again might get irritating by month two hundred. Have a discussion about what you notice about each other's invitations. Talk to each other about what you think and feel about the way each of you does it. Go gently on each other, as a less-than-satisfactory way of inviting may be a habit that one of you has fallen into as it's the easiest thing to say; it worked once so you just kept doing it. Talking about sex can be hard, so we need to give each other permission to not always get it right.

Over the next few pages, we'll explore some skills and techniques for communicating with your partner.

COMMUNICATION MAP

In the previous chapter, I spoke of a map to help you on your journey of developing more comfort with communication. You can find this map set out on the opposite page, along with a detailed key to accompany it on pages 252–254. The foundation levels are a good place to start, and I would suggest reviewing these and starting here if you don't feel confident with them. If you feel super confident here, or practise these skills and feel ready to move on, the next level includes comfort talking about sex in a way that isn't personal to you or your relationship. Advanced skills are possible once you have built these solid foundations, or if you already have a sound foundation of sexual communication. These include talking about your own sex life, inviting and turning each other down easily, and keeping talking about sex on the agenda often and in a variety of ways. I'd like to invite you to each plot a point on the map that is your current comfort level and consider the journey ahead. The journey does not have to be linear or follow my suggestions; plot a course that feels right for you and commit together to try this out, allowing each other to feel clumsy about it, a bit embarrassed or to 'get it wrong'. Continue to weave your way between levels in all directions as you build your confidence. Remember that a shift in any culture, whether it be in our culture of communicating or otherwise, can require effort and intentional action at first, then start to gather momentum and feel easier and more habitual over time.

ADVANCED SKILLS

Easy invites, easy turning down

Bring your motivations into your inviting

Notice anything you hold back

Practise linking your motivations to types of sex

INTERMEDIATE SKILLS

LEVEL 2

Review your sex life regularly

Reminisce about the first time you had sex

Practise different ways of inviting each other in

Practise directing sex in the moment using words

Share sexual thoughts, memories or fantasies you've had

LEVEL 1

Send suggestive texts

Send suggestive clips

Share your invitation preferences

Share your conditions for good sex

FOUNDATION SKILLS

LEVEL 2

Talk about sex straight after sex

Use non-verbal communication during sex more

Sex scene date night

Talk about sex as a topic

LEVEL 1

Learning more about good communication

Practise trying not to 'fix'

10-minute check-in commitment

When do you feel most heard?

Reflect on what you'd like to say

Foundation skills

General communication

The first level concentrates on general communication skills in your relationship, outside of sex, in order to lay the groundwork for what's to come.

Learning more about good communication: Both commit to learning more about aspects of good relationship communication. Listen to podcasts, read books, engage with accounts on social media related to this. The Gottman Institute (https://www.gottman.com) is a great place to start.

Practise trying not to 'fix': Avoid the temptation to solve or offer suggestions regarding whatever your partner is struggling with. Instead, spend twice as long as you would normally listening and empathizing.

When do you feel most heard? Discuss together when you feel, or have felt, most heard and understood by each other. What was it about that conversation that really worked for you? How can you each do more of that?

10-minute check-in commitment: Make a regular time/commitment to really connect with each other after a busy day or week. Commit to no phones, eye contact, really listening, showing understanding and empathizing. Ask curious questions of each other to expand your understanding (see page 182).

Reflect on what you'd like to say: Think about what you'd like to say to your partner about your sex life. What you'd like more

of, what you miss, what you'd like to try, what you would like
to ask for, who you'd like to be sexually, where you'd like your
sex life to go, plus the conditions which make sex good for you.
If you want a template on doing this for yourself, download my
free resource, 'Conditions for good sex', which you can find on
the resources page of my website, www.thehavelockclinic.com,
or in my book, *Mind The Gap: The Truth About Desire and How to
Futureproof Your Sex Life* (Headline Home, 2020).

Sexual communication

The next level is designed to increase your comfort talking about
sex in a non-personal way, or in a way with the least awkwardness
or difficulty.

Talk about sex straight after sex: Tell each other what you liked
  about it. This is easiest after sex that has gone well. At this stage,
  stay away from conversations about things you'd like to change
  (unless this feels urgent or pressing!).

Use non-verbal communication during sex more: Direct what
  you want to do during sex with non-verbal communication,
  such as moving your partner's hand where you'd like it to go, or
  using noise to communicate pleasure.

Sex scene date night: Search for a list of 'best sex scenes in
  films' online. Take turns choosing a film from the list to
  watch together as a regular date-night activity. After the film,
  take turns sharing anything you found hot, and anything you
  didn't like. The next date night, the other person chooses
  which film to watch.

Talk about sex as a topic: Make a commitment to talk more about sex generally (i.e. not your own sex life). For example, talk about books you have read, things you've heard people say, podcasts you've listened to. Consider art/theatre/performance dates with a sexual or sensual element and talk about them. Make talking about sex comfortably part of your relationship culture.

Intermediate skills

Ramping up your sexual communication

The next two levels are designed to promote an easy culture of communication about sex in your relationship, increasing the 'sexual currency' between you.

Send suggestive texts: If writing the words feels too hard, try communicating with emojis as a starting point, or by sending a link to some lyrics in a song that you found hot. Text each other the title of the song and perhaps the time the lyrics appear?

Send suggestive clips: Use audio erotica apps, such as Dipsea or Ferly. Listen alone and then send each other episodes that you enjoyed. If you want to, send them the time your favourite bit happens as well as the episode itself. (You can use written erotica, or porn for this also.)

Share your invitation preferences: What works best for you? (see page 195).

Share your conditions for good sex: Once you've completed your 'conditions for good sex' (see foundation skills), ask your partner to complete it too and arrange a date to discuss what you have each written.

Increasing confidence

If you're feeling confident with everything so far, try these more advanced skills:

Practise different ways of inviting each other in: Focus particularly on ones you never usually use. Use the list of categories on page 195 to help you consider how you can mix things up.

Practise directing sex in the moment using words: For example, where you'd like to be touched, what you'd like to happen next, what you are enjoying in that moment.

Share sexual thoughts/memories or fantasies you've had: If it helps, do this without eye contact, on a walk, in the dark, whatever works!

Reminisce about the first time you had sex: Ask each other questions, i.e. what did you think about _____? What surprised you the most? What do you remember feeling? How did you feel the next day? What did you tell your friends?

Review your sex life regularly: Ask each other two questions – what's going well? What would we like to do more of/try? (You can find a template to help you with this on my website, www.thehavelockclinic.com, under the resources section).

Advanced skills

These are aspects of your sexual communication that demonstrate easy, relaxed conversations about sex, and a culture of talking about sex which is established and comfortable. These ideas incorporate bringing conversations about your motivations into your invitations, as well as free and easy inviting and turning down.

Easy invites, easy turning down: Practise developing a culture of inviting each other in frequently and turning each other down with no pressure.

Bring your motivations into your inviting: For example, 'I'd really like to get my hands on your body as I want to feel close and I miss the feel of your skin'. This allows your partner to understand what you want and why.

Practise linking your motivations to types of sex: This means don't assume predictable sexual scripts or what you always do, but consider what is motivating you, and what type of sex act would meet that motivation, then make this explicit to a partner. For example, 'I'm missing having a bit of passion and feeling like you want me. I fancy a really hot kissing session – fancy it?'

Notice anything you hold back: If you find there is something about sex that doesn't feel easy to communicate, or you are keeping to yourself, notice it. Not everything needs to be shared, but it can benefit your intimacy if you can keep up an advanced level of sexual communication. For example, have you noticed yourself feeling an attraction to someone? Have you started to notice a new trend in the porn you watch? Many people feel fearful of discussing such things with a partner, but doing this can actually be beneficial for our sex lives and relationships. You will achieve this by continuing to privilege a culture of sexual communication.

Equity and mental load

One of the aspects I encouraged you to look at when you completed the sex-life barometer in Chapter 2 was whether one of you bears the brunt of the household admin and labour. As you are now aware, couples who have more equitable distribution of these roles have higher sexual satisfaction and sexual frequency. This dynamic has many ramifications on the emotional climate of your relationship, the sexual dynamic between you, your stress levels and the cognitive and attentional burden this has on you psychologically, impacting your available headspace for sex.

We have reviewed the research that this is not as straightforward as who does the cleaning, or who washes the car, but, rather, who carries the mental load for the family? Who is on all the WhatsApp chats? Who remembers everyone's birthdays and buys gifts? Who asks about allergies before a playdate? Who supports everyone emotionally? Which tasks weigh more heavily mentally? Which tasks are thankless, less visible and build resentment?

If one of you feels they have lost themselves and their self-hood in parenthood, and the other feels able to take time away from the home for hobbies or interests without concern, you absolutely need to put more thought into the division of domestic labour. It's unrealistic to expect one person to hold all of this in their head then still have the mental space for sex, and by now, hopefully, you understand why. Sex requires time, attention, ability to invest in oneself and our identities outside parenthood, being able to see our partner as an equal not another dependant, and a relationship climate low on resentment.

This conversation is a crucial one, as it is possible that one of you is unaware of the impact of this on the other. In fact, research suggests that the parent doing less of the household and childcare labour (men, as a rule, in relationships with women) often overestimate their contribution and underestimate the inequity.[20] Until now, you may have both been unaware of the potential impact of this on your sex life. Here's a change you can make that has nothing to do with sex, but will likely impact your sex life greatly.

When sex feels like a job on your to-do list

When your to-do list as a parent is weighty, it can feel like sex is another item on it. This can feel especially pronounced if sex is a higher priority on your partner's to-do list than yours. Look out for signs that you are seeing sex as something you are doing for your partner, and therefore a 'task' that can feel more like an obligation than a choice. Obligations can lead to resentment, and reduced motivation. If this feels familiar to you, spend some time reflecting on what you, or the relationship as a whole stands to gain from you prioritizing sex. This could be a sense of fun, connection, relationship satisfaction, feeling more like partners than co-parents for a while, for example. These are termed 'approach reasons', as discussed on page 28, and describe something we feel we will gain, rather than something we feel we will lose. Reframing sex this way, as a choice that will have positive benefits for us, rather than an obligation or a chore we are doing for someone else, can therefore have a huge impact on our feelings towards it.

Managing domestic drift

In Chapter 6, I shared the concept of domestic drift to explain the impact of housework and childcare on diminishing sexual desire that was there earlier in the day. How do we handle disappointment when our partners float the idea of getting it on later, perhaps with a text earlier in the day, and then domestic drift creeps in and they flop on the sofa, exhausted by bedtime with the kids?

This can be frustrating, particularly if you've spent the day thinking about what's to come, getting yourself in a sexual headspace, or if there is a frequent pattern of this. But what's the alternative? An invitation to get it on is, in essence, a communication of desire. Communications like these are the glue in sexual relationships, as they:

- express attraction and desire, making us feel wanted by another

- maintain a culture of easy communication about sex between us, which creates a virtuous cycle of easy communication over time

- put an idea in one or both of our minds, which then allows us to get further into the headspace/do whatever we need to create time or get physically, psychologically or practically ready

- create excitement in their own right, and a sexual charge between us (sexual currency), and this defines you as a sexual couple – it's you connecting sexually in the moment of the invite, regardless of what happens next

Domestic drift will sometimes derail all of this despite people's best intentions, and, yes, this can cause frustration. The alternative, though, is your partner never sending that message in the day for fear that they may not feel like it later and one or both of you will feel disappointed. You then lose out on all the benefits above. Creating a relationship climate where you feel free to invite, free to turn down, and the ability to let each other down gently is the key to sexual satisfaction as parents.

Relationship climate

There is a circular pattern that connects the relationship climate and the sex lives or sexual satisfaction of parents. A relationship climate that is favourable can make sex far more enticing, possible or wanted. A sex life that is favourable supports the relationship climate. What is key is that both feed into the other, strengthening the system over time.

Sexual satisfaction, as we have already discussed in Chapter 1, is known to increase relationship satisfaction. This pattern doesn't always follow in the opposite direction, so relationship satisfaction doesn't always lead to a good sex life. In that case, what are the features of relationship satisfaction which we know *are* correlated with good sex? What are the things that, by doing them, we are not only investing in our relationship but also in our sex lives? What things, even if we are not ready to work on sex, can we work on instead, knowing they will have a knock-on positive effect on our sex lives?

Relationship satisfaction and longevity is a huge topic that is outside the scope of this book, but let's look at some of the key aspects of your relationship culture that are most likely to benefit your sex life as a parent.

How you are with each other matters

If you subscribe to the idea of desire as being ever present and occurring out of the blue (not backed up by science but popular opinion, as you now know), then how you spend your time as a couple and how you relate to each other probably doesn't feel like it matters too much. You just get on with your daily life, including all its stresses, then feel like sex before you go to bed, right? Well, not really.

The time you spend together, and how you relate to each other in that time, *does* matter in its contribution to a relationship climate that leaves us feeling receptive to sex. In fact, it may matter *more* for people who are time-poor (parents) than it matters for anyone else.

It can be easy to think that, if you live with someone, then you spend a great deal of time with them, so there's that 'time together' box ticked. But time spent in the same building does not equal time to nurture your relationship, or time that could have a positive knock-on effect on your sex life. Added to this, parents have greater demands on their time, so when we're looking for places to borrow that time from, our relationship with our partner might well be the place that takes the hit. Let me explain.

The time you spend together may fall into one of several categories. Firstly, co-existing but not really noticing each other particularly. This might look like passing each other on the stairs and saying a quick 'morning!' while you are both rushing to work/getting the kids ready, being so preoccupied with your own day and tasks that you don't check in with each other or know what's happening in each other's days, and then sitting together of an evening, but being disconnected from each other (for example, one of you is watching TV, the other is scrolling your phone). This pattern can be especially tempting if you just want some alone time after a day with the kids, and interacting with anyone just feels too much. It can also be simply a habit your relationship culture has fallen into, so you both just do it, without conscious thought.

The second category is what I call 'giving each other the scraps'. Instead of an absence of connection, like the example above, here connection between you is characterized by gripes and quips about things you both wish the other had done, or stressful interactions between you, where you speak to each other in a way that you would never speak to another person (hence giving each other the scraps, as you've saved all the other versions of you – the more polite, more patient, more engaging, more interested you etc – to give to friends, colleagues and the lollipop person on the school run). This pattern of connecting can signal an overstretched and under-resourced parent/ couple and can put emotional distance and a sense of being on opposing teams into the relationship culture.

The last category is one of meaningful connection, empathy and interest for one another. For example, knowing that one of you has something on that day that they feel nervous or apprehensive about and taking the time to send a text: 'Hey, hope it went well?' Taking ten minutes when the kids have gone to bed to sit together, with full attention on each other, including eye contact, and saying, 'Tell me about your day.' Ask each other questions about the high points and the low points. For example, 'Why did that moment feel good?' and 'What was it about that moment that felt really hard?' Listen with empathy and interest about their day, giving them your full attention for this short period of time. Resist the urge to make it about you – 'I felt like that today too!' – or to offer solutions, but instead work hard at just validating how each other felt. Once one person has shared, you can swap over and ask the other the same questions and show them the same empathic, active listening. If you've had some harder moments of communication that day, you may also want to add a reparation on the end of your conversation as well. For example, 'I'm sorry I had a go at you about the bins not being out this morning, I was just feeling overwhelmed by getting the kids ready and it came out all wrong.' These reparative attempts can help us connect emotionally even over the inevitable negative quips that come out in times of stress (none of us are perfect, by any means).

Relationship gurus John and Julie Gottman write extensively about conversational styles that preserve and expand couple connection, as well as moments of emotional intimacy through really listening, such as this, sometimes called 'rituals of connection'. In fact, the

Gottmans have written about being able to predict relationship breakdown just by watching the interaction style between a couple.[21] Of course, life isn't simple, and you might find days characterized by one of these styles and days where you relate entirely differently. But notice if there's a trend here that might be less favourable for your relationship if it continues, and consider a daily check-in like this, for connection, support and emotional intimacy.

Let's discuss why how you connect matters so much for your sex life.

Emotional intimacy is a precursor to being open to the idea of sex, but patterns of connecting have other gains too. When we are connected, we can better understand and negotiate the differences between us around sex (such as one of us wanting sex, and the other not). We can also use our couple connection to make desire easier to access.

It has been suggested that good communication and active listening aids our sex lives by giving us a sense of really mattering to our partner when they listen attentively. Similarly, by hearing about their inner worlds we are fostering connection through self-disclosure and feeling connected to their inner worlds, nurturing a sense of chemistry.[22]

When parents who are sexual partners report greater 'dyadic empathy' (understanding the other's point of view and empathic concern for the other), they report greater sexual satisfaction regardless of how much sex they are having.[23] This research done by the wonderful team at CaSHlab was in relationships between cis men and women, but the principles are likely to apply to all couples.

Having more of this 'dyadic empathy' means we are more likely to feel understood and validated in our relationship, as opposed to feeling misunderstood, unimportant or feeling your partner's actions are insensitive. What's your experience of this? Do you notice the impact of feeling understood or feeling important to your partner in helping or hindering your sex life?

Saying 'yes', and saying 'no' gracefully

Alongside this idea that we are generally more satisfied, from a relationship and a sex life point of view, if we feel our partners understand us, sex research demonstrates that people who feel motivated to meet their partner's needs in this way have higher levels of relationship and sexual satisfaction than people who don't.[24] This has been called 'sexual communal strength', and it basically means meeting your partner's needs to have sex, when you may not necessarily be on the same page.

Fascinatingly, this also works the other way around, particularly for parents. A 2017 study[25] found that the motivation to show understanding about a partner's desire *not* to have sex also improved sexual satisfaction and relationship satisfaction for new parents. Interestingly, it didn't just improve sexual satisfaction for the person saying 'no', *but it also improved satisfaction for the ones being turned down*. The impact of this was significant for birthing parents (in this study, mothers), who the authors hypothesized might have more reasons why sex is not a priority in the first year of a child's life and appreciate their partners responding well to the news that they would rather not have sex than have it.

For example, Lou and Sal have two young kids and, on a Saturday night, Lou starts to notice that Sal is wanting to have sex. She doesn't really feel that sex is a priority for her right now, but she can see it's important to Sal, and she knows that, even if she doesn't feel like it right now, once they start, her desire will be triggered and it will be a positive experience for her. She makes it clear to Sal that she can see what he wants, and she may be convinced into it if he can support her to get in a sexual headspace . . . *

The week after, the same thing happens. Sal is feeling like sex on a Saturday night. He really, really hopes that Lou might be up for it. He makes a hint early in the day that sex is on his mind. Lou was up four times the night before with their youngest, who had a tummy bug. She lets Sal know that there is no way that sex is on the cards tonight: 'Babe, I'm sorry, but I'm exhausted and I just want to curl up in front of the TV with a glass of wine.' Sal shows empathy and responsiveness by sacrificing his own needs and wants for hers, just like she did the week before. 'Totally get it, darling. Another time. Let me know what you fancy watching, the choice is yours.'

Turning sex down is, of course, a communication, and one that can be done in a number of ways, all which may have different effects, and impact on the way a partner responds and feels. In Chapter 7 we talked about how the way in which we turn each other down matters. The message here is that both of you can feel more sexually satisfied in this phase of your child's life by being motivated to sometimes meet your partner's needs by saying yes, and sometimes showing greater understanding when your partner says no, not necessarily by having more sex. You can benefit your sex life greatly by reflecting on your own responses to a partner when you say no to sex. How do you usually do it? Is it with empathy, understanding and gentleness? Or is it with frustration, irritation and sharpness? It can be easy to get into a pattern of less-than-graceful relating when

---

* I hope by now you can see the potential impact of low pressure, an enticing invitation and comfort with them both occupying the space in between invitation and desire, feeling able to end the encounter (stress-free) if it doesn't feel right.

sex has felt like an issue, or when you feel your partner is lacking empathy for your position, or when you are simply exhausted. Modifying your 'no', as well as considering how you invite each other into sex, are two aspects of your relationship climate and your sexual communication that could have big results if you make slight changes of course.

A cautionary note here. Having sex that you don't want to be having to prevent conflict, a partner being frustrated or leaving you/having sex elsewhere does not fit into this theory of sexual communal strength. In fact, having sex for these reasons (termed 'avoidance' reasons) will deplete your desire to be sexual with that person over time.

It might feel important to have balance in this evident to both of you in your relationship. For example, it may feel harder to meet your partner's needs when you feel they never meet yours. In my work with couples, I notice how hard it can be for partners to respond with empathy when their partner doesn't want sex and they do. Accepting this but then sulking, being emotionally cold, or making jokes about how little sex you have is not showing empathy for your partner's lack of interest.

The relevance of all of this for your sex lives? Knowing your partner is motivated to meet your needs, whether that's to have sex, or to not have sex, leads to sexual satisfaction. This means that understanding each other's needs more, and expressing that understanding, as well as sometimes meeting them where they are even if you're not there yourself, could be the key to being happier with your sex life.

A relationship climate that promotes sexual satisfaction and good sex can be created in small acts of intentional action such as these – you don't necessarily have to be having more sex. Considering how you turn each other down (and how you respond to being turned down), as well as sometimes deciding to say 'yes' when your head isn't quite there yet, seeing your sexual relationship as something that needs to be worked on rather than something which should 'just work', sharing the mental load and creating a culture of high sexual currency, opportunities to connect above the mundane and comfort talking about sex are just a few of the ways that your sexual satisfaction can be improved based on the theme of relationship climate, even when sex itself feels out of reach.

Where are you at?

Review the sex-life barometer questionnaire you looked at in Chapter 2. By now, you should be able to see what category of changes each item falls into. For example, being able to talk about a good sex scene you've seen on TV is 'sexual communication' and falls into 'perfecting the relationship climate'. Reinstating passionate kissing that doesn't lead anywhere is 'sexual currency' and sits within 'expanding your relationship perspective'. Increasing sexual currency also addresses creating triggers for desire in the theme of 'harnessing motivation'. The point here is that, at this stage of the book, your answers to the sex-life barometer questionnaire should start to make sense to you in terms of what aspects of your current sexual relationship could benefit from small changes. Use it, if you like, at key points in your future journey as a couple, as a navigation tool to check your course, and tweak your trajectory if needed.

TASK: Bringing it all together

Spend some time together looking at the answers you gave for the sex-life barometer questionnaire. First, make a list of aspects of your sex life that would benefit from doing things differently. Second, asterisk the ones that don't require any additional time, but require you both to take a different action moving forward. For example, making sure sex doesn't always follow the same predictable pattern. For these, I want you to write down what you plan to do differently. For example, if you always have penetrative sex every time you have sex, you might write: 'We will try to make sure that about one in five of our sexual experiences doesn't involve penetration to mix it up.'

Next, I want you to list all the things we've talked about in this exercise that may be contributing. For example, one of you carries the mental load of everything that needs to be done around the house, so you get no time to wash your hair and do your nails, say, and it makes you feel unsexy, or your child is five and waking multiple times in the night and you are shattered. These are background contexts affecting your sex life and I want you to consider whether there are any solutions to them that you can come up with together (such as one of you giving the other one thirty minutes of uninterrupted time to pamper yourself, or dividing up the household tasks more equally).

Before you make any of the changes you have outlined, I want you to have a discussion together about what you feel the impact will be on you and your relationship. Here are some questions to ask yourself:

How would it make us feel about our sex life and relationship if we put in place some of the things we have learned
in this book?

What trajectory do we want our sex life to be on in five years
from now? How do these changes we are thinking about
making support this?

How will we check that we are on track periodically? (it can
be useful to set a date night to review how things are
going – essentially check the course you are on and make
adjustments if necessary).

As I mentioned at the very start of this book, part of maintaining a
good course is checking it from time to time, to ensure you haven't
drifted too far from where you hoped you might be. In this final
chapter I set about outlining the key small changes that can make a
big difference to your sex life, based on sex research and my extensive
clinical experience. My hope is that, even if you started this book
feeling like solutions to your sex life were one-dimensional (more
sex) and out of reach (as perhaps you don't actually want more sex!),
this chapter has demonstrated the variety of ways sexual satisfaction
can be improved that are accessible to all.

Not all of the suggestions in here are right for everyone, or will be
right for you, and not all of them will feel like an appropriate starting place. Your task, together, is to understand how and why these
things work, and decide what to commit to together with the intention of being intentional about the course you are taking, and your
final destination.

Conclusion

Parenthood creates challenges for your sex life that can feel insurmountable at times. Challenges that can threaten your relationship satisfaction and personal wellbeing to critical levels. Our societal narrative about the sex lives of parents creates an almost impossible narrative of declining sexual satisfaction and gendered resentment, with no talk of how to avoid, or resolve, the problems that emerge.

I hope by now you can see that it doesn't have to be this way. Sex can be a way to escape monotony, connect with yourself, invest in your relationship and nurture the family unit. Having kids can be an opportunity to take a close look at your sex life and use the restrictions and challenges now placed upon it to nurture, invest and attend to this important part of your couple relationship.

When I picture the sex lives of parents across the world, I picture a fleet of boats, all relationships in their own right, navigating these seas, and their onward journeys. I also picture a range of outcomes, depending on the stage of the journey they are at and what is happening onboard each of these vessels. On some, the crew are struggling. Blindly sailing on with a rip in their sail, hugely off course for where they originally planned to be, and not talking with each other about where they find themselves or what might be ahead. I see others, in the eye of the storm, protecting their boat as much as they can, simply trying to survive as they do so. They catch sight of another boat in the distance doing the same, and they are comforted, for a moment, by knowing that they are not alone. They make a plan together to get by, by making safe, and to review the damage to the boat later on, ready for the next phase. In doing so they come together as a team, not blaming one another for the damage, but seeing the conditions of the sea as something they are up against together.

Finally, I see boats getting tossed around by the waves and the wind, but utilizing every tool at their disposal to hold their position, and look for the path of least resistance through the water. This crew are working together, with an awareness of their shared destination, and an understanding that small tweaks to sails, small changes of position, and an awareness of the tides will come good over the long haul. They are aware that they will be at the mercy of the sea for some time, but that they do not have to remain powerless to its force. They know where they want to head, and they are intentional in their movements towards this destination.

I would argue that all parents at any stage of their parenting journey have the capacity to make at least one of these small changes, and many will be able to make several, without this taking away from their energy levels, or adding too much to their already significant to-do list. These changes do not need to take any more time, nor do they need to involve any more sex. I hope that you have felt empowered by these suggestions for change, and that this has left you feeling optimistic for the next leg of your journey. If you feel unable to make any change right now, I hope that the information I have shared has left you feeling less alone, and with the knowledge and skills to right your course when the time is right for you.

Together we have travelled a journey of the trajectory of your sex life as parents, from preconception to pregnancy, babyhood and the long haul of having small kids at home. Whether you are already a parent, or about to become one, I hope that you have recognized your boat somewhere in these pages and noticed some of the ways it may be drifting slightly off course. My hope in writing this book was that you might start to see the route ahead, and more than anything, might start to see the power that you have to make small but impactful changes, to captain your own boat well, and to move closer and closer to the sex life that you want.

Notes

1. Learning the ropes

1. Regan, P. C., 'The Role of Sexual Desire and Sexual Activity in Dating Relationships', *Social Behavior and Personality*, 28, 51–59 (2000).
2. Burleson, M. H., Trevathan, W. R. and Todd, M., 'In the Mood for Love or Vice Versa? Exploring the Relations Among Sexual Activity, Physical Affection, Affect, and Stress in the Daily Lives of Mid-Aged Women', *Archives of Sexual Behavior*, 36, 357–368 (2007).
3. Muise, A., Impett, E. A., Desmarais, S. and Kogan, A., 'Keeping the Spark Alive: Being Motivated to Meet a Partner's Sexual Needs Sustains Sexual Desire in Long-Term Romantic Relationships', *Social Psychological and Personality Sciences*, 4, 267–273 (2013).
4. Joel, S., Eastwick, P. W., Allison, C. J., Arriaga, X. B., Baker, Z. G., BarKalifa, E., Bergeron, S., Birnbaum, G. E., Brock, R. L., Brumbaugh, C. C., Carmichael, C. L., Chen, S., Clarke, J., Cobb, R. J., Coolsen, M. K., Davis, J., de Jong, D. C., Debrot, A., DeHaas, E. C. and Eller, J., 'Machine learning uncovers the most robust self-report predictors of relationship quality across 43 longitudinal couples studies', *Proceedings of the National Academy of Sciences*, 117(32), 19061 (2020).

5. Fallis, E. E., Rehman, U. S., Woody, E. Z. and Purdon, C., 'The longitudinal association of relationship satisfaction and sexual satisfaction in long-term relationships', *Journal of Family Psychology*, 30(7), 822–831 (2016).

6. Sprecher, S., 'Sexual Satisfaction in Premarital Relationships: Associations with Satisfaction, Love, Commitment, and Stability', *Journal of Sex Research*, 39:190–6 (2002); Heiman, J. R., Long, J. S., Smith, S. N., Fisher, W. A., S. and M. S. and Rosen, R. C., 'Sexual Satisfaction and Relationship Happiness in Midlife and Older Couples in Five Countries', *Archives of Sexual Behavior*, 40, 741–753 (2011); Debrot, A., Meuwly, N., Muise, A., Impett, E. A. and Schoebi, D., 'More than just sex: Affection mediates the association between sexual activity and well-being', *Personality and Social Psychology Bulletin*, 43(3), 287–299 (2017).

7. Beaulieu, Noémie, Bergeron, Sophie, Brassard, Audrey, Byers, E. Sandra and Péloquin, Katherine, 'Toward an Integrative Model of Intimacy, Sexual Satisfaction, and Relationship Satisfaction: A Prospective Study in Long-Term Couples', *The Journal of Sex Research* (2022).

8. Amato, P. R., Loomis, L. S. and Booth, A., 'Parental divorce, marital conflict, and offspring well-being during early adulthood', *Social Forces*, 73(3), 895–915 (1995).

9. Selvini, M. P., Boscolo, L., Cecchin, G. and Prata, G., 'Hypothesizing—circularity—neutrality: Three guidelines for the conductor of the session', *Family process*, 19(1), 3–12 (1980).

10. Lawrence, E., Rothman, A. D., Cobb, R. J., Rothman, M. T., & Bradbury, T. H. (2008). Marital satisfaction across the transition to parenthood. Journal of Family Psychology, 22, 41–50; Twenge, J. M., Campbell, W. K., & Foster, C. A. (2003). Parenthood and marital satisfaction: A meta-analytic review. Journal of Marriage and Family, 65, 574–583.

11. Leigh, B. C., 'Reasons for having and avoiding sex: Gender, sexual orientation, and relationship to sexual behavior', *Journal*

of Sex Research, 26, 199–209 (1989); Hill, C. A. and Preston, L. K., 'Individual differences in the experience of sexual motivation: Theory and measurement of dispositional sexual motives', *Journal of Sex Research*, 33, 27–45 (1996).

12. Mark, K. P. and Murray, S. H., 'Gender differences in desire discrepancy as a predictor of sexual and relationship satisfaction in a college sample of heterosexual romantic relationships', *Journal of Sex & Marital Therapy*, 38, 198–215 (2012).

13. Murray, S. H., Milhausen, R. R., Graham, C. A. and Kuczynski, L., 'A qualitative exploration of factors that affect sexual desire among men aged 30 to 65 in long-term relationships', *The Journal of Sex Research*, 54(3), 319–330 (2017).

14. Murray, S. H. and Brotto, L., 'I want you to want me: a qualitative analysis of heterosexual men's desire to feel desired in intimate relationships', *Journal of Sex & Marital Therapy*, 47(5), 419–434 (2021).

15. Birnbaum, G. E. and Reis, H. T., 'Evolved to be connected: The dynamics of attachment and sex over the course of romantic relationships', *Current Opinion in Psychology*, 25, 11–15 (2019); Dewitte, M., 'Different perspectives on the sex-attachment link: Towards an emotion-motivational account', *Journal of Sex Research*, 49(2–3), 105–124 (2012).

16. Hinchliff, S. and Gott, M., 'Intimacy, commitment, and adaptation: Sexual relationships within long-term marriages', *Journal of Social and Personal Relationships*, 21(5), 595–609 (2004).

17. Impett, E. A. and Peplau, L. A., 'Sexual Compliance: Gender, Motivational, and Relationship Perspectives', *The Journal of Sex Research*, 40:1, 87–100 (2003).

18. Muise, A., Impett, E.A. and Desmarais, S., 'Getting it On Versus Getting it Over With: Sexual Motivation, Desire, and Satisfaction in Intimate Bonds', *Personality and Social Psychology Bulletin*, 39, 1320–1332 (2013).

19. Gurney, K., *Mind The Gap: The Truth About Desire and How to Futureproof Your Sex Life* (London: Headline Home, 2020).

20. Impett, E. A., Muise, A. and Rosen, N.O., 'Is it Good to be Giving in the Bedroom? A Prosocial Perspective on Sexual Health and Well-being in Romantic Relationships', *Current Sexual Health Reports*, 7, 180–190 (2015).

2. Chart your position

1. Uppot, A., Raposo, S., Rosen, N. O., Corsini Munt, S., Balzarini, R. and Muise, A., 'Responsiveness in the Face of Sexual Challenges: The Role of Sexual Growth and Destiny Beliefs', *The Journal of Sex Research* (2023).
2. Reviewed in ibid.

3. Taking stock of the journey

1. Gagnon, J. and Simon, W., 'Sexual Conduct: The Social Origins of Human Sexuality', *Aldine* (1973).
2. Klusmann, D., 'Sexual Motivation and the Duration of Partnership', *Archives of Sexual Behavior*, 31, 275–287 (2002); Sims, K. E. and Meana, M., 'Why Did Passion Wane? A Qualitative Study of Married Women's Attributions for Declines in Sexual Desire', *Journal of Sex & Marital Therapy*, 36(4), 360–380 (2010).
3. Rhoades, G. K., Stanley, S. M. and Markman, H. J., 'The impact of the transition to cohabitation on relationship functioning: cross-sectional and longitudinal findings', *Journal of Family Psychology*, 26(3), 348 (2012).
4. Herbenick, D., Mullinax, M. and Mark, K., 'Sexual Desire Discrepancy as a Feature, Not a Bug, of Long-Term Relationships: Women's Self-Reported Strategies for Modulating Sexual Desire', *The Journal of Sexual Medicine*, 11, 2196–2206 (2014).
5. Mitchell, K. R., Mercer, C. H., Ploubidis, G. B., et al., 'Sexual Function in Britain: Findings from the Third

National Survey of Sexual Attitudes and Lifestyles',
The Lancet, 382 (2013).

6. Cawood, E. H. and Bancroft, J., 'Steroid Hormones, the Menopause, Sexuality and Wellbeing of Women', *Psychological Medicine*, 26, 925–936 (1996); Cain, V. S., Johannes, C. B., Avis, N. E., Mohr, B., Schocken, M., Skurnick, J. and Ory, M., 'Sexual Functioning and Practices in a Multi-Ethnic Study of Midlife Women: Baseline Results from SWAN', *The Journal of Sex Research*, 40:3, 266–276 (2003); Avis, N. E., Zhao, X., Johannes, C. B., Ory, M., Brockwell, S. and Greendale, G. A., 'Correlates of Sexual Function Among Multi-Ethnic Middle-Aged Women: Results from the Study of Women's Health Across the Nation (SWAN)', *Menopause*, 12, 385–398 (2005).

7. Chivers, M. L. and Brotto, L. A., 'Controversies of Women's Sexual Arousal and Desire', *European Psychologist*, 22(1), 5–26 (2017).

8. Dawson, S. J. and Chivers, M. L., 'Gender Differences and Similarities in Sexual Desire', *Current Sexual Health Reports*, 6: 211–219 (2014).

9. Dawson, S. J. and Chivers, M. L., 'Gender Differences and Similarities in Sexual Desire', *Current Sexual Health Reports*, 6: 211–219 (2014).

10. Both, S., Everaerd, W., Laan, E. and Janssen, E., 'Desire Emerges from Excitement: A Psychophysiological Perspective on Sexual Motivation', in Janssen, E. (ed.), *The Psychophysiology of Sex* (Bloomington, Indiana: Indiana University Press, 2007), pp. 327–339; Toates, F. M., 'An Integrative Theoretical Framework for Understanding Sexual Motivation, Arousal, and Behavior', *The Journal of Sex Research*, 46:2–3, 168–193 (2009); Singer, B. and Toates, F. M., 'Sexual Motivation', *The Journal of Sex Research*, 23:4, 481–501 (1987).

11. Toates, F. M., 'An Integrative Theoretical Framework for Understanding Sexual Motivation, Arousal, and Behavior', *The Journal of Sex Research*, 46:2–3, 168–193 (2009).

12. Basson, R., 'The Female Sexual Response: A Different Model', *Journal of Sex & Marital Therapy*, 26, 51–65 (2000); Basson, R., 'Using a Different Model for Female Sexual Response to Address Women's Problematic Low Sexual Desire', *Journal of Sex & Marital Therapy*, 27, 395–403 (2001).

13. Elaut, E., Buysse, A., De Sutter, P., Gerris, J., De Cuypere, G. and T'Sjoen, G., 'Cycle-Related Changes in Mood, Sexual Desire, and Sexual Activity in Oral Contraception-Using and Nonhormonal-Contraception-Using Couples', *The Journal of Sex Research*, 53:1, 125–136 (2016).

14. Murray, S. H. and Milhausen, R. R., 'Sexual desire and relationship duration in young men and women', *Journal of Sex & Marital Therapy*, 38(1), 28–40 (2012); Graham, C. A., Mercer, C. H., Tanton, C., Jones, K. G., Johnson, A. M., Wellings, K. and Mitchell, K. R., 'What factors are associated with reporting lacking interest in sex and how do these vary by gender? Findings from the third British national survey of sexual attitudes and lifestyles', *BMJ open*, 7(9), e016942 (2017).

15. Bouchard, K. N., Cormier, M., Huberman, J. S. and Rosen, N. O., 'Sexual script flexibility and sexual well-being in long-term couples: a dyadic longitudinal study', *The Journal of Sexual Medicine*, qdad067 (2023).

16. Gurney, K., *Mind The Gap: The Truth About Desire and How to Futureproof Your Sex Life* (London: Headline Home, 2020).

17. Anderson, A. B. and Hamilton, L. D., 'Assessment of Distraction From Erotic Stimuli by Nonerotic Interference', *The Journal of Sex Research*, 52:3, 317–326 (2015).

18. Madore, K. P., Khazenzon, A. M., Backes, C. W., Jiang, J., Uncapher, M. R., Norcia, A. M. and Wagner, A. D., 'Memory failure predicted by attention lapsing and media multitasking', *Nature*, 587(7832), 87–91 (2020).

19. For a review, see Banbury, S., Lusher, J., Snuggs, S. and Chandler, C., 'Mindfulness-based therapies for men and women

with sexual dysfunction: a systematic review and meta-analysis',
Sexual and Relationship Therapy (2021); Stephenson, K. R. and
Kerth, J., 'Effects of Mindfulness-Based Therapies for Female
Sexual Dysfunction: A Meta-Analytic Review', *The Journal of Sex
Research*, 54:7, 832–849 (2017).

20. Selice, L., & Morris, K. L. (2022). Mindfulness and sexual
dysfunction: a systematic research synthesis. *Journal of Sex &
Marital Therapy*, 48(4), 323–342

21. For example, Hoge, E. A., Bui, E., Mete, M., Dutton, M. A.,
Baker, A. W. and Simon, N. M., 'Mindfulness-based stress
reduction vs escitalopram for the treatment of adults with
anxiety disorders: a randomized clinical trial', *JAMA psychiatry*,
80(1), 13–21 (2023); da Silva, C. C. G., Bolognani, C. V., Amorim,
F. F. and Imoto, A. M., 'Effectiveness of training programs
based on mindfulness in reducing psychological distress and
promoting well-being in medical students: a systematic review
and meta-analysis', *Systematic Reviews*, 12(1), 1–28 (2023); Meyers,
M., Margraf, J., and Velten, J. 'Subjective effects and perceived
mechanisms of change of cognitive behavioral and mindfulness-
based online interventions for low sexual desire in women',
Journal of Sex and Marital Therapy, 1–15 (2023).

4. Action Stations!

1. von Sydow, K., 'Sexuality during pregnancy and after
childbirth: A metacontent analysis of 59 studies', *Journal of
Psychosomatic Research*, 47, 27–49 (1999).

2. Meston, C. M. and Buss, D. M., 'Why humans have sex',
Archives of Sexual Behavior, 36, 477–507 (2007).

3. Summary in Jawed-Wessel, Sofia and Sevick, Emily, 'The
Impact of Pregnancy and Childbirth on Sexual Behaviors:
A Systematic Review', *The Journal of Sex Research*, 54:4–5,
411–423 (2017).

5. Batten down the hatches

1. Dawson, S. J., Vaillancourt-Morel, M. P., Pierce, M. and Rosen, N. O., 'Biopsychosocial predictors of trajectories of postpartum sexual function in first-time mothers', *Health Psychology*, 39(8), 700–710 (2020).

2. Rosen, Natalie O., Vannier, Sarah A., Johnson, Matthew D., McCarthy, Leanne and Impett, Emily A., 'Unmet and Exceeded Expectations for Sexual Concerns across the Transition to Parenthood', *The Journal of Sex Research* (2022); Ahlborg, T., Dahlöf, L-G. and Hallberg, L. R. M., 'Quality of the intimate and sexual relationship in first-time parents six months after delivery', *Journal of Sex Research*, 42:2, 167–174 (2005).

3. Schlagintweit, H., Bailey, K. and Rosen, N. O., 'A new baby in the bedroom: Frequency and severity of postpartum sexual concerns and their associations with relationship satisfaction in new parent couples', *The Journal of Sexual Medicine*, 13(10), 1455–1465 (2016).

4. Barrett, G., Pendry, E., Peacock, J., Victor, C., Thakar, R. and Manyonda, I., 'Women's sexual health after childbirth', *British Journal of Obstetrics and Gynaecology*, 107, 186–19 (2000).

5. Jawed-Wessel, S. and Sevick, E., 'The Impact of Pregnancy and Childbirth on Sexual Behaviors: A Systematic Review', *The Journal of Sex Research*, 54:4–5, 411–423 (2017).

6. Summarized in ibid.

7. Hipp, L. E., Kane Low, L., & van Anders, S. M. (2012). Exploring women's postpartum sexuality: social, psychological, relational, and birth-related contextual factors. *The journal of sexual medicine*, 9(9), 2330–2341

8. Hyde, J. S., DeLamater, J. D., Plant, E. A. and Byrd, J. M., 'Sexuality during pregnancy and the year postpartum', *Journal of Sex Research*, 33, 143–151(1996).

9. Lewis, R. and Marston, C., 'Oral Sex, Young People, and Gendered Narratives of Reciprocity', *Journal of Sex Research*, 53:7,

776–787 (2016); Pinkerton, S. D., Cecil, H., Bogart, L. M. and Abramson, P. R., 'The pleasures of sex: An empirical investigation', *Cognition and Emotion*, 17(2), 341–353 (2003).

10. Craig, Lyn and Bittman, Michael, 'The incremental time costs of children: An analysis of children's impact on adult time use in Australia', *Feminist Economics*, 14:2, 59–88 (2008).

11. Kalmbach, D. A., Arnedt, J. T., Pillai, V. and Ciesla, J. A., 'The impact of sleep on female sexual response and behavior: A pilot study', *The Journal of Sexual Medicine*, 12(5), 1221–1232 (2015).

12. Kling, J. M., Kapoor, E., Mara, K. and Faubion, S. S., 'Associations of sleep and female sexual function: Good sleep quality matters', *Menopause*, 28(6), 619–625 (2021).

13. Richter, D., Krämer, M. D., Tang, N. K., Montgomery-Downs, H. E. and Lemola, S., 'Long-term effects of pregnancy and childbirth on sleep satisfaction and duration of first-time and experienced mothers and fathers', *Sleep*, 42(4), zsz015 (2019).

14. Ahlborg, T., Dahlöf, L-G. and Hallberg, L. R. M., 'Quality of the intimate and sexual relationship in first-time parents six months after delivery', *Journal of Sex Research*, 42:2, 167–174 (2005).

15. Kahn, M., Barnett, N. and Gradisar, M., 'Let's Talk about Sleep Baby: Sexual Activity Postpartum and Its Links with Room Sharing, Parent Sleep, and Objectively Measured Infant Sleep and Parent Nighttime Crib Visits', *The Journal of Sex Research* (2022).

16. Ibid.

17. von Sydow, K., 'Sexuality during pregnancy and after childbirth: A metacontent analysis of 59 studies', *Journal of Psychosomatic Research*, 47, 27–49 (1999).

18. Ahlborg, T., Dahlöf, L-G. and Hallberg, L. R. M., 'Quality of the intimate and sexual relationship in first-time parents six months after delivery', *Journal of Sex Research*, 42:2, 167–174 (2005).

19. Iles, D., Khan, R., Naidoo, K., Kearney, R., Myers, J. and Reid, F., 'The impact of anal sphincter injury on perceived body image', *Eur J Obstet Gynecol Reprod Biol*, 212:140–143 (May 2017).

20. Signorello, L. B., Harlow, B. L., Chekos, A. K. and Repke, J. T., 'Postpartum sexual functioning and its relationship to perineal trauma: A retrospective cohort study of primiparous women', *American Journal of Obstetrics and Gynecology*, 184(5), 881–890 (2001).

21. Al-abri, K., Edge, D. and Armitage, C. J., 'Prevalence and correlates of perinatal depression', *Soc Psychiatry Psychiatr Epidemiol* (2023).

22. Ibid.

23. Rosen, Natalie O., Vannier, Sarah A., Johnson, Matthew D., McCarthy, Leanne and Impett, Emily A., 'Unmet and Exceeded Expectations for Sexual Concerns across the Transition to Parenthood', *The Journal of Sex Research* (2022).

24. Barrett, G., Pendry, E., Peacock, J., Victor, C., Thakar, R. and Manyonda, I., 'Women's sexual health after childbirth', *British Journal of Obstetrics and Gynaecology*, 107(2), 186–195 (2000).

6. Weather the storm

1. Ahlborg, T., Dahlöf, L. G. and Hallberg, L. R. M., 'Quality of the intimate and sexual relationship in first-time parents six months after delivery', *Journal of Sex Research*, 42(2), 167–174 (2005); Rosen, N. O., Dawson, S. J., Leonhardt, D. N., Vannier, S. A. and Impett, E. A., 'Trajectories of sexual well-being among couples in the transition to parenthood', *Journal of Family Psychology* (2020).

2. Doss, B. D., Rhoades, G. K., Stanley, S. M. and Markman, H. J., 'The effect of the transition to parenthood on relationship quality: an 8-year prospective study', *Journal of Personality and Social Psychology*, 96(3), 601 (2009).

3. Summarized in Rosen, N. O., Dawson, S. J., Leonhardt, D. N., Vannier, S. A. and Impett, E. A., 'Unmet and Exceeded Expectations for Sexual Concerns across the Transition to Parenthood', *The Journal of Sex Research* (2022); Cowan, C. P. and Cowan, P. A., *When Partners Become Parents: The Big Life Change for Couples* (Mah Way, NJ: Lawrence Erlbaum Associates, 2000).

4. Hipp, L. E., Low, L. K. and van Anders, S. M., 'Exploring women's postpartum sexuality: Social, psychological, relational and birth-related contextual factors', *The Journal of Sexual Medicine*, 9, 2330–2341 (2012).

5. Richter, D., Krämer, M. D., Tang, N. K. Y., Montgomery-Downs, H. E. and Lemola, S., 'Long-term effects of pregnancy and childbirth on sleep satisfaction and duration of first-time and experienced mothers and fathers', *Sleep*, 42(4) (1 April 2019).

6. Glass, J., Simon, R. W. and Andersson, M. A., 'Parenthood and Happiness: Effects of Work-Family Reconciliation Policies in 22 OECD Countries', *AJS*, 122(3):886–929 (Nov. 2016).

7. Mikucka, M. and Rizzi, E., 'The Parenthood and Happiness Link: Testing Predictions from Five Theories', *Eur J Population*, 36, 337–361.

8. Hamilton, L. D. and Meston, C. M., 'Chronic stress and sexual function in women', *The Journal of Sexual Medicine*, 10(10), 2443–2454 (2013).

9. See summary of data in Lockman, D., *All the Rage: Mothers, Fathers, and the Myth of Equal Partnership* (New York: HarperCollins Publishers, 2019).

10. 'In a Growing Share of U.S. Marriages, Husbands and Wives Earn About the Same', Pew Research Center (April 2023).

11. Ciciolla, L. and Luthar, S. S., 'Invisible Household Labor and Ramifications for Adjustment: Mothers as Captains of Households', *Sex Roles*, 81, 467–486.

12. Van Anders, S. M., Herbenick, D., Brotto, L. A., Harris, E. A. and Chadwick, S. B., 'The heteronormativity theory of low

sexual desire in women partnered with men', *Archives of Sexual Behavior*, 51(1), 391–415 (2022); Harris, E. A., Gormezano, A. M. and van Anders, S. M., 'Gender inequities in household labor predict lower sexual desire in women partnered with men', *Archives of Sexual Behavior*, 51(8), 3847–3870 (2022).

13. Goldberg, A.E., Smith, J. Z. and Perry-Jenkins, M., 'The division of labor in lesbian, gay, and heterosexual new adoptive parents', *J Marriage Fam*, 74:812–828 (2012); Perlesz, A., Power, J., Brown, R., McNair, R., Schofield, M., Pitts, M. and Bickerdike, A., 'Organising work and home in same-sex parented families: Findings from the work love play study', *Australian and New Zealand Journal of Family Therapy*, 31(4), 374–391(2010).

14. Harris, H. A., Gormexano, A. M. and vam Anders, S. M., 'Gender Inequities in Household Labor Predict Lower Sexual Desire in Women Partnered with Men', *Archives of Sexual Behavior*, 51:3847–3870 (2022).

15. Leistner, C. E. and Mark, K. P., 'Attitudes toward Mothers as Sexual Beings (ATMSB): Scale Development and Associations with Satisfaction and Desire among Parents with Young Children', *The Journal of Sex Research*, 1–12 (2022).

16. Johnson, M. D., Galambos, N. L. and Anderson, J. R., 'Skip the dishes? Not so fast! Sex and housework revisited', *Journal of Family Psychology*, 30(2), 203 (2016).

17. Harris, H. A., Gormexano, A. M. and vam Anders, S. M., 'Gender Inequities in Household Labor Predict Lower Sexual Desire in Women Partnered with Men', *Archives of Sexual Behavior*, 51:3847–3870 (2022).

18. Craig, L. and Bittman, M., 'The incremental time costs of children: An analysis of children's impact on adult time use in Australia', *Feminist Economics*, 14:2, 59–88 (2008).

19. Muise, A., Harasymchuk, C., Day, L. C., Bacev-Giles, C., Gere, J. and Impett, E. A., 'Broadening Your Horizons: Self-Expanding Activities Promote Desire and Satisfaction in Established

Romantic Relationships', *Journal of Personality and Social Psychology, 116*(2), 237 (2019).

20. Bareket, O., Kahalon, R., Shnabel, N. and Glick, P., 'The Madonna–Whore dichotomy: Men who perceive women's nurturance and sexuality as mutually exclusive endorse patriarchy and show lower relation-ship satisfaction', *Sex Roles, 79*(9), 519–532 (2018).

7. Navigating together

1. Mallory, A. B., Stanton, A. M. and Handy, A. B., '"Couples" Sexual Communication and Dimensions of Sexual Function: A MetaAnalysis', *Journal of Sex Research* (2019).
2. Murray, S. H., Milhausen, R. R. and Sutherland, O., 'A Qualitative Comparison of Young Women's Maintained versus Decreased Sexual Desire in Longer-Term Relationships', *Women and Therapy,* 37, 319–41 (2014).
3. Merwin, K. E. and Rosen, N. O., 'Perceived partner responsiveness moderates the associations between sexual talk and sexual and relationship well-being in long-term relationships', *The Journal of Sex Research, 57*(3), 351–364 (2020).
4. Kim, J. J., Muise, A. and Impett, E. A., 'Not in the mood? How do people reject their partner for sex and how does it matter?', paper presented at the Canadian Sex Research Forum, Kelowna, Canada (September 2015); Muise, A., Maxwell, J. A. and Impett, E. A., 'What theories and methods from relationship research can contribute to sex research', *The Journal of Sex Research,* 55: 4–5, 540–562 (2018).
5. Zebroff, P., 'Questionnaire for Turn-on Initiation Preference: Development and Initial Reliability and Validation', *The Journal of Sex Research, 58*(8), 1019–1034 (2021).

6. Rhoades, G. K., Stanley, S. M. and Markman, H. J., 'The impact of the transition to cohabitation on relationship functioning: Cross-sectional and longitudinal findings', *Journal of Family Psychology*, 26(3), 348–358 (2012).

8. Plain sailing

1. Mitchell, K.R., Mercer, C. H., Prah, P., Clifton, S., Tanton, C., Wellings, K. and Copas, A., 'Why Do Men Report More Opposite-Sex Sexual Partners Than Women? Analysis of the Gender Discrepancy in a British National Probability Survey', *The Journal of Sex Research*, 56:1, 1–8 (2019).

2. Wellings, K., Palmer, M. J., Machiyama K. and Slaymaker, E., 'Changes in, and factors associated with, frequency of sex in Britain: evidence from three National Surveys of Sexual Attitudes and Lifestyles (Natsal)', *British Medical Journal*, 365:1525 (2019).

3. Gurney, K., 'The surprising truth about desire everyone needs to know', TEDxRoyalTunbridgeWells, TED Conferences (February 2020).

4. Gurney, K., 'The truth about faking orgasms', TED Conferences (April 2022).

5. Frederick, D. A., John, S., Kate, H., Garcia, J. R. and Lloyd, E. A., 'Differences in orgasm frequency among gay, lesbian, bisexual, and heterosexual men and women in a U.S. national sample', *Archives of Sexual Behavior*, 47(1), 273–288 (2018).

6. Laan, E. and Both, S., 'What makes women experience desire?', *Feminism and Psychology*, 18, 505–514 (2008).

7. Frederick, D. A., John, S., Kate, H., Garcia, J. R. and Lloyd, E. A., 'Differences in orgasm frequency among gay, lesbian, bisexual, and heterosexual men and women in a U.S. national sample', *Archives of Sexual Behavior*, 47(1), 273–288 (2018).

8. Wetzel, G. M., Cultice, R. A. and Sanchez, D. T., 'Orgasm frequency predicts desire and expectation for orgasm: Assessing the orgasm gap within mixed-sex couples', *Sex Roles*, 86(7–8), 456–470 (2022).

9. Blumenstock, S. M., 'Expectations and sexual desire in romantic relationships: An experimental investigation of pleasure and emotional closeness expectancies among young adults', *The Journal of Sex Research*, 59(3), 1–21 (2021).

10. Wetzel, G. M., Sanchez, D. T. and Cole, S., 'Feasibility Cues during a Sexual Encounter Impact the Strength of Heterosexual Women's Orgasm Goal Pursuit', *The Journal of Sex Research* (2023).

11. Blair, K. L., Cappell, J. and Pukall, C. F., 'Not all orgasms were created equal: Differences in frequency and satisfaction of orgasm experiences by sexual activity in same-sex versus mixed-sex relationships', *The Journal of Sex Research*, 55(6), 719–733 (2018).

12. Cohen, J. N. and Byers, E. S., 'Beyond lesbian bed death: Enhancing our understanding of the sexuality of sexual-minority women in relationships', *The Journal of Sex Research*, 51(8), 893–903 (2014).

13. Ibid.

14. Kleinplatz, P. J. and Ménard, A. D., *Magnificent Sex: Lessons from Extraordinary Lovers* (Routledge, 2020).

15. Kovacevic, K., Tu, E., Rosen, N. O., Raposo, S. and Muise, A., 'Is Spontaneous Sex Ideal? Beliefs and Perceptions of Spontaneous and Planned Sex and Sexual Satisfaction in Romantic Relationships', *The Journal of Sex Research*, 1–15 (2023).

16. Ibid.

17. Kinsey, A. C., Pomeroy, W. B., Martin, C. E. and Gebhard, P. H., *Sexual Behavior in the Human Female* (W. B. Saunders, 1953).

18. Blair, K. L. and Pukall, C. F., 'Can less be more?: Comparing duration versus frequency of sexual encounters in same-sex and

mixed-sex relationships', *The Canadian Journal of Human Sexuality*, 23(2), 123–136 (2014).

19. Wetzel, G. M., Sanchez, D. T. and Cole, S., 'Feasibility Cues During a Sexual Encounter Impact the Strength of Heterosexual Women's Orgasm Goal Pursuit', *The Journal of Sex Research* (2023).

20. Erickson, R. J., 'Why emotion work matters: Sex, gender, and the division of household labor', *Journal of Marriage and Family*, 67(2), 337–351 (2005).

21. Gottman, John, *The Seven Principles for Making Marriage Work* (Orion, 2000).

22. Park, H. G., Suk, H. W., Cheon, J. E. and Kim, Y. H., 'Darling, come lay with me or talk with me: Perceived mattering and the complementary association between sex and communication within marital relationships', *The Journal of Sex Research*, 60(3), 336–348 (2023).

23. Rosen, N. O., Mooney, K. and Muise, A., 'Dyadic empathy predicts sexual and relationship wellbeing in couples transitioning to parenthood', *Journal of Sex and Marital Therapy* (2016).

24. For a summary, see Muise, A., Impett, E. A., Kogan, A. and Desmarais, S., 'Keeping the Spark Alive: Being Motivated to Meet a Partner's Sexual Needs Sustains Sexual Desire in Long-Term Romantic Relationships', *Social Psychological and Personality Science*, 4(3), 267–273 (2013) and Muise, A., Kim, J. J., Impett, E. A., Rosen, N. O., 'Understanding When a Partner Is Not in the Mood: Sexual Communal Strength in Couples Transitioning to Parenthood', *Archives of Sexual Behavior*, 46(7):1993–2006 (Oct. 2017).

25. Muise, A., Kim, J. J., Impett, E. A. and Rosen, N. O., 'Understanding When a Partner Is Not in the Mood: Sexual Communal Strength in Couples Transitioning to Parenthood', *Archives of Sexual Behavior*, 46(7):1993–2006 (Oct. 2017).

Acknowledgements

Writing this book has been fun. Much like having a second child, I have learned that a second book is much less stressful than the first. Like second children, they come at a time when you know what you're getting yourself into, what to expect at different stages, and (dare I say it) feel slightly more relaxed that they'll turn out alright.

Saying that, they say it takes a village, and books are no different.

First, I want to thank Anna Steadman, editor extraordinaire at Headline Home, who hadn't had enough of me after working on *Mind The Gap*, and had the idea to do this book. Between her and my wonderful agent, Julia Silk, they managed to convince me over a lovely lunch that I could fit writing this book into my life and I am glad that they did. I was also graced with not one but two wonderful editors, due to Anna's maternity leave, and wish to extend huge thanks to Zoë Blanc, who in stepping in for Anna provided a brilliant sounding board, ideas tester and clarity machine from the first draft to the finish. It's been an enormous pleasure and privilege getting to work with you, Zoë, and you are just as good as Anna and Julia said you would be. Thanks also to Anna Hervé for being a copyedit marvel and for being so enthusiastic about my work, again! Thanks also to Federica Trogu in publicity, and Caroline Young, who designed the fantastic cover, which encapsulates the book so well.

Part of what enthuses me are the people I work with who are nothing short of exceptional. I wish to thank every single person at 56 Dean Street (the Beyoncé of sexual health clinics) for being so freaking fabulous. My other team, The Havelock Clinic, are just as awesome, love you all. Particular thanks to Dr Ali Mears and friend, colleague and all-round inspiration Prof Kirstin Mitchell for their words of solidarity over gin and tonics and 2 a.m. swims. Big thanks to Lori Brotto for your cheerleading and words of support, it means a lot. Thanks to Katy Harrad for saving my bacon all the time.

Big thanks to my pals and cheerleaders. The Sandgate Parent Crew for making me feel so welcome this past year, and the MODS for not forgetting me! Thanks to Rae Langford, Kate Baxter, Lindy Fittall and Chloe Potter for being there even from afar. The Queer Writing group for solidarity, swims and silent space. Rob Taliesin Owen for eternal optimism and motivational words. Fi and Ros Undersmith, Charlotte and Emily Weatherall, Kaye Maguire and Gemma Caney, Paul Lawrenson, Steven Thwaite and Rick Shultz for the enthusiastic cheerleading.

Huge thanks also to all my clients over the years, who, in our therapy sessions together, are the sounding boards for my ideas, and allow me to test out what works for parents with busy lives, in getting their sex lives on the right trajectory.

Writing any book takes you away from the world for a while to retreat into your own one, and the only way I could do this is with the support and encouragement of my family. Thanks especially to my two boys for being patient with me (again!). The last and always the biggest thanks to my partner, AJ, whose capacity to simultaneously take over the running of the house, solo parent and be my biggest supporter seems to know no bounds.

Resources for parents

Association for Post-Natal Illness (APNI) – www.apni.org . A charity providing support with mental health problems in the perinatal period.

Cashlab (Couples and Sexual Health Lab) – www.natalieorosen.com. You can also visit www.postbabyhankypanky.com for short animations explaining key findings about the sex lives of new parents.

Dr Emma Svanberg – www.dremmasvanberg.com, or on Instagram at @mumologist. Emma, a perinatal clinical psychologist, is the author of two excellent books, *Why Birth Trauma Matters* (Pinter & Martin Ltd, 2019) and *Parenting for Humans: How to Parent the Child You Have as the Person You Are* (Vermillion, 2023).

Emma Brockwell – www.physiomum.co.uk and on Instagram as @physiomumuk. A pelvic health physiotherapist and author of *Why Did No One Tell Me? How to Protect, Heal and Nurture Your Body Through Motherhood* (Vermillion, 2021).

Make Birth Better – www.makebirthbetter.org, or on Instagram at @birthbetter. A community with resources to support parents after birth trauma.

MASIC Foundation – www.masic.org.uk, or on Instagram @masicfoundation. A charity supporting people with injuries after childbirth.

POGP (Pelvic Obstetric and Gynaecological Physiotherapy) – www.thepogp.co.uk. Find a qualified pelvic health physiotherapist in your area, or download resources on pelvic health.

Index

Note: 'n' indicates that the reference relates to a footer note.

Index